Green Ghost, Blue Ocean

No Fixed Address

Jennifer M. Smith

POTTERSFIELD PRESS

Lawrencetown Beach, Nova Scotia, Canada

Library and Archives Canada Cataloguing in Publication

Title: Green Ghost, blue ocean : no fixed address / Jennifer M. Smith.
Names: Smith, Jennifer M. (Adventurer), author.
Identifiers: Canadiana (print) 20200171798 | Canadiana (ebook) 20200171836 | ISBN 9781989725054
    (softcover) | ISBN 9781989725061 (HTML)
Subjects: LCSH: Smith, Jennifer M. (Adventurer)—Travel. | LCSH: Adventure and adventurers—Canada—Biography. | LCSH: Voyages around the world. | LCSH: Sailing.
Classification: LCC G540 .S57 2020 | DDC 910.4/5—dc23

Front cover credit: Alex Nikolajevich

Cover design: Jennifer M. Smith

Pottersfield Press gratefully acknowledges the financial support of the Government of Canada for our publishing activities. We also acknowledge the support of the Canada Council for the Arts and the Province of Nova Scotia which has assisted us to develop and promote our creative industries for the benefit of all Nova Scotians.

Pottersfield Press
248 Leslie Road
East Lawrencetown, Nova Scotia, Canada, B2Z 1T4
Website: www.PottersfieldPress.com
To order, phone 1-800-NIMBUS9 (1-800-646-2879) www.nimbus.ns.ca

Printed in Canada

Pottersfield Press is committed to preserving the environment and the appropriate harvesting of trees and has printed this book on Forest Stewardship Council® certified paper.

Table of Contents

FIGURES

Author's Note

Green Ghost, Blue Ocean is a true story told from my point of view. From scribbled journals, salt-stained logbooks, ragged calendars, and the hundreds of e-mails I sent home, I have reconstructed the story of our sailing adventure. Naturally, many stories from the seventeen-year period have been left out as have many of the wonderful people we met along the way. To fellow sailors not included in this book, we remain deeply thankful for your camaraderie, cold beer, and spare parts, and for your comforting voices over the long-distance radio. Nobody sails the world completely alone.

Also missing from my story are tales of the family members and friends who flew to far-flung corners of the earth to support us with their company and their enthusiasm for sampling a small part of our adventure. We are thankful for the privilege of visiting foreign countries and for the gracious hospitality of the local people. Warm and friendly interactions far outweighed any difficult exchanges we had. Of course, more dramatic stories arise from the more challenging situations and some of these stories are told here.

I have tried to recreate our conversations and experiences to the best of my imperfect memory. Others' memories of the situations I describe will, no doubt, be different from my own. While the people in my story are real, some character identities are composites and, in some cases, I have changed the name and/or the identity of individuals.

I hope you enjoy going to sea with *Green Ghost* on the blue ocean.

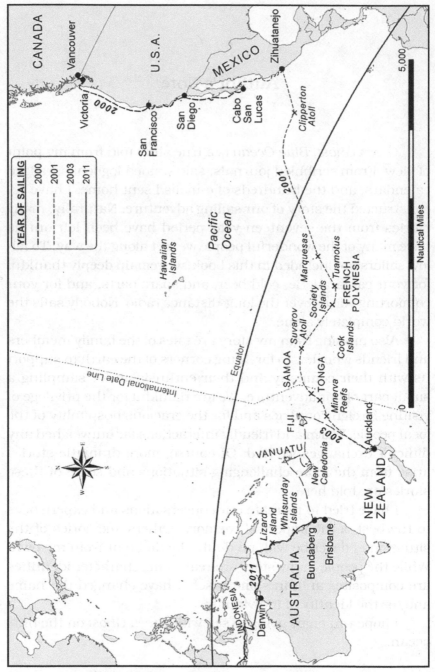

Figure 1. Pacific Ocean Route Map

CHAPTER 1

Departure

(late August – early September 2000)

We sold the car. We couldn't go back. We couldn't go back because we sold the car. These weren't reasonable thoughts for a sensible, analytical person like me. But in that deafening dark moment I wasn't making sense. I was certain it was the sale of our car that had done it. That immutable act had changed everything. The car was the last connection to our Vancouver land life and we'd willfully, recklessly severed it. We sold the car, we couldn't go back, and I didn't know the way forward from here.

But we were moving forward even as I lay there fretting in my berth. We were hurtling forward in fact. We were pitching and rolling and yawing. We were violently thrown around. As each wave took us up, up, up, it felt as though an unseen hand had grabbed *Green Ghost* by her transom, tossing her onward without a thought to her well-being. Then, that giant roller would pass under us, lowering us into a trough so deep our horizon line became the back of that passing wave and the crest of the next one to come. Big weather – it wasn't in the forecast.

None of what was happening had been in my forecast. So much had gone into this, so much education, preparation, and planning. Nine years earlier the plan to change our lives had been a dream. But now, I lay worrying in my bunk, listening to the dark noise of wind and the rush of water hurtling past the hull. Just three days in and our dream felt more like a nightmare. It wasn't supposed to be this way. I thought it was going to be fun.

I lay on a cushioned bench seat in the main salon. Six feet away, my husband Nik lay on the port-side bench incapacitated by seasickness. He was a huddled mass, dressed in fleece, and covered in a blanket. He'd wedged a large stainless steel stockpot between his body and the lee cloth that held him in his bunk. Even if he wanted to, he couldn't stand up.

My mind was reeling and helpless. I was unable to contemplate solutions, to see a way out. I stopped thinking about the car for a moment and focused on a single word: undo. I wanted to undo all of this. I wanted to reverse the hundreds of decisions we'd made that had brought us here, to this heaving patch of ocean, to these towering seas, to the forty-knot winds rushing us south. I wanted daylight. I wanted land. I wanted us to jump in our car and drive away. But we couldn't do that. We couldn't go back because we'd sold the car – forward was the only way from here.

❈

I should have known we were doomed, we'd had such an inelegant departure. I'd imagined Nik and me, poised and nautical in Breton stripes, gliding out of our slip shipshape and unruffled. Instead, with short tempers and long faces we were furiously addressing our to-do lists. With only hours left before a tide-imposed sailing time, gear lay everywhere waiting to be stowed. Nik needed a haircut. I needed to go to the bank. Our landline and garden hose were still connected to the dock. A knock on the hull drew our attention. Neighbouring sailors who'd lived their offshore dream years earlier recognized that our harried expressions and frenzied pace could mean only one thing: Departure Day.

Handing us a bottle of champagne, they assured us, "It won't always be like this. Eventually you'll relax. You'll love Mexico! And the Pacific is fantastic! You'll have a wonderful time!"

A bottle of bubbly and a couple of goodbyes at the dock were all we had. There was no other fanfare, no tearful crowd waving handkerchiefs, no band playing. Midday, midweek, there were no witnesses as we backed out of our Coal Harbour berth. In the late August sun, we slowly motored into the view I'd had from my Vancouver office a month earlier. It was a big moment, but if I told you it was the consummation of years of dreaming, I'd be lying. Dreaming only gets you started. That day was the outcome of deciding, followed by a decade of doing.

Two people, a cat, and a sailboat were leaving the big city behind. Unacknowledged, I felt small and alone in the face of what lay ahead. I thought that this massive undertaking deserved some sort of inauguration. Just then, my thoughts were startled by three blasts from a nearby boat. It was the tourist vessel, *Constitution*, out on a harbour cruise. Captain Jim, our neighbour for four and a half years at Harbour Ferries Marina, was at the helm. As we rounded the navigation marker beyond the fuel barges, he gave us a proper send-off. Those three cheerful blasts lifted my spirits. Our departure was not so anonymous after all. With that one proper farewell salute, we were on our way.

It was a two-day trip to Victoria, where we would pick up crew. A strong westerly wind made for an exhilarating sail down Haro Strait. With twenty-three knots blowing on our quarter, *Green Ghost* flew at hull speed, racing toward our starting line. I was at the helm and loving it, believing the brisk day was a good test. But Nik felt ill and apprehensive, and our long-haired calico cat, Tuzo, felt the same. She vomited on the floor below decks. Ah, the romance of offshore sailing – it had already begun.

Three friends, who were interested in going offshore in their own boats someday, joined us in Victoria. Kathleen and Tiro, friends from the mining industry, were outdoorsy types and excited to be a part of the inaugural leg. Jordan, a colleague of Nik's, was an engineer and a keen power-boater, but not a sailor himself. Tiro was the only one of us who knew what he was getting into. Two decades earlier, at the age of thirteen, his parents had taken their family cruising through the South

Pacific aboard their home-built sailboat. Of *Green Ghost*'s five-man crew, Tiro was the only one with any offshore experience. The rest of us were there to get it.

Over two days we made last-minute preparations and contemplated the weatherfax information received through our HF radio and PACTOR modem. Each time the radio sprang to life with the latest weather report, Captain Nik silenced our noisy, giddy excitement. When the forecast indicated that the winds would switch from southwesterly to northwesterly with no wind over twenty-five knots predicted for the following week, all systems were go for a downwind run to San Francisco. Sunday, September 3, 2000, would be our departure day.

We eased into the trip, motoring up a windless Juan de Fuca Strait and making good progress toward the cape. Everyone was feeling fine but we were hedging our bets. To combat seasickness Kathleen and Tiro were taking a drug called Stugeron, a motion-sickness medication. Nik and I were each using half of a scopolamine patch, a transdermal anti-nauseant and anti-emetic. Even ship's cat Tuzo was drugged up on a tiny dose of a children's Gravol. Only Jordan tempted fate.

With the chaos of departure behind us, we settled into the trip, each one of us keen for the adventure. We passed around the binoculars when orcas arced off the port side. Camera shutters clicked when a U.S. Navy submarine passed us heading out to sea.

When Dall's porpoises leaped from the water and crisscrossed our bow, I held on tightly to the bow pulpit, beaming. No matter how often we saw them, I always marvelled at their antics. Their playful nature, their leaps of delight, filled me with joy. I believed their visit was a happy send-off and the best possible kind of omen.

For dinner on that first night, we warmed frozen beef stew and the five of us ate like children, with spoons from bowls, as we rounded Cape Flattery and headed south. A ten- to fifteen-knot northwest wind filled in behind us exactly as the forecast predicted. In a light swell, the engine went off, the sails were set, and our mechanical self-steering gear was engaged. Nik poured a tot of rum into the sea in a toast to Neptune, the sun sank in the western sky, and the first night was upon us. We planned to sail eighty nautical miles (NM) offshore to stay out of the shipping traffic. With 750 NM to go, we anticipated a week at sea to reach San Francisco.

Nik and I had both plenty of experience and no experience at all. We knew our boat inside out. We'd lived aboard and had sailed locally for four and a half years before our departure. Every piece of equipment we'd added had been painstakingly installed ourselves. We'd done cruises on the inside passage up to Desolation Sound; we'd crossed open water on a trip to Bella Bella. We'd done a month-long circumnavigation of Vancouver Island. We'd crossed Georgia Strait in the dark. We had over 1,300 NM under our belts. Courses in basic and intermediate sailing, celestial navigation, and coastal navigation had been completed. We'd read many offshore sailing books, even the disaster-at-sea stories, thinking we might learn something from them. We'd passed government exams in Safe Boating, Maritime Radio, HAM Radio, and Morse Code. More coursework was completed in diesel engine repair (Nik), sail repair (me), spinnaker sailing, weather for sailors and heavy-weather sailing tactics. Yes, we had experience – we had day-tripping coastal sailing experience. But when it came to multi-day, non-stop offshore voyaging, we had no experience at all. The conundrum of a blue-water sailing experience is that you may not want to go offshore without it, but you can't get any of it until you go offshore.

Prior to departing Victoria, I'd wondered how it would feel to spend nights at sea. I had a vague notion that we might stay up late in the cockpit discussing the meaning of life over steaming cups of hot chocolate. Or perhaps a game of cribbage would be played by the red glow of the night-lights below decks. My ideas were more romantic than fearful. I pictured a cozy scenario akin to a gathering around a cottage campfire. In reality, at nightfall on that first night at sea, grabbing a bunk was like a game of musical chairs. When the sun went down, the music stopped and anyone who wasn't required on deck dashed below to grab a berth. The off-watch crew was in bed, lights out, by eight p.m. So much for deep thoughts over hot chocolate.

We had five berths, but only three of them were comfortable at sea. No one wanted to sleep in the V-berth because there was too much motion in the bow. We planned a two-man watch at all times, which meant there was a berth for each person on the off-watch crew – just not a fresh one. We were hot-bunking.

We agreed that no formal watch was required by day. We simply took turns. If you were up and you felt like it, you were on watch. This pleased the captain and his laid-back ways. For the nights, we agreed on a schedule. This pleased me, as I am more punctilious than the captain when it comes to, well, when it comes to just about everything.

Things went well for the first few days. We had clear skies, smooth seas, and a remarkably constant fifteen-knot north-westerly on our quarter. We sailed with the mainsail up and the large foresail, the genoa, poled out. At night, to be conservative, we put one reef in the main and retired the downwind pole. Our Cape Horn mechanical self-steering gear, which we had nicknamed Digger, was performing flawlessly. The five of us were happy to let Digger steer.

Nik found the night shifts challenging. To keep nausea at bay it was best to focus on the distance, but it was difficult to see one another in the cockpit, let alone see the far-off horizon line. The darkness was disorienting and through his moonless shifts, Nik was in a perpetual state of nausea. We'd been foolish to cut the scopolamine patch in half. It wasn't a proper dosage and it was not working. He soon switched to Stugeron.

When the winds began to build midweek, we were not concerned. The forecast called for a fifteen- to twenty-knot northwesterly, peaking at twenty-five knots in the night, then easing back the following day. As the conditions became more boisterous in the late afternoon, we enjoyed our increased speed. Before sundown we put two reefs in the main, and furled the genoa in favour of using the smaller staysail. We thought ourselves quite smart – but we were not smart enough. It was on this night that it all went to hell in a handbasket.

Nik and I stood watch on the early shift. Despite a sliver of moon now lighting the horizon, neither one of us felt well. It was cold. Our body temperatures were falling as the wind speed steadily rose. We sat huddled and braced in the cockpit, hanging on for the ride.

At the end of our watch at two a.m. we were chilled through and shivering. The winds were thirty knots and we were beginning to consider reducing sail further but we were too cold and too tired to take action. Kathleen and Tiro were on watch next and, as pathetic as it may sound, although we were the boat owners, we decided to let the fresh crew, our guests, assess the situation. We wanted to believe that it was only our fatigue overriding our ability to cope with the elements.

Below deck we tried to get some sleep. I tried the mantra I'd used when we'd been in uncomfortable conditions in B.C. *This won't last, this won't last, this won't last*, I repeated to myself, hoping to slide into sleep. But I couldn't settle and I got up to pee. I didn't see the open hatch in the dark. As I sat on the toilet, a wave hit the boat and five gallons of freezing cold seawater poured in over my head, then sloshed back and forth on the floor before swirling down the drain hole into the bilge. Swearing bitterly, I changed out of my wet clothes in the wild motion of the V-berth. With damp hair, I collapsed into my bunk. It was then that I began to fret about the car, about everything. Every thought I had ended in *go back, go home, undo*. But we couldn't go back – because we'd sold the car.

CHAPTER 2

Gale Force

(September 2000)

The wind increased and the hum of the water flying past the hull got ever louder. There were cheers and exclamations from the crew on deck as spray exploded over the rails and rushed astern. At times a wave curled over and boarded *Green Ghost*, swishing about the cockpit floor before draining back into the sea. A wave slapped the port quarter hard enough that a geyser of cold saltwater shot up through the cockpit drain. From my bunk, it sounded as if Kathleen and Tiro were on a carnival ride, laughing and swearing in astonishment. Then they got quieter and their remarks were less jovial and more urgent, which only increased my worries. What was going on?

Suddenly Tiro opened the companionway doors. "Guys," he said, "we've got to get some sail down. We need you on deck." It was three a.m.

I abandoned the mental hand-wringing I'd been doing, swung my legs over the settee, and sat there. *Undo.* I was tired and desperately cold. I felt sick. I hadn't slept at all. *Undo.* I was shivering in whole-body shudders. I couldn't bear the thought of going out there. *I can't*, went through my mind, and *I don't want to* followed in close succession. I wanted someone else to do it. But there were only the five of us. There was no one else to do it. And this was my boat, our boat. If anyone should be doing it, it should be me, it should be us.

We donned our foul-weather gear and went on deck. The wind had reached gale force with a sustained speed of thirty-nine knots and gusts to forty-five. The seas had picked up too, and we crested on frothing white rollers fifteen feet high.

Nik took the helm and started the engine. I put the spreader lights on so we could see what we were doing. The bright light was great for anyone handling lines or wresting-in sails, but it was hell on the helmsman. The blinding light created a sense of detachment. In the dark, with the lights off, you saw less detail, but you saw farther. Night vision allowed you to orient yourself in the larger setting of the boat and its position in the sea. But with the spreader lights on, Nik had only the instruments for orientation. This exacerbated his seasickness and soon he was repeatedly retching overboard, flinging himself astern to port or to starboard, whichever way the boat was rolling.

We didn't have the lines rigged for a third reef in the mainsail, so our aim was to take the mainsail down altogether and run before the wind with staysail only. We needed to head up, to point the bow into the screaming winds, to get the mainsail down and to get the boom secured in the gallows. As Nik tried to head up, I saw him steer the boat through the eye of the wind and set us on the opposite tack.

"You've got to keep it into the wind for us!" I yelled at him.

I watched the needle on the wind indicator. He tacked back, again over-steering. I stopped looking at the instruments and looked at Nik. It was then that I realized how sick he was. He was pale and green.

"Jenn, take the helm!" he yelled as he flung himself aft. With his head over the stern he violently heaved. For weeks before the trip Nik had been concerned about being overcome by motion sickness. Now his worst fear was rocketing up through his gut and hurtling itself into the sea.

It frightened me. I'd never seen him that sick before. I steered into the wind while the rest of the crew dropped the mainsail and secured the boom in the gallows. I returned us to our southerly course, running downwind with only the staysail deployed. Without the mainsail, we were rolling a little more, but we were under control.

Nik went back to bed and I went below with him. Jordan offered to take the helm while Kathleen and Tiro donned warmer clothing before continuing their watch.

I went forward to brace myself against the hanging lockers to peel off my heavy-weather gear. Tiro and Kathleen were standing below the companionway. Suddenly the boat lurched violently to starboard and I saw Kathleen flung six feet across the width of the cabin. She put her hand out as she went hurtling into the galley stove. She popped back up as the boat lurched to port. Tiro was standing behind her and she slumped into his arms. She was holding her head. I felt sure that she was passing out. I expected a bleeding forehead but, thankfully, there was no broken skin. She'd hit her hand and her head on the metal rim of the galley stove. It was her hand that was injured.

"My hand! I think I've broken it," she gasped.

To add insult to injury, as she was thrown into the galley Kathleen had landed in the cat box that had slid there during the sail change. Her damp clothing was covered in clumping kitty litter.

I felt a rising panic. Nik lay in the port-side berth, incapacitated by seasickness. He was clutching the stockpot and retching into it. Kathleen remained slumped in Tiro's arms. *Two down, three left*, I thought to myself. Maybe I'd been reading too many disaster-at-sea books but I couldn't stop thinking that this was how bad things happened. It's rarely one terrible event where everybody gets done in at once; it's usually a sequence of small accidents, little turning points that lead to total failure. At that moment, I looked up through the companionway to see Jordan at the helm, the only non-sailor among us. I cursed aloud. It wasn't supposed to be like this.

Tiro helped Kathleen remove her gear and climb into the starboard bunk. She needed ice for her swelling hand and drugs for the pain. I dug some ice out of the freezer, put it in a Ziploc bag, and gave it to her. Then I set about finding the Tylenol No.3 with codeine. I grabbed the prescription medicine box and read a dozen labels before finding the right bottle. I gave Kathleen two pills and a glass of water. At that moment, the reading of fine print caught up to me and I rushed to vomit into the galley sink. Fortunately for me, this was only task-oriented seasickness. I recovered as soon as I went back on deck into the refreshing forty-knot breeze.

Tiro crouched beside the port bunk to discuss storm tactics with Nik. Nik believed we had more control with some sail up and some speed. He knew that *Green Ghost* liked her stern to the wind. With the staysail alone in the current conditions we were not over-canvassed. Because we had plenty of sea room to run, there was no need to attempt to slow or stop the boat. Tiro agreed and went back on watch to spell Jordan off at the helm.

"Jenn!" Nik yelled at me from his bunk. "I think we should call the Coast Guard!"

"What?" I said, balking at the idea. "How would that change anything?" I was embarrassed at the thought of it. I didn't want to be one of those pathetic uninformed rookies who brazenly bit off more than they could chew, then expected the Coast Guard to come to their rescue.

"It's not a call for help. It's a call to give and receive information. We should let them know our position and our conditions and ask if them if they have further weather information. They might be able to tell us if conditions are predicted to deteriorate. If they are, we can plan accordingly."

Nik was right. Despite his seasickness he was still coming up with good ideas.

"I can't believe it's come to this." I continued to grumble some resistance as I turned on the radio.

Normally a simple task, operating the radio became a difficult endeavour in the violent motion on board. To move around safely we all needed two hands to remain upright. Seeing that I was going to have to forfeit a handhold in order to hang onto the microphone, Jordan gripped the navigation table on either side of me, pinning me in place so that all I had to do was hold the mic, think and speak clearly.

It was nearly five a.m. when, with a shaky and emotional voice, I called, "United States Coast Guard, United States Coast Guard, United States Coast Guard, this is the sailing vessel *Green Ghost, Green Ghost.*"

The reply came back, "Sailing vessel *Gringo,* this is the United States Coast Guard, go ahead."

Gringo? We laughed with comic relief.

"Negative, not *Gringo. Green* as in the colour, *Green,* and *Ghost* as in phantom. This is the sailing vessel *Green Ghost,*" I corrected him.

I gave them our position and our heading as well as details of the people on board and their state of health. The Coast Guard read us the weather forecast including that cute little bit about the maximum twenty-five-knot wind speeds.

"Bad forecast," I complained into the mic. "It's sustained near forty and gusting forty-five out here."

They suggested we set up a schedule with them and call them at the top of the hour every hour until conditions abated. Unlike us, they'd done this before and they knew a little hand-holding would go a long way.

Eventually, Jordan went back to bed to salvage what was left of his off shift. Tiro and I stayed up until daylight. The radio schedule with the Coast Guard alleviated our distress and gave us a distraction as the hours passed.

All seemed better in the light of day and we quit our schedule with the Coast Guard by nine a.m. Finally, Tiro and I got a chance to sleep when Kathleen got up and sat in the cockpit in the morning. While her one-handed status made it difficult for her to do much, she was still able to stand watch for other marine traffic.

Conditions eased through the following day but this didn't change anything for the captain. Nik remained horizontal for another twenty-four hours.

"So I guess things are going to change for you," Jordan said to me.

"What do you mean?"

"Well, you're going to have to change your plans. Look at him," he said, nodding at Nik comatose in the bunk with the stockpot of dried barf beside him.

I looked at my husband lying there and wondered how Nik and I would ever be able to do long-distance voyages alone. Jordan's comments were pointed. How could I think we would make it to Mexico, let alone cross the Pacific as we'd hoped? The scopolamine patch had not worked for Nik, nor had the Stugeron. Considering these were two of the most widely used anti-seasickness drugs among offshore sailors, his prospects weren't looking very good. If Nik became that sick when we had no other crew on board, I would be left to sail the boat alone. I wasn't sure I could do it.

Jordan's question was reasonable but I didn't like it. This was a private matter. If I was going to talk to anyone about our plans changing, it was Nik, and I wasn't going to have that discussion in front of three friends in forty-two feet of space. Our dream and its possible demise was not up for public scrutiny. It was something we would figure out together after the crew left the boat in San Francisco.

⊕

On our fifth day at sea the captain returned to a vertical position. In gentle conditions, we set the spinnaker and enjoyed a beautiful downwind run through a warm and sunny afternoon. But the delightful conditions, as with all things at sea, were not to last.

The winds began to build again toward the end of the week and naturally it was nightfall when wind speeds reached thirty knots. This time we were unfazed. With those few days of experience we'd fallen into a proactive routine. For this second round of rising winds we put the mainsail away to run with the genoa alone for the night.

This proved to be a brilliant decision as the winds continued to build. On the two-to-six a.m. watch I was looking at gusts to forty-five knots again. It was remarkable how relaxed we were this second time around. The difference was that we were ready, and we had the right sail plan implemented before the worst of the weather hit. We were chuffed that we managed the second gale so readily, without calls to the Coast Guard, without any issues at all.

The wind blew at gale force for twenty-four hours. We flew south with the genoa furled to the size of a tablecloth. After sundown on our sixth day, Nik spotted the light at Point Reyes. We were closing in on San Francisco.

On our seventh day at sea, overwhelmed with a sense of achievement for getting through those dark and stormy nights and for managing the longest sustained gale-force conditions we'd ever experienced, we sailed under San Francisco's Golden Gate Bridge and into our new life. It was then I realized it didn't matter that we'd sold the car. I knew *Green Ghost* was all we needed to find our way forward from here.

CHAPTER 3

A Steamer Trunk with a Mast

(before 1996)

There were steamer trunks in the basement of my child-hood home. They were the real deal, complete with tarnished brass knobby corners, hefty locks, and faded stickers from far-off places haphazardly slapped on all sides. I was fascinated by the trunks and often emptied their contents to sift through old letters, tarnished school awards, and 78 rpm vinyl records. They'd belonged to my grandad, from his days travelling the world as the china buyer for Eaton's, once Canada's largest department store. Or maybe they'd belonged to his brother, my great-uncle Don, an author and a bit of a playboy, who'd also travelled the world.

I imagined the trunks perfectly packed for a journey. The idea of reducing your possessions down to the contents of a steamer trunk thrilled me – the delicious efficiency of it! I loved the thought of being nimble, of being ready to go. But to go where exactly, I didn't know.

☸

At eighteen, feeling both adventurous and rebellious, I en-rolled in Geology, Energy & Fuel Science at Lakehead University in northern Ontario, a thousand miles from home. Ever since my grade two teacher had taught us about the discovery of King Tutankhamun's tomb, I'd wanted to be an archaeologist. But a high school aptitude test had strongly suggested a career in engineering for me. The results left me in a quandary. I wasn't really sure what engineering was. After reading the description of a career in geological engineering, I decided the geology part sounded pretty good. It seemed the right combination of physical geography and science – both subjects I loved. And besides, the subject retained the air of a treasure hunt – there might still be some digging for gold.

I followed my undergraduate studies with a master's degree in geology at the University of Alberta, a farther thousand miles away. In 1987, halfway through my graduate degree, I took a summer job working for a junior mining company doing gold exploration near Rankin Inlet, Nunavut, not far from the Arctic Circle. There, in a tented bush camp on the icy shores of Happy Lake, I met my future husband, Alex Nikolajevich, a geology graduate from the University of Toronto. His friends in the camp called him Nik and since meeting him that summer, I've never called him anything else.

Nik's dark brown, almond-shaped eyes twinkled with mischief under his knitted Mongolian hat. His brunette hair and sun-browned skin, together with his sloping eyelids, carried a hint of Asian ancestry. In that setting, there on the tundra, there was something almost Inuit in his looks, but a mass of facial hair said otherwise.

Nik had a physicality about him, a body-confident presence that seemed to shout: "Bring it on!" With his unruly hair, unshaven face, and rough bush clothes, he looked like he'd stepped from the pages of my favourite public school textbook, *Breastplate and Buckskin: A Story of Exploration and Discovery in the Americas*. But he was no illustration of a man: he was the real thing. At the day's end, when he entered the camp kitchen for dinner, he didn't merely step across the threshold – he burst in with a swirl of Arctic air, carried on a gust of potential. As I sat in the cozy cook-tent watching his dramatic entrance, my heart leapt. Whenever Nik arrived in a room, it felt like something exciting was about to happen. There was an immediate mutual attraction and once we'd admitted it to each other, it took him only three days to tell me he was going to marry me. I was a bit more cautious.

We endured a long-distance romance between Edmonton and Toronto for a year while I completed my master's degree and then the two of us set off to Australia to backpack with a working-holiday visa.

In Sydney, we bought an old orange Toyota HiAce van that we affectionately dubbed The Tangerine Dream. Our job hunt began in Sydney and we continued our search in every major city on a route south and west. Three months later we landed contract jobs as drill geologists at an open-pit gold mine in Kalgoorlie, Western Australia. After six months of work, we enjoyed another three months on the road completing our circumnavigation, venturing north up the Western Australian coastline and then east across the sunbaked top of the country. In Darwin, we exchanged engagement rings and planned our wedding for December 1990, several months after returning to Canada.

We married in Oakville, but settling in Ontario was not for Nik. He saw life in Toronto as a materialistic rat race and yearned for the more laid-back outdoorsy west coast. Immediately after our marriage, we moved to Vancouver, our new home.

Little did I know of the faint flicker of a dream that Nik carried west in his heart. Although we had much in common, Nik had enjoyed some experiences in his youth that I'd never had – in particular, sailing. Long before we'd met, Nik had attended the Toronto Boat Show where he stood patient and shoeless in a long queue to view the beautiful Whitby 55, a self-sufficient cruising sailboat that could take you anywhere. The lovely Whitby fanned his sailing interests into a small flame, a pilot light to his heart's desire.

In our first year on the west coast, Nik tossed me an idea.

"The Pacific's on our doorstep," he said. "We ought to take advantage of it. We should take sailing lessons."

It was a simple thing to say, a little idea pitched to me randomly one day, an idea that changed our lives.

✵

We set about establishing ourselves in Vancouver. In March 1991, we bought a modest raised ranch home in a family-oriented suburb in North Delta, an hour from downtown Vancouver.

We took our first Canadian Yachting Association beginner level sailing course in the fall of that year. With thoughts of the Whitby in mind, we learned to sail on keeled boats, 30-footers, large enough to take a group of six students and complex enough for us to learn the ropes on a vessel with a mainsail, a foresail, and a spinnaker. Below decks I took in the sleeping berths, the head and shower, the icebox and the stove. The layout was efficiency perfected. I recognized it immediately – this was a steamer trunk with a mast.

Through the short days of winter, while we toiled in the Vancouver offices of our respective employers, Nik fuelled his fire buying *Cruising World* magazines. At lunch, he'd read articles about sailors in exotic places and come home announcing, "Listen to this! Listen to what these people did!"

"Do you think *we* could do it?" I asked.

"Probably," he answered. "We've got more to learn, but yeah, I think we probably could."

We began to imagine a future where, together with our children, we would sail off into the sunset discovering the world. We became obsessed with the vision of a life not defined by the norm and we seized upon sailing as the perfect way to journey down a road less travelled.

✵

As exploration geologists, we spent months working in the bush, away from home, but when work schedules allowed we educated ourselves with further sailing courses. As required by law we got our pleasure craft operator's certificates and our VHF radio operator's licenses. We read books, went to seminars, and joined the Bluewater Cruising Association in Vancouver, a club that held courses, slide shows and social nights for their membership base of what they called Dreamers, Doers and Doners. We immersed ourselves in all things to do with long-distance offshore sailing, or "cruising," as it is commonly called.

In the early '90s, a downturn in world metal prices resulted in staff reductions in the mining sector. Our careers stalled when Nik's contract ran out and I was laid off. Paying our mortgage, saving for a sailboat, having children, and setting off on our cruising adventure? None of it seemed possible then. We were thirty years old and every one of our ambitions was looking like a dead-end road. We recognized quickly that financial stability was the key to everything we hoped for.

The life we were living was not what we wanted for the long haul. Exploration geology work wasn't well suited to family life and it wasn't easy making financial plans based on intermittent employment. While many of our mining colleagues began heading for jobs in South America, we hung up our hiking boots, and retrained with the hope of gaining more control over our future.

Nik took the Canadian Securities Course to learn more about the stock market as well as a few courses in sales to test his interest. I was tired of being laid off by accountants and decided that if you couldn't beat them, you might as well join them. I began taking business courses.

The chances we took paid off and our redirected careers began in earnest in the fall of 1993. Nik landed a job as a technical sales representative with a North Vancouver company selling specialized groundwater monitoring systems. I was accepted into the School of Chartered Accountancy and landed a position in downtown Vancouver with Price Waterhouse, a work environment that was the polar opposite to living in a bush camp in northwestern B.C. It was a big change but also a great relief to be living year-round in Vancouver, to be freed from the seasonal market-sensitive mining industry, and to be a two-paycheque family again.

With our employment situations stabilized, we began to focus on our other aspirations. Having passed two sailing courses, we confidently rented boats for a day or a weekend. After chartering a NonSuch thirty-foot sailboat for a week in Desolation Sound, we decided it was time to buy a boat of our own. We thought we loved sailing, but we hadn't had to address gear failures and maintenance issues, nor take on the costs of insurance and year-round marina fees. We needed to test ourselves. We wondered if the responsibilities of boat ownership would prove too much for us, so, we bought a 1972 twenty-seven-foot C&C 27 to find out.

We called her *Tethys*, the Titan-daughter of Uranus and Gaia, and sister and wife to Titan-god Oceanus. Tethys was also the name given to a mid-sized moon of Saturn and to the first ocean formed by plate tectonics. Our new boat had an image of Saturn on its spinnaker and, with our geological background, we thought the name suited both the boat and us perfectly. Every long weekend we made the 25 NM trip across Georgia Strait to the Gulf Islands. Every summer holiday we sailed for weeks in Desolation Sound. There was no doubt about it: we were hooked. More sailing was all we wanted.

But how to sail more was the problem. We were diligently paying down our mortgage and putting every other spare penny into our Registered Retirement Savings Plans, maximizing our contributions annually. We saved, not for the far-off retirement years, but to build a cruising kitty that we hoped to use sooner rather than later. But how much money did we need? We couldn't find an answer to that question anywhere, so we defined our own goal. We decided we needed to purchase and pay for an offshore sailboat and we needed C$100,000 put away into each of our retirement savings plans before we could go.

Most cruising sailors are retired. Very often they have been involved in sailing their whole lives and have waited to go cruising in their retirement years when their children have grown up and their house has been paid off. We were impatient. Our cruising dream was an opportunity pounding on the front door of our hearts. It never occurred to us to wait. We wanted to sail *with* our children, not wait until they were grown and gone. Paying off our house, however, was another matter. How could we do that quickly? We wanted to go offshore but we wanted something to come back to as well.

I spent spare time constructing spreadsheets trying to come up with the golden formula that would allow us to go sailing *and* keep our house, but no matter how I did the math, there was no way we could make it work. While we worried over wealth, we were lucky to have access to wisdom.

During my work in the mining industry I met a woman who did contract work in our office. She and her husband were sailors. They lived aboard their sailboat in Vancouver. They had even raised their children aboard a boat. Twenty years my senior, she was a wealth of knowledge. Nik and I were invited to tea where we met her husband and sat in rapt attention asking question after question about their boat, their experiences, and their thoughts on offshore sailing. They became our friends and mentors. We put them on a pedestal and hung on their every word.

Whenever we got together they would ask us questions too, testing us and seeking answers on the progress of our sailing dream. Listening to our verbal hand-wringing about the financial side of cruising, our mentor-friend put it bluntly: "Listen, guys, there are not many people who are wealthy enough to own a sound cruising boat in the forty-foot range and own real estate, especially in Vancouver and especially at your age. You have to ask yourselves if you want to work that hard. You have to ask yourself if you want to wait that long. If you want something bad enough, usually you have to give something up to get it. How bad do you want it? That's the only question here. I think you know what you want. Why don't you go out there and get it?" He did what good mentors do: they pose questions that make you focus. They make you think.

The cruising dream was about travel and adventure, but it was also about simplicity. It was about boiling life down to the essentials and focusing on the most important things. The rewards in the corporate world were always the same – more money to buy more things. But I regarded free time as the biggest reward, the greatest luxury. The way I saw it, there was always one more dollar you could be making, but you never got to make another minute.

For us, it was an easy decision. We put our house on the market and listed *Tethys* with a broker while we searched for a well-built offshore sailboat.

We found her in Vancouver in the spring of 1996. She'd been called *Romanichel* by her first owner, meaning gypsy or bohemian. Her second owner repainted her black hull a dark green. He was a horse veterinarian, who told us that because of his green farmer's jacket, and his green boots and gloves, and because he'd appear at the racetrack to tend to injured horses at all hours of the day or night, people began calling him The Green Ghost. When he learned of his nickname, he thought it a good name for his boat, and *Romanichel* became *Green Ghost*.

It was love at first sight and our new life took shape quickly.

We sold the house.

We sold *Tethys*.

And we bought *Green Ghost*.

CHAPTER 4

First Steps in San Francisco

(September 2000)

Nine years after our first sailing lesson and four and a half years after buying *Green Ghost*, we'd thrown off the dock lines and sailed away from Vancouver. After one week of offshore sailing, the first leg of our trip was completed. The crew departed, flying back to their homes in Vancouver and Calgary while we idled at anchor in Sausalito Bay, a short distance but a long journey from the world we'd left behind. It was just the two of us now and that was significant. We had no children.

Our departure was many things: the beginning of an adventure, the realization of a dream, the result of many years of hard work. It was also a turning point. We had wanted to go sailing with children, but several months before we bought *Green Ghost* a ruptured ectopic pregnancy ended our hopes for our first-born child and nearly took my life. At thirty-two years old, I was left with diminished chances for natural conception.

"You're all right and that's the main thing!" sympathy cards and well-wishers gushed when I was released from hospital.

But I was far from all right. I was hopeless. I felt that all my children had died before I had a chance to meet them. I felt that any luck I'd had in life was lost. In a surge of grief and despair we were swept into the world of infertility and struggled in that heartbreaking rut for five years. While our cruising plans slowly took shape, our dream of becoming parents suffered torturous discouragement. A family and a sailing life – in our hearts the two paths were inseparable. Without children, what would become of our dream? For a time, a great emptiness engulfed us. We were paralyzed. Acceptance was a difficult journey. Finally, we made a choice to move forward and find peace in our fate. At thirty-seven, we began to see ourselves differently: not childless, but childfree.

☸

Sometimes finding peace means getting a tattoo from a one-legged First Nations artist named Percy. One might argue that a sailor ought to earn a tattoo and get inked up upon arrival in some faraway port. But for me it was important to get a tattoo before departure. I believed I'd earned it in a different way. The way I saw it, with all my surgical scars, my body had plenty of marks on it that I never wanted. I wanted to choose a mark that meant something positive to me. I wanted to mark the time when I turned away from sadness and moved forward to a happy future.

Before we left Vancouver, I got my tattoo. Inked on my left ankle is a Haida-styled dolphin with two drips of salt water streaming from its tail. With a dolphin at my bow and tears in my wake, I chose to go sailing.

☸

But what about Nik? After his dazzling display as Captain Upchuck on the trip south, I had my doubts about his choices. Alone in San Francisco after our friends departed we had a serious discussion. What I learned was both a relief and an aggravation. As far as I knew, Nik had tried two of the strongest and most commonly used anti-seasickness medications but neither had worked. What I didn't know was that in the pleasant conditions early in the voyage, Nik had stopped taking medication. He was not drugged-up during the gale. Learning this was a great relief to me, but I was angry too. His decision was both covert and careless. I felt strongly that all people on board had a duty to maintain themselves as fully capable crewmembers. After his dreadful seasickness, I'd worried for days about our future sailing plans, not knowing how we could possibly continue. Meanwhile, Nik had quietly come to the conclusion that the next time he went to sea he would stay medicated. I resented that he had rolled the dice and left me to worry in the dark without knowing his decisions.

Staying angry for long wasn't an option. Forty-two feet long and twelve and a half feet wide, less than three hundred square feet – that was our living area. It wasn't new to us to live aboard our boat. What was new was finding ourselves transplanted hundreds of miles from home. We had our long-haired calico cat Tuzo. We had each other. We had *Green Ghost*. Everything else was different. We had no job, no car, no friends, and no family nearby. We had no Internet. We had no phone. In San Francisco an overwhelming sense of "Now what?" descended upon us. We'd taken the big step of letting go, but we didn't really know how you went about doing the cruising thing.

☸

"Oh, you must see the Delta!" locals told us in San Francisco. "It is so beautiful up there!"

While we shopped for boat supplies in the chandleries, we picked the brains of local sailors and took their advice on local cruising. We headed inland to the confluence of the San Joaquin and Sacramento rivers. We found it unusual to be in such shallow water. In British Columbia, most of our sailing had been in deep water; we'd venture into shallower water only for anchoring. But here, cruising up a river basin, we travelled for two days in depths that would be considered decent anchorages in B.C. We proceeded into Grizzly Bay, a place we'd been told was a lovely stop. We pressed on up a narrow channel farther than we should have. With our depth sounder showing one foot of water under our keel and with clouds of mud being churned up by our propeller, we felt sure we would run aground and we chickened out. Grizzly Bay was not for us.

This was a problem because sundown was near and we had no backup plan. The winds had been building all day and by late in the afternoon they were blasting inland at fifteen knots. We looked at the chart and decided we would go upriver to Honker Bay where we could seek some refuge from the wind behind a couple of islands.

Nautical charts provide a great deal of information about the water but very little information about the land. We were used to reading nautical charts for B.C. where an island was actual land. We didn't understand that in the Delta area, islands were barely land at all. Islands shown on the charts were mounds of mud just high enough above the water's surface to grow grass. Locals called them "toolies" – they were not islands at all and they offered no protection from the building winds.

Our options were diminishing as quickly as the light. We had no other choice but to anchor in Honker Bay behind the toolies fully exposed to the building wind. It was embarrassing. We looked like total novices anchoring in this place that was not an anchorage at all.

The wind built to twenty-five knots by the time darkness fell and a horrific chop developed. *Green Ghost* was bucking so dreadfully at anchor that neither one of us could bear to sleep in the bow so we curled up separately on the settee benches. It was back to the sea berths again.

We fully expected that our anchor would drag that night but we weren't too worried about it. There was a mud bottom and a wide expanse of gently shoaling water astern. There wasn't another boat for miles. In this uncomfortable spot, that was hardly a surprise. Nik got up and checked our position every couple of hours through the night. We did drag, over one hundred feet. With our heavy ground tackle, an oversized sixty-five-pound plow type anchor on an all chain rode, *Green Ghost* had never dragged anchor before. It wasn't until morning that we saw a nearby hilltop lined with massive power-generating windmills.

We made a mental note for future reference: anchoring within clear view of a wind farm (and completely unprotected from the wind) was not a good idea.

Our second day up the Delta got us safely into Potato Slough where we dropped the hook and spent nine days peacefully at anchor in a very un-peopled part of the world. As for the boast that the Delta was beautiful I wasn't so sure. The place was flat. From the deck of our boat we looked out at the levees that surrounded the below-water-level farmers' fields. In the near view, there were piles of dirt. In the distance, there were radio towers and power lines. Beautiful B.C. with its snowy peaks and deep fjords had spoiled us.

At Potato Slough a man in his mid-sixties came alongside in a small open Boston Whaler.

"Hi, I'm Chris!" he said.

We introduced ourselves and a lengthy conversation ensued. His forty-three-foot sailboat was tied up in a marina not far away. He explained to us that he had cruised for ten years with his wife; they had circumnavigated the Pacific and returned home to San Francisco. His wife had recently passed away and he was finding it difficult to manage as a single hander. Standing in his tender and hanging onto the toe rail of our boat, he asked about our plans.

"We're going to cross the Pacific to Australia," we told him.

"But you're so young," he replied. "I can't figure out how you've done it. How can you afford this boat, this trip, at your age?"

We explained that we'd sold our house to buy the boat, that we had enough money to get to Australia, and after that we didn't really know what would happen, but we believed we would figure it out when we got there.

"Ah, retirement by installment then! Sounds like a good plan because you're the perfect age for this," he said. "It's physical – it gets harder as you get older. But you're still young and strong. I can't believe you've figured it out at your age, but you have. You're going to have the most fantastic time!"

The following morning, he was back and after another lengthy conversation he asked Nik to help him bring his sailboat out of the nearby marina and sail it up to Potato Slough so that he could anchor nearby. We were taken aback. Both Nik and I tend to be slightly introverted and reticent around newcomers, letting our Canadian reserve rule us a little too readily. We both found it a bit strange that this complete stranger wanted to take Nik away in his Boston Whaler to points unknown, leaving me behind, alone on *Green Ghost*. Somewhat reluctantly Nik agreed. The trip took much longer than I expected and for a time I wondered if I would ever see my husband again. But all went well and soon Chris was anchored beside us in Potato Slough.

The next day, in thanks for Nik's help, Chris invited us to his boat for coffee. The day after he was back alongside *Green Ghost* in his tender, inviting himself aboard for the return favour. We chatted daily for a week. He gave us what he called "constructive criticisms" about our gear and our plans. We gave him company.

We were slow learners, but after nine days in the Delta, Chris had educated us on the social norms of the cruising life. You don't leave someone standing in their tender clinging to the toe rail alongside your boat. "You invite them in out of the sun," he told us. "You offer them a drink."

"You'll be asked for assistance and you'll give it because sooner or later you'll need assistance yourself," he told us. "It doesn't matter if you've never met the person before in your life." Chris pointed out that from this point forward everyone we met would be a stranger, so it was up to us to make that stranger a friend. He told us we would find the cruising community fantastic, and that we would form bonds out there on the water that would last the rest of our lives. We will always remember him. He is the first new friend we made.

We enjoyed the hot weather, wallowing lazily in the gentle current of the fresh water river. We jumped in and floated with the life rings, idle in the cooling water. We zipped about in the dinghy clad only in bathing suits, not minding the spray in the heat. We toured the sloughs and investigated the marinas. We ate ice cream. We got tanned.

By the end of our week in the Delta we'd begun to see the beauty in the stand of eucalyptus trees that grew on the toolie beside our anchorage. We were charmed by the nightly symphony of frogs and crickets and bewitched by the resident owl gently hoo-hoo-hooing at dawn. The Delta had grown on us.

After Chris's tutelage, we'd learned that it was okay to dinghy up to another boat, introduce ourselves, and practically invite ourselves on board. With this knowledge, back in Sausalito we made more new friends. When a couple of American cruisers came by and invited us over to play board games one night we were not surprised, though we felt we had to decline as I was in the middle of making cinnamon buns and they were due to go into the oven exactly at the hour of invitation. "We'll put our oven on and you can bake them at our place while we play," they said. So we accepted their invitation and enjoyed a very social evening and freshly baked cinnamon buns when the gaming was done.

After a month in the San Francisco Bay area we were starting to get the hang of the cruising life, but it was time for us to move on. It was time to head out on our own, harbour-hopping southbound down the California coast. We hoped to be in Mexico for Christmas.

CHAPTER 5

California Cruising

(September – December 2000)

I'd had some romantic notions of California cruising. I'd imagined we'd glide across the liquid surface of this remarkable planet, resting in each peaceful bay, wandering through every quaint harbour town on our route. In reality, by the day's end, the only exploring we did was through binoculars. After a half-hearted look at the shoreline we'd retire below, too exhausted from sailing to do anything more. On our first day out of San Francisco, we made Half Moon Bay where we anchored for the night but didn't go ashore. Next up was Santa Cruz and we didn't set foot there either. We were boat-bound.

It wasn't that we didn't want to get off the boat – it was just that we were cheap and lazy. Tying up to a dock at a marina costs money. Back then, it was US$20 or more for one night in a slip. Twenty dollars isn't much, but anchoring is free and to the cost-conscious cruiser, free is always better. But there is a different cost to free. If you anchor out, the only way to get ashore is by dinghy.

Green Ghost is a cutter rigged sloop, which means she has a single mast and two foresails: a genoa and a staysail. Our staysail had a self-tacking boom that took up a great deal of space on our foredeck, the very place to store a dinghy. If we'd purchased a tiny dinghy it might have fit on the bow. But we didn't have a tiny dinghy – we had a huge one.

Everything we'd read during the yearning years told us that when cruising, you needed a good dinghy. It was the cruising equivalent to a car and would be used to haul everything: groceries, laundry, water, fuel, bicycles, and people. Buy the biggest dinghy you can they said. So we did and we didn't regret it.

We loved our eleven-foot Avon inflatable with a hard-bottomed roll-up floor. The upside was that with a fifteen horsepower outboard, we could plane with four adults on board. The downside was that we had to partially deflate it to stow it on the foredeck every time we went to sea. There was some work involved before every dinghy launch and this frustrated Nik.

When we pulled into an anchorage, in order to use our "car" we'd have to go through a twenty-minute routine of preparation. The dinghy had to be untied, pumped up, then hoisted off the deck using a halyard and the electric winch (windlass) on the bow. Once in the water, it was pulled aft to where the outboard engine was stowed on the stern rail. The outboard was then lowered onto the dinghy transom using another lift/winch set-up. Then the dinghy was kitted out with the gas tank, the fuel line, the seats, the oars, and the life jackets, then filled with any other items we wanted to take ashore. There was no way around it: launching the dinghy was a process. To give it a land-based perspective, it is like having to change a tire on your car every time you want to go for a drive. It was no wonder that after a long day on the water, when the anchor went down with the sun, when we were cold and tired and hungry, putting the dinghy in the water was the last thing we wanted to do.

Unlike the quiet coves we'd come to love in B.C., the anchorages on the California coast were open roadsteads subject to the heaving Pacific. It was hard to relax when being at anchor felt so much like being at sea.

We noticed some odd aches and pains developing. It was less from the sailing itself, the grinding of winches and the hauling up of sails, and more the result of being at sea and the continual hanging on tight in a seaway. And it wasn't just exercise we got during the day; we flexed through the night as well. At times, I woke to find that my legs were swinging back and forth across the sheets with each swell that passed under the hull. My neck was stiff from gripping the pillow, my face fatigued from teeth-clenching, and my arms sore from supporting my body on its side, the way I've always liked to sleep. The free and easy life of the cruising sailor was proving to be a tense affair in ways we never expected.

I was wound up about food as well. Since provisioning in Vancouver, where I'd gone wild filling *Green Ghost* with groceries, I'd been unable to cut back on my obsession for lockers filled with food. Each time I was in a grocery store I stocked up as if I was expecting a nuclear war. If I used one can of tomatoes I would feel compelled to buy four more cans, one as a replacement and three others, just in case. Nik didn't think much of my squirrelling behaviour. Now that we were cruising, every item we bought had to be carried home on our backs.

It wasn't only me. Captain Nik was amassing his share of stuff too. The tendency to stockpile is a natural one for cruisers and it goes well beyond the pantry. Bits and bobs and scraps and spare parts are jammed into the lockers of cruising boats worldwide. It's a problem we have. What if I need this? What if I run out of that? What if I can't get another one? We think these thoughts quite desperately, as though our very lives might depend upon them, and they might. So we keep that last can of whatever it is, that last little bit of anything and we stuff it away in a special place, just in case. This leads to another odd little commonality among cruisers: we can't find anything.

A good offshore boat is designed for efficient use of space and *Green Ghost* has plenty of storage. Every inch of space is used to the utmost advantage. There is a place to put everything and if only everything was put in its place there wouldn't be any trouble. But it took me a while to figure this out.

Making a simple meal like spaghetti was like playing a game of *Concentration*. Meat was stored at the bottom of the freezer, the coldest spot. Cans (tomatoes) and other heavy items were stored in lockers down low, the better for stability. Glass items (tomato sauce) were either in a bin or on a shelf, but never on a shelf that did not have a lipped edge for fear they might fly out in a seaway. Dried goods (pasta and spices) were stored high to stay dry. Wine bottles were stuffed into cheap tube socks – black socks for red wine, white socks for white – and nestled into bins in the bilge.

To keep it all straight, I made an Excel spreadsheet detailing the quantity and location of every grocery item I had on board. I could sort my list by locker or by food type and find what I was looking for fairly quickly. Soon, I had the food inventory under control.

Underwear inventory was another thing. We needed a lot of underwear. This had nothing to do with moments of fear. It was just that laundry was another one of the chores that couldn't be done with ease. With both water and power in limited supply, laundry was done ashore. We tended to put it off for weeks, but once we were out of clean undies, we had to step up to the task.

Back in Vancouver when we'd first moved out of our house and onto *Green Ghost* I'd had a hard time adjusting to doing my laundry in a public laundromat. Getting it done was a biweekly affair that took up most of a Saturday morning. On one occasion a fellow live-aboard sailor came into the launderette while we were tediously pairing socks at the folding table.

"You guys actually do your own laundry?" she asked. "Why don't you drop it off? Get them to do it for you. It's not that expensive."

"I don't want some stranger handling my undies," was my prissy reply.

"Ha! My weekend is too precious," she said. "They can sniff my undies for all I care!"

I laughed out loud at her bawdy response, thinking how liberating it was to care less about things that didn't matter. Right then and there I decided I had to be more like her. I had to lighten up.

I'd become uninhibited about airing our dirty laundry, but the sheer volume of it was always daunting. Without a car, moving the mountain of laundry and our two folding bicycles ashore in the dinghy was a chore in itself. Three weeks of laundry barely fit on our bikes and on our backs. Like a couple of pack mules, we'd set out to find the nearest launderette. Getting it home again unsoiled and dry was no small task either.

As we sailed south to Monterey and beyond we were schooled daily in the cruising life. Some things were the same; sleeping, eating, laundry, and taking the garbage out (ashore) were no different than the chores of a land-life, but the physical effort and the time required to complete them was.

Our minds, on the other hand, were free. There were no more commuting stresses or long days at the office. We were detached from the rivalry for promotion, released from the tedium of meetings, and free from the pressures of work, but our heads were far from empty. Watching the weather had become a constant in our lives. Monitoring the various systems on the boat was ongoing. Planning our next move was discussed every night.

⚓

"How long is your stay in California?" we were asked on shore when our Canadian accents were revealed in conversation with the locals.

When we answered, "Well, that depends ..." we usually ended up explaining our situation and giving details about our trip. This often led to curious looks and probing questions.

"What does your husband do?" was a question that often came up when I was being addressed individually.

It took me aback every time. I felt fully engaged as an equal partner in our new cruising life and I was always surprised to realize that that was not how I was seen by others.

Most cruising sailors are retired, and as Chris had fairly pointed out, we looked young for the part. I understood that now. But it hadn't occurred to me that I looked like I didn't have a part at all. By leaving my high heels, business suits, and briefcase behind and donning deck shoes, shorts, and a backpack my image had been transformed. No longer a contributing member of society, in California, it was assumed I was not a contributor to much at all. Who I was or what I did had already vanished. My husband was obviously successful, and now he was the captain, that was something at least. But me? I was perceived as a tag-along, a person who was living a life provided by "what my husband does." When I quit work to go cruising, it hadn't occurred to me how quickly I'd be erased. I began to detect an increasing uncertainty in who I was even as I experienced an increasing certainty in what I was doing,

We met other cruising sailors along the way. Their questions were much easier. Among the cruising fleet, everyone knew who you were. Obviously, you were a long-distance sailor and that counted. What you'd done in your life before cruising didn't seem to matter one whit. Among cruisers, after answering the inevitable "What boat are you on?" and an introduction of first names, conversations continued on one of these three topics: your location – where had you come from and where were you going; the weather – how did it look; your boat – what was broken or about to break? On the last two topics, the skippers could talk for hours.

⚓

From Monterey, we hoped for good weather to do our first overnighter with just the two of us on board. We planned to round Point Conception and make our way to the northern Channel Islands.

Point Conception is the inflection between the north-south trending northern California coast and the east-west trending southern California coastline. This geographic turning point promises accelerated winds and rough seas. The Pilot Book for the area refers to Conception as the "Cape Horn of the Pacific," and from all the reading we'd done, we'd developed a healthy respect for it.

Eighteen hours out of Monterey we found ourselves on a windless sea in a heavy fog. The idea of motoring all day around the Point and crossing the busy shipping lanes in a dense fog was unappealing. We were tired and decided to rest in the next port, near San Luis Obispo.

Port San Luis was alive with wildlife. Sitting on our deck at anchor was like having a front row seat at Marineland, only better. Humpback whales gracefully circled the anchorage, diving, surfacing, and snorting their salty breath into the air. Among them pelicans fell from the sky like bombs, surprising their underwater prey. Pacific white-sided dolphins capered about while the seals performed synchronized swimming routines. Chasing prey or running from it, they appeared dolphin-like as they repeatedly leaped in unison in elegant arcs above the surface. It was a remarkable place.

And it was a good thing that it was remarkable because our plan to stop for a night became a week of waiting for bad weather to abate. The foggy flat calm that we'd chosen to forgo turned into a spell of wicked weather that we were not willing to test. We'd ducked into Port San Luis due to a lack of wind and we got stuck there because of too much of it. When we finally departed, the windless weather pattern was repeating itself. We ended up motoring around the dreaded Point Conception on flat seas – the very thing we'd wanted to avoid a week earlier.

Despite the easy sea conditions, our night passage was not without drama, both wondrous and frightening. It was a moonless night and the slate black sky met the obsidian sea in a barely visible horizon line. Suddenly, bullets of light came streaking through the inky black water straight at our hull. Twinkling torpedoes bore down upon us. Just as we were thinking, My God, what is that? a sound – *phhhhsssstttt!* – burst into the air. A pod of dolphins exhaled loudly beside the cockpit. We nearly jumped out of our skin. The dolphins were enveloped in phosphorescence. Their whole bodies aglow, individually they were Pacific white-sided comets, together, an aurora borealis of the sea. Dolphin sightings were pure joy by day, but this nighttime visitation was even more wondrous. We crept forward and watched them in the pressure wave at the bow. Bathed in glittering light, they were like shooting stars showing us the way.

Other lights were less wondrous and far more concerning. Shipping traffic received more serious attention. On my watch, I saw a freighter leave the coast behind us. The red light on her bow indicated she was presenting her port side to me. For a long while I could not tell if she was headed north up the coast or angling south in my direction. My depth perception was failing me. She was not yet on the radar screen, but as long as I could see the red port light, I knew I was on her port side and all was well. She would be crossing my stern and heading out to sea.

All at once it became obvious that she was moving south when suddenly there were two lights: red and green. That meant only one thing: we were directly in its path. The freighter had turned south and was bearing down upon us. My pulse rate increased as I stared down those lights, my heart beat quickly, red-green, red-green, red-green. When the bow of the behemoth crossed our stern and only the green starboard light of the freighter's bow was visible, relief washed over me. I knew then there was no collision course – she would pass me on my port side. We were okay. That ship looked the size of an aircraft carrier, an immense wall of darkness a mile and a half off, blotting out the lights of the coastline as she passed.

After a stop in each of the northern Channel Islands our plan was to sail south straight to the southern group to bypass the sea of humanity on the mainland, but the winds were against us and we were blown to Oxnard instead. Similarly, we left Oxnard for Catalina Island and found ourselves blown to Marina Del Rey, another unplanned stop. With each little hop that we made, each harbour we entered, each overnighter we did, we gained confidence. By San Diego, Nik and I had settled into a good routine.

But our furry companion Tuzo was not settling in well at all. We had adopted her from the SPCA nine years earlier. She reluctantly took part in all our short coastal sailing trips, and when we moved aboard *Green Ghost* in Vancouver she moved with us. With no children to fuss over, we showered Tuzo with affection. Simply put, we loved her.

We loved her, but we did not want to take her offshore. With a landfall in Australia in our sights we felt that a pet on board was not smart forward thinking. Quarantine issues could be problematic. We'd decided that she should remain in Vancouver but we'd been unable to find her a suitable home, so she came with us.

At anchor, Tuzo was captive. At a dock, she was a flight risk. She was seasick every time we went to sea. On longer voyages she did get her sea legs, but we still felt it was a cruel life for her. The relentless swell, the cramped conditions, and never a chance for a walk – it all seemed very unfair. In San Diego, we made a phone call to a Vancouver friend who had expressed a slight interest earlier. We asked if she would consider taking Tuzo. She agreed and we had a new home for our cat.

Looking back now, I realize how large our next steps loomed in our minds. Bit by bit we were letting go of everything our lives had been, but we had not yet fully released our grip. We were still in the United States, still speaking English, still in a culture we largely understood. Venturing into Mexico meant we were one step closer to heading offshore, westbound across the Pacific. It would be a full year before we reached Australia. We'd severed the umbilical cord to our Vancouver life but we had not severed our ties to the continent. We were still coastal cruising. In San Diego, we both felt the need to touch our home bases one more time. Tuzo was flown to Vancouver. Nik visited his parents vacationing in Florida and I flew to Toronto. This time it was a bigger goodbye. We had no idea when we'd be home again.

CHAPTER 6

Mexico

(December 2000 – January 2001)

In mid-December 2000, we checked out of the U.S.A. and departed for Bahía de Tortugas (Turtle Bay), Mexico. We'd dawdled in San Diego and were feeling left behind as many of the other cruisers we'd met were well ahead of us farther south.

Our route took us 35 NM offshore and 320 NM due south over three days and two nights. For this leg, we both used a proper dosage of seasickness medication and donned a scopolamine patch. While this anti-seasickness drug works well for many people it can produce undesirable side effects. Using the patch, we both experienced a dry pasty palate, morning-mouth twenty-four hours a day. We also experienced disturbing auditory hallucinations. Nik was certain he heard bagpipes in the distance while I heard a far-off radio playing at low volume all the time. Unfortunately, I also developed another side effect, blurred vision, which was a problem because it kept me from reading – a favourite pastime when underway.

Nik also loved to read through his night shifts but by day he was all about fishing. It all started with a book, *The Cruiser's Handbook of Fishing* by Scott Bannerot and Wendy Bannerot. He'd read it cover to cover before our departure and so revered the text that it came to be known as *The Sacred Scrolls* aboard *Green Ghost*. After reading *The Scrolls*, Nik gave up on using the simple term "lures" and began using the term "presentations." He named his fishing rod The Red Devil and began to speak in dramatic ways.

The fishing fixation spread from his reading habits to his shopping habits and to his navigational habits as well. All courses he plotted arced offshore over any bank he could find on the charts.

Southbound we continued 230 NM from Turtle Bay to Bahía Santa Maria and on to Bahía de Magdalena via the Uncle Sam Bank. It was okay with me since fishing was one of the few things that got Nik excited about the longer passages. Besides, I was very interested in landing more fish. A lot of money had been spent on fishing gear. According to my cost-per-pound analysis, we had a C$700 albacore caught off the Oregon coast and two US$35 mackerels caught in California. After the San Diego shopping spree and the Mexican fishing license, we were another US$400 in. As far as I was concerned, we needed to catch more fish to lower our cost per pound.

On our first day out of San Diego, we were boldly flying our spinnaker when The Red Devil shrieked. How does one slow a boat down to land a fish when a lofty spinnaker filled with a steady twelve-knot breeze is billowing out before the bow? We had to douse the spinnaker of course. Nik pulled the tubular sock down to snuff the wind out of the sail. In his haste to rush astern to deal with the catch he didn't secure it. I went to the helm to start the engine to give us some control in the swell. When I looked forward, I saw the spinnaker sock creeping up, up, up, and the spinnaker beginning to fill with wind once again. The unsecured snuffer line was blown high out of reach in the breeze, so the only way to get the spinnaker down was the old-fashioned way, lowering the halyard while rapidly pulling the sail in at the bow. We made a complete mess of it, dropping the sail into the water, driving over it, filling it with water and losing the sheets overboard where they dragged astern, nearly getting caught in our spinning propeller in the process. Meanwhile, the fish was bleeding all over the starboard side deck. In the end, after plenty of yelling, the sail was recovered, the fish was cleaned, and another lesson was learned. Spinnaker flying and fishing don't mix.

On the second day of our trip south we passed over hallowed ground, the Uncle Sam Bank. Nik pulled two salted ten-inch mackerel carcasses from the fridge.

"This is the ultimate bait presentation!" he announced excitedly.

"Okay," I said, disinterested.

"Prepare for the second coming of the Tuna God! These presentations are known to disappear in an explosion of white water stirred by the behemoths of the deep!"

He was into it.

Six yellowfin tuna and several smaller bonito later he stopped fishing because he was tired of reeling them in. We had fish in the freezer for a Christmas feast and plenty to give away to friends.

We pulled into Bahía Santa Maria on our tenth wedding anniversary. We had not been off the boat in eight days and I was antsy to go for a walk on Frisbee Beach, so named for the thousands of large sand dollars lying in the sand. The beachcombing was fantastic but the beach landing was another story. It was our first attempt at taking our dinghy in through the surf. *How hard could it be?* I thought. The dinghy was inflatable, like a rubber duck, so it would float no matter what, right? Besides, we had fold-down wheels on the transom. As soon as we were in shallow water, we could jump out, flip the wheels down, then lift the bow and drag the dinghy up the beach on its two-wheel assembly.

The trouble was that we hadn't stopped to think about the moment the dinghy touches bottom and comes to a stop. We hadn't thought about the waves – they keep coming. They broke over the transom and filled the boat with water. A 130-pound dinghy filled with seawater was pretty hard to drag up on a beach, wheels or no wheels.

The landing was a miserable failure, but the launch was worse. The waves broke over the bow and beat us back against the beach as we took on more and more water. We failed and bailed and tried again. On our second launch attempt a set of waves took the dinghy sideways and beat it hard against the sand bottom, bending a strut on the deployed wheel apparatus. Being a surfer, Nik was disgraced by our discombobulating in the surf and frustrated that we'd broken his home-built dinghy wheels on our first-ever landing. We made it out on our third attempt.

We joined a number of other Canadian cruising boats in Magdalena Bay for Christmas. On Christmas Eve, we rafted up with friends aboard the trimaran, *Paudeen*, and together dinghied over to a party held on one of the larger boats in the bay. Christmas carols and colourful lights made the evening festive and there was no shortage of potluck goodies and cruiser camaraderie among the two dozen sailors on board.

On Christmas morning, we zipped into the town of San Carlos to find a phone to make calls to family celebrating in the traditional way back home. For us, this was no ordinary Christmas. After our long-distance well-wishing, we flew back to the *Ghost* at high speed in the dinghy, passing a gray whale in the channel on our way. The rest of our day was spent in the water and on the beach where another potluck was held. A boisterous beach soccer game followed Christmas lunch. I wasn't sorry to miss a wintery turkey dinner back home. I loved where we were and what we were doing – playing with fellow cruisers in Magdalena Bay was everything I thought a cruising Christmas would be.

As we turned our bow south once again, heading to Cabo San Lucas for New Year's Eve, friends in Mag Bay hailed us on the VHF radio to wish us a boring trip as all good sailing friends do. And that's exactly what we had; with light winds under sail we had a perfectly boring run down to the tip of the Baja.

The ever-changing sea enthralled us. On this low-speed leg to Cabo we had small squid land on the deck in the night. Their limp little bodies left inky stains on the white fibreglass of the coach house. Perhaps they were attracted to the boat's navigation lights and had flung themselves moth-to-a-flame toward the light or perhaps our passing had startled them from the water.

Another day, we found ourselves sailing through sapphire blue water with thousands of tiny scarlet crustaceans floating by. I scooped one up in a bucket for a better look. They were bright red, like miniature Atlantic lobster, only an inch long. We later learned that the locals called them tuna crabs.

With turtles drifting by and whales breaching in the distance, the sightings of wildlife kept us entertained by day and other natural phenomena amused us by night. There were shooting stars so bright I ducked in reflex as they streaked across the sky. There were other more mysterious lights as well.

In the wee hours of a night watch I identified two white lights on the horizon directly off the bow. *A ship!* I thought. But two white lights? It didn't make sense. Through the binoculars I thought I could see a pinkish glow. Perhaps it was a very poorly lit port light. Whatever it was seemed to be coming closer very quickly. It was directly in front of us – a collision course? I stared into the binoculars trying to understand what it was. It was getting larger and brighter. It was barrelling down upon us, and yet white navigation lights signified the stern of a vessel, not the bow. Confused, I contemplated waking Nik. Then the two lights merged into a line of light along the horizon and I realized what it was. The two lights were the tips of a crescent rising on the distant horizon. We were on a collision course with the moon. I was embarrassed at my momentary panic but glad I'd not woken the captain for the "emergency." I never would've lived it down.

Unharmed by the shooting stars and without a scratch from our close call with the moon, we arrived in Cabo ready to take on officialdom. Although we'd been on the Mexican coast for over two weeks, we had not cleared in with Mexican customs. In Cabo, we paid our anchorage fee at the port authority, then went to the bank to pay our tourist visa fee. After that, it was over to the port captain's office to check in to the port, then to the immigration office to check in to the country. There was yet the tonnage fee to pay, so we went back to the bank and then finally back to the port captain's office to complete our check-in by showing all our receipts from the various offices. Some cruisers grumbled loud and long about the paperwork in Mexico. There was no doubt it was a red tape jungle, but we found if we made an outing of it and did the rounds with friends we could figure it out together, share costs if taxis were necessary, and have some fun along the way. We tried to see it as more of a cultural experience and less of an administrative nightmare.

⚓

La Paz, La Paz, everybody said so much about La Paz.

"Forget Cabo," they said, "that horrible tourist town. La Paz is where it's at. La Paz is the real Mexico."

When we voiced concern that La Paz might be too small-town for our boat maintenance needs they insisted, "Don't worry! You can get anything you want in La Paz!" From all this raving about La Paz by seasoned American cruisers we built up our expectations for a cultural experience. What we found was that although Cabo was clogged with sunburned one-week North American tourists, La Paz was equally encumbered. The difference was the La Paz tourist was the well-tanned North American RV camper who stayed for several months or the leathery cruising sailor who stayed for several years. From the numbers of gringos crowded into the local bars, La Paz appeared to us as less of an adventurous frontier and more of an affordable place to drink yourself to death. In expat circles we found it somewhat depressing.

Of course, it's possible that it wasn't the town that was bringing us down. We were dealing with some difficulties on board that probably influenced our judgement. Nik had become concerned about the water pump on the engine. On a routine inspection, he noticed that the pulley was wobbly and he suspected that the bearing was deteriorating.

We might have splurged on a slip at a marina while these repairs were being made but there were none available. The repair, if it could be done, would have to be done at anchor. It is risky to take your engine apart while at anchor for the simple reason that if anything goes wrong in the anchorage – if the wind comes up, if your anchor drags, or if your neighbour's anchor drags – you cannot easily get out of trouble. One might think a sailboat could always sail its way to safety, but that was not the case in La Paz.

Sailboats naturally sit bow to the wind even in a light breeze, but the La Paz anchorage is subject to strong currents and strong winds, often in opposing directions. This wreaks havoc among the anchored boats as different hull designs respond to the wind direction in various ways and different keel designs react individually to the underwater forces. Instead of being neatly aligned in the prevailing wind direction, in La Paz the boats lie helter-skelter, oriented every which way in the close-packed anchorage. They call it the "La Paz Waltz." At times, *Green Ghost* sat stern to a twenty-knot wind, held in that position by the several-knot current.

There were many windy days and the Waltz caused a few boats to collide, resulting in minor hull damage. Often we didn't feel comfortable leaving our boat unattended. When the boats swung erratically we wanted to be on board to fend off collisions with neighbours. I volunteered to stay while Nik went ashore to find a mechanic. This may have seemed brave of me, but the truth is that I'd fallen victim to Montezuma's revenge (the result of a meal out the evening before). Being at home in an engineless boat in an unpredictable anchorage was okay by me – at least I was near my own toilet.

Besides, Nik was better suited to dealing with the water pump. He took it around town on his bicycle and managed with broken Spanish, wild hand gestures, and much laughter to find a shop that could fix it. He was so pleased he was able to remove the pump, have it repaired and reinstalled in less than twenty-four hours. One thing they said about La Paz was true: you *could* get anything repaired there, quickly and inexpensively.

With the water pump fixed we were ready for our next destination, mainland Mexico's west coast. We had Zihuatanejo in our sights.

CHAPTER 7

Crew

(March 2001)

We were getting pretty good at it and we were getting it right. Down the Mexican coast our confidence was building, so much so that we invited family and friends to join us at various ports along the way. We'd cruised the west coast of North America for seven months, facing each challenge presented to us. We saw ourselves as increasingly intrepid even though our insurance company still considered us newbies.

We sailed as far as Zihuatanejo, or "Zee-town" as so many cruisers called it. It was our jumping-off point. From the golden shores of Mexico, we were Australia-bound. Setting out across the Pacific was a huge step for us. It's a great step for every sailor, travelling nearly 2,800 NM from Mexico to the Marquesas (the easternmost island group in French Polynesia); it's the longest offshore leg of many circumnavigations. From this point on, there was no easy way to get home. In my mind, the Pacific crossing was nothing short of an expedition and the first leg was a daunting one.

Our insurance company was firm – if we set out alone, we were uninsurable. They insisted we have a minimum of four people on board and that at least two of the crew be experienced open-ocean sailors. At the time, *Green Ghost* represented a significant portion of our personal wealth. If we suffered a total loss and survived it, we wanted coverage. We wanted to insure the boat, but our desire to mitigate our financial risk was at odds with the way we wanted to live. Having experienced a crowd of five aboard for the one-week trip to San Francisco, the thought of having a four-man crew for many weeks did not appeal to us; twice the provisions, twice the water consumption, twice the personalities, twice the sweaty bodies taking up space, and half the privacy. It was not how we wanted to travel.

Besides, who did we know who had both the time and the money to fly one way to Mexico, sail for a month, and then buy a one-way ticket home from a tiny island in French Polynesia? We weren't in a position to pay crew to join us. Anyone who accompanied us on the journey would have to be willing to pay their own way.

We put the word out to would-be offshore sailors while simultaneously looking for a new underwriter, one that would trust our sailing skills. Our Vancouver mentor and friend put his hand up. Retired, he had both the time and the budget to join us. He wrote to say that if we needed another crewman for insurance purposes, he was up for the passage. Meanwhile our broker found us coverage for a two-man crew. We didn't need another body after all, but having incited our friend to join us, we did not want to revoke the invitation. If he had a passionate desire to join us for a unique opportunity, our offer remained open. But we didn't want to take on crew who thought they were doing us a favour. We didn't want one whit of obligation to influence his decision. We made a long-distance phone call from Mexico to explain the situation and to give him an easy out. His commitment was firm. He was in. *Green Ghost* was getting a crewman.

To make it easy for our friend to find us, we made a booking at a local marina. In a slip for three days we got some chores done. I went to work with the garden hose on deck, desalting *Green Ghost* with the first endless supply of fresh water that we'd had in two months. We erected the sun awning to combat the heat but it made little difference to our crewman. Just arrived from Canada, pale-skinned and streaming with sweat, he took a pair of scissors to his jeans and the electric shears to his full head of thick hair within hours of his arrival.

Despite all the long-term preparations made before our departure from Vancouver, there was plenty to do in Zihuatanejo. On foot, by bicycle, or by bus we made daily forays into town to search for parts and provisions, to run errands, and, on occasion, to have a little fun. We used our best sleuthing skills to find plumbing hose, a dinghy anchor, funnels, spark plugs, engine oil, padlocks, and fabric for flags. I was sure it would be nearly impossible to find electrical contact cleaner at the hardware store and truly impossible to ask for it. But when it came to language challenges Nik was always up for it, summoning the few words he remembered from our Vancouver Spanish courses, improvising with French, or tossing out a fictitious word instead.

"Leave it to me," Nik said, moving toward the middle-aged man at the counter. "Donde esta electrico ppfssst ppfssst?" he said with confidence.

In return, he got a huge smile, a "Si, señor," and a spray can of exactly what he wanted.

"See? My Spanish works like a peach!" Nik boasted.

"Like a charm," I said.

"What?"

"Works like a charm. Everything is peachy or something works like a charm, but you can't say something works like a peach – that doesn't make sense."

"Whatever," he said. "I got the contact cleaner, didn't I?"

At the marina, we carried on with the chores. The latch on the port-side cupboard was fixed, the oil filters were replaced, and the knot meter was pulled and cleaned. The rig was inspected and tuned; the gas-powered emergency bilge pump was tested; the gas tanks and water tanks were chemically treated. The dinghy was scrubbed of barnacles, and the bicycles and surfboard were stowed. Meanwhile, I was cooking, filling the freezer with pre-made meals for the crossing. My feet became so swollen from standing in the heat I felt like I was walking on gel-pad shoe liners. The business of getting ready was so tiring that I felt no apprehension about departure. Just the opposite was true: I couldn't wait to go to sea, to have nothing to do but eat, sleep, and watch.

Back at anchor, we were down to the last few errands before departure: buying food and fuel and making phone calls home. Of the three items, food was by far my greatest worry. In remote circumstances, where the daily demands are high, entertainment scarce, and pleasures few, there better be some good grub on the table. If an army marches on its stomach, so does a mining bush camp (as we'd already learned), and so does a ship at sea, particularly a short-handed crew on a small yacht. Of the small prizes we had to look forward to – food, sleep, comfort, and the entertainment of the voyage itself – food was the only thing we could control. I didn't want to get it wrong, but I didn't want the sole responsibility for getting it right either.

We agreed that breakfasts and lunches would be an each-man-for-himself affair. For the evening meal, we would eat together. But this was an expedition, not a dinner party, and I saw myself as a crewmember just like everyone else. So when our crewman suggested that we take turns preparing supper, I was pleased, happy for the team approach to galley duties.

We expected a twenty-three-day crossing, but to be safe we provisioned for thirty days. I'd made and frozen a dozen dinners already, so we needed another eighteen dinners planned out. Thinking up eighteen more meals was overwhelming but with the workload divided, thinking up six dinners each was not so bad. Thinking up only two meals to serve each one three times should have been easy.

For our final provisioning run we went on a three-hour grocery shop at the local Comercial Mexicana, tediously pushing two carts up one aisle and down the next at a slow crawl. I reminded the guys to think about the items that were needed for their six dinners and to make no assumptions about what was already on board. If you wanted to eat it in the next month, you had to put it in the cart.

Provisioning was challenging in part because the volume of food we needed was astounding and in part because we had to think of everything. Imagine doing that at home, purchasing enough inventory to be completely self-sufficient for an entire month: no run to the corner store when you've got a sudden urge for chocolate, no drop in at the supermarket when you're out of milk, no borrowing an egg from your neighbour.

And it wasn't just meals to contend with. What about snacks? Nik liked eating ramen noodles on his night shift. If he wanted to be sure there was one package available to him every night of the crossing he needed to put two dozen packages in the cart. If our crewman enjoyed the same snack, another two dozen packages were required. If I wanted one on occasion I needed to grab a dozen more. Sixty packages of ramen noodles seemed absurd, but I did the math and added more to the pile.

"What are you going to make with that?" I asked, seeing soup cans being pulled from the shelf.

"You can make almost anything as long as you have cream of mushroom soup," our crewman answered.

"Yeah, but if *all* you have is cream of mushroom soup, then that's *all* you're having," I pointed out, wondering about the other ingredients for his meal plan.

I could see that the concept of shared responsibilities was headed for failure. If you weren't in the habit of doing it, planning out every ingredient required for any given meal was no small task. On the grocery run, I sensed a subtle shift in the "team approach" – when it came to galley duties, it seemed the finer details were on me. Frustrated, I made a second sweep through the store to find the missing ingredients that had been overlooked on the first pass.

I had a flashback to childhood vacations – an image of my mother packing for a trip to the family cottage on Georgian Bay.

"Two weeks at the cottage," she'd say, perspiring in the summer heat, exasperated by what didn't fit into the squeaky Styrofoam cooler. "It's a holiday for everyone but Mom."

Now, I understood her.

Back on board I packed away the mountain of inventory, taking notes on my spreadsheet as I went. Canned corn?

Port side, midship cupboard behind the settee. Rice? Starboard side, aft cupboard, behind the settee. Olive oil? Starboard side, lower shelf. I printed the list, alphabetically sorted, so we all had equal access to the food. I didn't want to be woken up to be asked where things were each time someone was hungry.

There were more challenges to our joint undertaking. Every boat has its eccentricities. As pedantic as it may sound, there are best practices, if you will – certain ways to do everything. The fridge door needed a little bit of a slam; the freezer lid, although square, fit only one way. You had to watch not to bump your head in certain places. If you turned on the tap just right, you'd get a nice slow flow of water, wasting little. There were strict rules for the galley: never put the produce on the top shelf of the fridge. Never put a glass container there either. The beer will freeze if it touches the refrigeration plate; so will the eggs. Pack the cheese and butter there instead. If you wanted a shower, the switch for the sump pump was over here. If you wanted a coffee, the switch for the propane solenoid was over there. If you wanted toasted bread, you had to fry it because the toaster used too much power. If you wanted fresh air, one sliding porthole worked and one didn't – it was stuck closed, and we didn't know why.

Our friend understood a boat's eccentricities, but of course he was used to his own. I wondered if the odd glitches we tolerated aboard *Green Ghost* would irritate him. The stuck porthole didn't bother us. We'd tried several times to fix it but nothing we tried had worked. Stuck closed really didn't matter; on the other hand, broken open did. Worried that further efforts might break the glass or damage the frame, we left the porthole stuck shut. But what we saw as a reasonable decision, our friend might have seen as maintenance apathy.

But now we were off, filled up with food, water, and diesel. The paperwork cleared with the officials, we were ready to go. In the late afternoon of the Fool's Day, 2001, we departed from Zihuatanejo Bay, the mighty Pacific before us. Our tensions and misgivings were hidden behind farewell smiles as we waved goodbye to fellow sailors in the anchorage. We had nearly 2,800 NM of open ocean ahead, at least three weeks at sea. Our petty grievances and irritants were carefully stowed away. We thought we could keep them locked up for the crossing, but we were wrong. The sea has a way of shaking everything loose.

CHAPTER 8

The Long Crossing

(April 2001)

The crossing didn't start well.

As we departed the coast I made up the bunks. Our crew-man had settled in the aft cabin. Nik and I were to sleep in the sea berths in the main salon. There would be no hot bunking. In the tropical heat, with limited water for personal hygiene, thank goodness, we didn't have to share. But, on the first night at sea, when I climbed into bed I found I was sharing anyway. There was a cockroach between my sheets. In our four months in Mexico we'd been vigilant about keeping our boat insect-free, but there must have been a slip-up during the final harried days. Bug-free on departure, we hadn't thought to purchase pesticides. We were on our way to French Polynesia in a floating roach motel.

We'd been watching the weather for weeks, listening to discussions among the fleet of Pacific crossers, contemplating good weather windows for departure. Gun-shy from the hammering we'd taken off the Oregon coast, we chose to leave when there was no bad weather on the horizon. Again, our inexperience was showing: we left with no weather at all.

Wind. A sailboat needs wind. Sure, you can run your engine and motor along, but on any long passage fuel conservation is always on your mind. We didn't dare to motor-sail so early in the voyage. We used the engine sparingly. For an hour or more each day, we ran the engine at low rpm only to charge our batteries. The rest of the time, because of the very light winds, we made slow progress, racking up only 75 NM daily. We knew we were in for a long haul.

We agreed on three-hour watches, which meant there were eight watch periods in twenty-four hours. With three people on board, we cycled through a schedule that repeated every three days. With this system, each one of us sampled the romance of the sunset hour, the tedium of the graveyard shift, and the wonder of dawn. Our watch system also worked perfectly for the agreed-upon galley duties: every three days you found yourself off watch between three and six p.m., free to cook the evening meal.

The first few days at sea are always the hardest. Our slow progress tormented us. We were endlessly tweaking the sails trying to find another fraction of a knot of speed. At the rate we were going, it would be a thirty-seven-day trip, an unbearable thought. I worried about the provisions. I lay awake at night thinking, Pasta! Why didn't I buy more pasta?

Our crewman had some suggestions to increase our speed. While a captain needn't endorse an idea simply to flatter the crew, Nik sensed the rising frustration and agreed to try the proposed sail changes, even though he was quite certain they wouldn't work. We executed the proposals one by one, show-ing by demonstration the limitations we already knew. At over seventeen tons, *Green Ghost* wasn't a light-air boat. In the end, after many changes to the sails, we solved nothing, achieving no greater speed, only greater frustrations all around.

"My boat has limitations, but I love it anyway," the captain defended himself.

Chastened, the crewman made a stinging comeback.

"Well, I'd never buy a boat that can't do better than that."

Boat insults. Ouch. You might as well tell a man that his dog bites and his children are ugly. Short words were starting to fly. Though none of us had acknowledged it, there'd been a shift, perhaps even a role reversal, in our mentor-mentee rela-tionship and it wasn't sitting well. After only four days at sea, I suddenly understood the necessity of rank aboard a boat. It is not a democracy. In the years since we'd owned *Green Ghost*, we'd become kings of our own castle.

   Toward the end of our first week at sea we had a problem
with our roller furling. Nik came off shift before sunup and told
me he'd been unable to furl the genoa, but there was no immediate danger. It would be a problem only if the wind picked
up. Nik wanted to wait until full daylight to take a close look
at it, but in the meantime he wanted to get some rest. When I
handed the watch over to our crewman at nine a.m., I relayed
the information that the genoa roller furling was jammed and
that Nik would address it when he came on shift well-rested at
noon. Our crewman went forward to inspect the apparatus at
the bow then came back to the cockpit.

   "Jenn, I can see what's wrong up there. The line is jammed
and I think I could just pop it out with a screwdriver ..."

   "I don't know – Nik asked us to wait. Let's leave it and let
him get some sleep," I suggested.

   The chatter woke up the captain. In his zest to address
the problem, our friend took Nik's semi-consciousness as an
invitation for further discussion. A foggy-headed Nik mumbled
agreement to his plan.

   As our crewman went forward tool in hand, Nik bolted upright in his bunk and turned to speak to me in the cockpit.

   "I just remembered, sometimes the furling drum jams when
the halyard tension is wrong. Just wait on the fix. It might just
be the halyard."

   But it was too late. Our crewman returned aft with a handful of broken parts and the news that ball bearings were rolling
around on the foredeck. The captain spoke harshly.

   "If you think I broke it, I didn't," our crewman responded,
backpedalling. "That roller furling has not been properly main-
tained," he said, insinuating that poor maintenance on Nik's
part had brought about this equipment failure.

   I was taken aback that our crewman could not see the
situation from Nik's point of view. What if Nik had gone forward on his boat and come back with a handful of parts? And
here, about 400 NM from the Mexican coastline and 2,400
NM from our destination, it was particularly poorly received.

The roller furling bearing failure was not something we could repair at sea.

It was not a good day. Trust was trampled. Morale took a beating. The captain was angry, the crewman was in the doghouse. There was some permanent damage done to the on-board relationships and we were not even one week in.

Thankfully we soon picked up some consistent wind that ended our light-air frustrations. With the higher winds and larg-er waves all tasks on board became more difficult. The waking hours were spent hanging on for the ride. The constant en-gagement with the environment left us bone-tired, but in the relentless motion, we slept less soundly. Nobody wanted to do anything extra. Through the day the deep galley sinks became stacked with dirty dishes from breakfasts, lunches, and snacks. They were piled so high that they began launching themselves across the cabin in the swell. When a bowl went flying, it sug-gested to me that it was time to get the lot washed, dried, and put away. The guys were blind to the pile. Rather than do the dishes, dirty projectiles were picked up off the floor and wedged back in the sink a little more snugly. I had the lowest tolerance for mess and found myself doing most of the washing up. It was a petty irritation, but in that environment of heat and fatigue, the very kind that festers and grows.

When booby birds circled overhead, we knew we were clos-ing in on Clipperton. Nik had been hell-bent to sail by Clipperton Atoll, 671 NM from Mexico and one of the most remote places on earth. He had tuna on the brain.

At first sight, it appeared to be nothing more than a couple of coconut palm groves growing straight up out of the ocean. The ring reef itself has negligible topography, being only about six feet above sea level around most of its seven-and-a-half-mile circumference. The barren volcanic Clipperton Rock juts nearly one hundred feet out of the water at its southeast end. A couple of wrecks on the beach stood like monuments to the dead.

It was both thrilling and terrifying to close in on Clipperton. Land beckons you with thoughts of swinging gently at anchor, folded into the arms of a safe harbour for a good night's rest. But when the land is a dangerous unprotected shoreline, at best it's a menacing obstacle and at worst a potential graveyard. Land is a seductive temptress, offering a comfortable bed for a night of sweet dreaming or a nightmarishly wicked end. Other sailors we knew had anchored off the sheltered side of the atoll in uncommonly calm conditions. Nik was keen to try the same, but first, some fishing.

He put his lures in the water as we closed the distance in the late afternoon. The Red Devil soon shrieked and we were in for a battle. The sails came down, the engine went on, and we chased his prey around in circles for more than half an hour. The catch was huge – at least a sixty-pounder – the largest yellowfin tuna Nik had ever caught. We were not going to be short of food.

We swung in close to shore on the leeward side of the atoll. The depth sounder, having not touched bottom in a week, started flashing readings of two hundred feet and less as we approached. Even on the leeward side of the island, the swell was notable. The steep bottom was not ideal for anchoring – this was no place to stop for a rest.

I turned the bow back out to sea. In a very short distance, the bottom no longer sounded due to the steep slope of the submarine volcanic cone. For some reason, our crewman believed that the on-again/off-again readings indicated that the depth sounder wasn't working at all.

With the sun low on the horizon we left Clipperton in our wake and sailed on.

Southwest of Clipperton conditions changed yet again. We passed through the Intertropical Convergence Zone (ITCZ, the doldrums). We were fortunate to get through this band of windless, rolly conditions quite quickly and soon found ourselves in consistently strong trade winds. The downside to the increased wind was the increased sea state. The seas built up, becoming the large heaving Oregon Coast sort of monsters we so loathed.

The relentless motion wore us down. None of us felt well,

each with a touch of motion sickness and considerable fatigue. We craved comforts. We all wanted to sit and be handed a plate full of good food. For captain and crewman this was a possibility. For me, not so much. As the days wore on, the dinner duties began to disintegrate. I was on for an extra meal when the fishing took place. I was asked to step up when conditions were rough. I was asked what to make when it wasn't my turn. I didn't mind doing some extra work in the galley. I made bread, cookies, cinnamon buns, special treats for morale. I didn't mind tackling a more complicated meal when it was my turn. But I did expect to have dinner handed to me two out of every three nights just like everyone else. I was hungry and tired too. But the more I stepped up in the galley, the more my expedition mates stepped back. I was increasingly put out.

One afternoon I was on watch in the cockpit. Our crewman had gotten up and was preparing a cup of tea before he relieved me of my duty. Holding the kettle, he turned to me with a bewildered look and said, "Jenn, I don't know if I've boiled the kettle or not." For a moment, I couldn't understand what he was asking.

"Touch it," I said. "If it's hot, you've boiled the water already and if it's not you'll need to put it on the stove." This interaction alarmed me. Was he still quite sleepy? Or was something else at play?

In the still boisterous conditions I saw our crewman apply another scopolamine patch. It was his fourth consecutive dosage since leaving Mexico. I was concerned. As well as its intended effects as an anti-nauseant, scopolamine can cause a number of side effects, including mental changes.

"You know, I think you might be experiencing adverse side effects to the patch," I said, voicing my concerns. "On our packets, it says that a single patch can be applied behind one ear and left on for three days, followed by a second patch applied behind the other ear and left on for three days, then it says, 'After six days DISCONTINUE USE.' It says that in three places in capital letters."

He was taken aback by my implication that he could be overdosing and countered that he had never heard of a recommended dosage. His was a different brand. Defiantly he read some of the fine print aloud in an effort to prove me wrong.

"I'm concerned, that's all," I said. "Nobody should be taking a potential overdose of any drug out here, particularly a drug that can cause hallucinations and confusion. I hope you'd be concerned for me if you thought I was overdosing. I figure, not only would it be your right, but it would be your duty to question me."

No doubt my interrogation left our crewman feeling policed and picked on. My interference resolved nothing. His response had not assuaged my concerns and my questions did not dissuade him from continuing to apply a new scopolamine patch every three days for the duration of the crossing.

As the trade winds wavered slightly in direction, we sailed some days gaining more westing and others gaining more southing. When conditions settled, our spirits picked up. When things got boisterous, we were less jovial. Our hands were tired from constant gripping, forever hanging on. We walked around like Sumo wrestlers – feet placed widely apart, knees bent, compensating for the motion with every step. I'd planned to journal my thoughts each day, but I was in a fog. It was one long passage of time; one three-hour period on, followed by a six-hour period off. It didn't matter what day it was or what hour it was, all that mattered was "Am I on?" or "Am I off?" I wrote nothing in my journal.

We were putting up with squall activity. The tropical rains rinsed the salt from the boat and from our bodies but they were a nuisance. If we didn't get the cockpit cushions stowed in time they got drenched. Hatches and portholes not closed in a hurry made for damp beds and, once sealed up against the monsoon rains, the boat became a sweltering sweatbox in the tropical heat. Often a downpour would coincide with the very moment I had the oven on to bake bread, creating a sauna-like atmosphere below decks.

Nik started monologue-ing. His topic was stable platforms. He announced that suburbia wasn't such a bad place after all. He avowed that he was not ever going to cross the Indian Ocean. He dreamed of electric bread makers, air conditioners, Jacuzzi tubs, big-screen TVs, and freighters carting *Green Ghost* back to Vancouver. After listening to his dissertation on how wonderful it would be to be cool and dry, sitting in a car in Vancouver traffic while he sipped his Starbucks coffee, I decided he was slowly going mad.

I was being beaten down in a different way. After years of dreaming and saving and months of preparation, I'd expected to come to a point where we got to do it, to go sailing and enjoy. The getting ready had exhausted us both, that was to be expected. I'd believed that eventually we would emerge from the hectic "get ready" years into the idyllic "go" years. But there had never been a graduation from "get ready" to "go." There was always maintenance to be done or breakages to attend to; there were always system improvements that could be made. It was a tiring state to be in, to be always *getting ready*.

Since the incident with the screwdriver, the genoa roller furling was broken, but we could still use it. Unfurling was relatively easy, but furling the foresail was a difficult task. With the line guard broken, the furling line slipped off the drum and wrapped itself around the base of the forestay. To prevent this, when we wanted to furl the sail, someone had to go forward to manually guide the furling line onto the drum. We were going to have to replace the entire furling system in Tahiti. At a cost of several thousand dollars, it would be a significant hit to the cruising kitty.

It would've been manageable if it was the only thing that broke, but it wasn't. Our telescoping downwind pole had also broken. A rivet had snapped, corroded through by the salty environment. We could no longer use it to pole out the genoa, making the sail less efficient. Without the downwind pole, the foresail repeatedly filled and collapsed as *Green Ghost* tossed in the swell. Our nerves jangled every time we heard the sail crack loudly when the wind filled it or thud against the rig in collapse.

We'd broken the top batten on the mainsail. We'd damaged a dorade box. We lost one fishing hand line overboard. We had three Malmac dishes fly out of a cupboard and shatter on the galley floor. The screen on our binnacle-mounted Garmin GPS took one too many downpours, water got in to it, and it was finished. At one point, I peered over the port side and I was astonished to find that the paint job, commissioned by the boat's second owner, was failing. The beautiful dark green paint was peeling up from the waterline in sheets, exposing grey blotches of undercoat. I was trying hard not to think about it all. I told myself that most of it was superficial, none of it was catastrophic, but taken together there was a significant amount of maintenance and repair to be done. It was going to be expensive.

While the conditions were beating Nik down, and the breakages were wearing on me, our crewman was also suffering. About ten days off the coast of Mexico, second thoughts were creeping in.

"We have a broken roller furling, a broken downwind pole, and the depth sounder isn't working. Are you thinking of turning back?" he asked one morning.

"What?"

"No!"

Our replies overlapped. His question was unfathomable to us. We closed ranks.

"The foresail is annoying but we're making it work. And even if we couldn't use it, we still have a mainsail, a staysail, and a spinnaker. We'll get to French Polynesia, just not as quickly as we'd hoped. As for the downwind pole, it's a bummer that it's broken, but it's not a necessity – some boats don't even have one. And the depth sounder? There's nothing wrong with the depth sounder," Nik countered.

We weren't ten days into the passage, we were ten years in. How could he think that two gear failures would be all it took for us to give up? We were in it for the long haul, he was in it for a month. Who was he to call it quits? We invalidated his concerns and quashed the one-man rebellion in seconds. It wasn't even a discussion. We were not turning back.

The conversation disquieted us, each in our own state of unease. Our flagging fellowship demoralized us and our state of agitation grew in the ever-increasing heat.

Nearing the equator, it was too hot for clothes. We stripped down to the bare essentials: the captain was in surf trunks, the crewman in his jockeys, and I wore a T-shirt and underwear. Bra? Forget about it. Too hot. My shirts were all stained with the slop from mugs of tea filled too high. My hair was a frightening mass of tangled waviness in the moist tropical air. My makeup was 30+ SPF sunscreen piled on the layer that had been plastered on the day before.

Our salt was the consistency of packing snow. Our refrigerator had grown an inch of ice on the plate despite being frost-free on departure. The upholstery was damp, our sheets were soggy, our faces were an oily sweaty slick. We were constantly hungry, constantly scrounging for something to eat and often headachy for lack of food. We were all losing weight. The only contented life forms on board were the cockroaches that were by then plentiful.

In the heat of the lowest latitudes we had a bad night. Nik was woken by the crewman noisily digging around for a snack at three a.m. Later we both jumped from our bunks to batten down hatches when rain came pouring in. It was all hands on deck for a short period when a violent squall overtook the *Ghost*. Caught off guard by the intense wind and heavy rain, we were all shaken and sleepless with adrenaline.

It was not surprising that tempers flared the following day. In no uncertain terms, Nik made it clear that disturbing the off-watch to rummage for snacks was unacceptable. Our crewman responded that he felt unappreciated. At that moment, I was up to my elbows in dirty dishes (again). I'd continued to stew over my unmatched hours in the galley and the word "unappreciated" was like putting out my fire with gasoline.

"Excuse me?" I said sarcastically. "*You* feel unappreciated?" I ranted about all the dishes that had been left in the sink, all the cooking and baking I'd done during my off-watch hours. "You're telling me that *you* feel unappreciated?" I said again. "Give me a break!"

"I never wanted any of that stuff anyway," he threw back.

"Fine then," I retorted, throwing down the gauntlet. "From here on in you can feed yourself."

It was a shameful display on my part. Out of patience, I lost my temper. We were supposed to be a team – the three of us. We were supposed to have mutual respect for one another. Perhaps we'd all failed to communicate our expectations. Maybe our expectations were out of line to begin with. I didn't know. All I knew was that things had gone terribly wrong between us and I didn't know how to fix it.

☸

"Land, ho!" Nik yelled at midday on our twenty-sixth day at sea.

I remained so dejected I didn't even rush outside to see it. When I finally did go on deck, the island of Hiva Oa looked so small it surprised me we'd found it at all. At the same time, it felt like destiny, as though it had been waiting there forever just for us to come upon it on that day.

Atuona Bay was an impressive sight with steeply sloped volcanic terrain, great pinnacles of pyroclastic rock, lush tropical vegetation, and misty peaks enclosing a snug anchorage.

Friends from the sailing vessel *Layla* greeted us. They zipped over in their dinghy and helped us set our stern anchor in the crowded bay. It was thrilling to have made landfall and intoxicating to be talking to other people again. I was so excited that I stood and chatted for some time, bending low over the lifelines to accept congratulations before realizing with some embarrassment that I was still in my offshore uniform, bra-less in a scoop-necked T-shirt and underwear.

Our friends suggested that we join them at a local French restaurant for dinner. We jumped at the chance but our crewman declined the invitation. He felt our crossing had not been a success. Although we implored him to join us, he didn't want to celebrate.

The following morning, we all went ashore. Amid mutterings of "Never again," our crewman literally hugged a tree as he whispered a private prayer to the wind. We suggested he stay with us for a week or two to enjoy the island for a while, but he wasn't interested. He couldn't wait to get away. He unabashedly kissed the release form he received from the Gendarme, the paperwork that officially removed him from our crew list and landed him in French Polynesia. In town, he found a hotel room and bought an airline ticket home. Our long-time friend and wise mentor couldn't stand another minute with us, not even in paradise.

We have not heard from him since.

CHAPTER 9

Two Percent Sheer Terror

(April – June 2001)

We needed a few things upon our arrival in Hiva Oa. You may be thinking a marriage counsellor, a boat broker, and a couple of airline tickets. But no, it wasn't that bad. We needed some time off the boat, some undisturbed sleep, and the company of others.

There was a celebratory buzz amidst the sailors in Atuona Bay. The longest leg of a circumnavigation was behind us and for novice west coast North Americans it was the completion of our first open ocean crossing. Arrival made us members of an unofficial club. There was a special camaraderie among us; we shared a strong sense of accomplishment, a deep satisfaction, and a great sense of relief.

"I'll never feel the same way about flying to an island paradise," Nik mused. "This!" he said as his gaze swept across the anchorage to the palm fringed shore. "We have *earned* this."

Passage stories were on the tips of every tongue. What port did you leave from? How long did it take? How was your crossing? Our twenty-six-day trip had been a long one. Most others had made their passage in three weeks or less. When we told of our three-man crew others envied us the extra rest but when we confessed our team's dysfunction, they knew it hadn't been worth it. No one wants to sacrifice a decade-long friendship for a little extra sleep. We wondered if we hadn't sailed aggressively enough, if our boat was a poor performer, or if we were. Our depressed spirits subdued the exhilaration of arrival and we continued to feel low while our divided hearts mended.

The twenty-five cruising boats in Atuona Bay was the convergence of two fleets: those boats that had departed from the west coast of the United States or Mexico and those that had come through the Panama Canal. In Mexico, the cruising community had been mostly Americans. This group was different. The fleet of boats that had crossed from Panama was an international crowd comprised of east coast North Americans, sailors from the United Kingdom, Europeans, South Africans, and world-weary antipodean circumnavigators sailing their last long leg home. The crowd was different for another reason also. Compared to the demographic of cruisers in Mexico, the offshore cruisers were, on average, younger by ten to fifteen years.

We quickly fell in with a clique of thirty- to forty-something cruisers. Our social schedule was crammed with potluck dinners, days at the beach, games nights, and festive welcome parties for others who arrived in Hiva Oa shortly after us.

We sailed to the nearby island of Tahuata and anchored in Hana Moe Noe Bay, noted in some cruising books as one of the most beautiful anchorages in Polynesia. We spent hours in the water. In the lee of the trade winds we lay floating near shore, lifted up and let down gently in the swell, never having to worry about being caught in a breaker. We went on group snorkelling expeditions, played Frisbee in the surf, and got together for meals in the evening. We enjoyed many happy hours, sipping cocktails in the cockpit watching the sun set over the Pacific, waiting wide-eyed for the green flash.

Nik's goal on Tahuata was to find a tattoo artist. This too he felt he had earned. Fati on Tahuata was reputed to the best tattooist in the Marquesas. He had all the modern tattooing equipment complete with autoclave-sterilized needles. He explained to us in simple French and elaborate hand gestures that tattooing was in his family, in his blood. Two hours and C$60 later, Nik was sporting a circular symbol on his right shoulder that incorporated the Marquesan cross, two warriors, and an artistic representation of sunbeams and flower petals. It wasn't just a tattoo, it was a work of art.

Back at the waterfront, we were shocked to see a commotion aboard *Green Ghost*. While we were away, our staysail had unfurled itself and was flapping wildly in the brisk afternoon wind. By the time we got back on board, the sail had beaten itself up so badly that the aluminum block sewn into the clew of the sail had ripped out. The block lay on the deck still attached to the sheet while the sail flapped furiously in the breeze.

My attempt at repair was unsuccessful. I got a few stitches in but the fabric at the clew of the sail was so thick an industrial machine was needed to complete the task. We left the block partially attached and wrapped the sail around the foil, securing it with a bungee cord. We'd have to see a professional sailmaker in Tahiti.

From Tahuata we sailed windward to the famous Baie des Vierges on the island of Fatu Hiva. The anchorage is one of the most spectacular anywhere in the world. Beyond the head of the deep bay, brown castellated outcrops of pyroclastic rocks rise skyward and verdant, weathered-out dykes form daring razorback ridges. Nestled in this volcanic crown is the tiny village of Hanavave.

Beyond its sheer beauty, Fatu Hiva is known as the wettest, lushest, and most remote island in the Marquesas. With no airport on the island, the only tourists arrived by boat. The Hanavaveans were not shy. They demanded goods, things, stuff of any kind. They would trade fruit for almost anything we had. The little children wanted candy. The women wanted lipsticks, nail polish, jewelry, and perfume. The men wanted CDs, fishing gear, and rum. Some things are the same the world over.

Everywhere in the Marquesas we found the people warm and smiling, helpful and charming. If they saw us walking, they stopped to give us a lift. They were proud and self-sufficient, appreciating our attempts at French and often trying out a little English on us.

We'd planned for a month of island hopping in the Marquesas but after lingering on the islands of Ua Pou and Nuku Hiva, five weeks slipped by. It was time to make the next jump, a four-day sail south and west toward the Tuamotu Archipelago. We weren't sure which one of the seventy-eight islands we would head for. We would wait and see where the wind blew us.

⚓

It is said that offshore sailing is 98 percent boredom and 2 percent sheer terror. We had well-developed trade winds with fifteen to twenty-five knots blowing us steadily toward our next landfall. It was exhilarating sailing. The usual tropical squalls made for a little drama now and then, but for the first thirty-six hours of our trip we enjoyed the 98 percent, all was under control.

On the second night at sea Nik transferred the watch to me just before midnight. A couple of brief rain showers had occurred during his watch, but otherwise he'd had no drama. Too wet to sit in the cockpit, I took up my watch at the navigation table below. There I could monitor the radar screen and sit comfortably dry while I read my book. Every eight minutes I poked my head up to scan the horizon for ships.

Just after midnight I saw a large dark blob marching across the radar screen, and no, it wasn't a cockroach. It was the outline of a rain squall and it was rapidly bearing down upon us. I put my book down. The boat shifted as we heeled over in the already increased winds. I took a moment to put the laptop computer away. As I stowed it, the boat lay over a little more and the rain began. I scampered up on deck as quickly as I could.

Nik awakened, conscious of the increased angle of heel.

"Do you need some help up there?" he shouted from the comfort of his sea berth.

"No, I think it's going to be okay, but I think I better be in the cockpit for this. I might need to hand steer through it – it's probably a little much for the autopilot." I took the helm.

Nik appeared in the cockpit. "You're going to need some help out here," he said. "I didn't tell you that the wind was so light on my watch that I fully unfurled the genoa. You've got a full headsail up there."

I was already finding the boat hard to steer. We had too much sail up and *Green Ghost* was trying to round up into the wind. Nik eased the mainsheet to spill some wind out of the mainsail. He tried to furl the genoa but of course it wouldn't roll in. The wind burst from the night sky, punching us with wicked forty-five knot gusts. I swore as I fought with the helm. By now the rain was blinding. I could barely make out the instruments above the companionway ten feet in front of me. Nik put the spreader lights on to see what was going on forward. As usual, the overhead lights were disorienting and I quickly lost my bearings.

"We've got to get some sail down!" Nik shouted over the roar of the wind. I steered downwind as Nik eased the sheet to allow the sail to billow out in front of us. We hoped we could coax it to furl around the foil without one of us having to go to the bow. There was very little line left on the winch and suddenly the sheet got away on him. The line was ripped from his hands and whipped forward – the sail was now loose and flapping wildly in the wind. The stop knot at the end of the sheet kept it from passing through the block amidships, but it was out of reach of the cockpit, unrecoverable without going out on deck.

Nik was about to dash out to grab at the stop knot to regain control of the sheet and the sail. But he wasn't wearing a harness – he wasn't tied on. I didn't want him out there. The thought of a man overboard in those conditions terrified me. Dramatic thoughts raced through my head and I screamed above the wind, "Do not go out there! I will never find you!"

Annoyed with me for playing the safety officer, Nik reluctantly grabbed a harness, clipped the tether to the jackline, and stepped out onto the deck. My white knuckles on the wheel were all that secured me to the boat. I braced my bare feet against the walls of the cockpit well. Ill-equipped for the weather, in a T-shirt and undies, I was soaking wet, and I shivered in the cold dark downpour.

In the brief time it took Nik to harness up, the unsecured sail and the sheet attached to it had been thrashing in the squall. The sheet had whipped itself into a tangled mass that got wrapped around a nine-foot stainless steel pole. The pole, an inch in diameter, was part of an awning system. It had been stored vertically, neatly tied to the shrouds, never in our way and never catching on anything all the way from Vancouver. Suddenly it was a serious liability. As the foresail continued to flap uncontrollably, the knotted sheet shook the awning pole and that in turn shook our rigging like a dog shakes its prey.

As he went out on deck, Nik heard the rip of sailcloth. He was frantic to stop the violent shaking of our rig. He tried to dislodge the knotted sheet from the pole, but it shuddered just out of his reach, about eight feet off the deck. Unable to grab the sheet, he decided to untie the pole from the shrouds. It wasn't such a good idea because when he did, he found himself holding a nine-foot pole, caught up in the tangled genoa sheet, attached to 640 square feet of sailcloth buffeted by the forty-five-knot squall. It was a terrifying moment. He barely had the strength to hang onto it, but letting go was not an option. To let go would've allowed the pole to whip around freely, to be flung through the shrieking black night against the boat, against the rig, or worse, against him.

Within seconds that same reckless, random wind that had tangled the line around the pole in the first place miraculously whipped the line off, leaving Nik standing on deck holding only the once straight pole that was now bent like a pretzel. He quickly lashed it to the deck while the sail continued to wallop the sky. By this time it was torn and useless. Rolling it up no longer mattered; we wanted only to get it down.

"Let's drop the halyard!" Nik instructed me. "Put a wrap on a winch, take the line brake off! Ease it down when I get to the bow!"

I did as instructed, but when I released the halyard nothing happened. The sail appeared to be jammed in the foil. Nik pulled at the sailcloth. Nothing. Just then I saw that a small twist in the halyard had jammed at the line brake, and without thinking, I took it off the winch and gave it a flick to release the snag. *Bam!* With one flick of my wrist I'd cleared the obstruction and the halyard flew out of my hands. The entire sail dropped instantly, landing half in, half out of the water. There was some yelling. With great effort Nik managed to drag the torn salty sail back on board.

With the shredded genoa on deck and the wind speed dropping, thinking we were finally under control, I put the boat on autopilot, harnessed up, and went forward with bungee cords to help Nik tie the genoa down. At that moment, the staysail unfurled. The bungee we'd used to secure it in Tahuata let go and now the loose staysail was battered by the wind. Our 2 percent sheer terror wasn't over yet.

The big weather we'd experienced at the very start of our voyage off the coast of Oregon had been unnerving, but I'd never felt in imminent danger then. This was different. The metal block I'd partially reattached to the clew of the staysail was whipping through the air at head level in thirty knots of wind. We were both trying to grab hold of the staysail, trying to bring it under control. I was certain a head injury was seconds away. I might have screamed for strength or luck but I didn't bother because I knew I was out of both. What frightened me most was, worse than being at the edge of my limit, I could see we were at the edge of Nik's, and Nik's strength was always my fallback. It took everything he had. He wrapped himself around the inner forestay and controlled the sail with his whole body. He instructed me to get back to the helm and to bring the boat into the wind so that we could drop the staysail also.

Our foredeck looked like a war zone. Both our foresails were piled in crumpled heaps among bungee cords, knotted sheets, and a twisted metal bar. We were exhausted and soaked to the skin. We were so spent, we could have sat down and cried. Instead we took turns getting out of wet clothes. Nik crawled back into his bunk and I resumed my watch as stars reappeared in the now clear sky. The squall never looked back.

She marched on through the black Pacific night, unleashing her
fury on all that lay in her path.

We arrived in Makemo Atoll in the Tuamotu Archipelago
with the boat a shamble after four days of travel. Aside from the
squall activity, we were fortunate to have terrifically consistent
winds that kept us travelling briskly south even when all we
had left was our mainsail. If it had not been for that one terrible
midnight hour, it would've been the best four days of sailing on
the whole trip.

CHAPTER 10

French Polynesia

(July – September 2001)

I had a preconceived idea of what it would be like anchored in the inner lagoon of a Tuamotuan atoll: peaceful, calm, serene, as though anchored on a pond. It was not like that atoll (sorry, I couldn't resist). But seriously, it wasn't. Not at first anyway. At Makemo Atoll we anchored off the village of Pouheva and found ourselves exposed to a brisk southeast wind. It was blowing across a 10 NM fetch, creating a notable wind wave inside the reef. Our bow bounced wildly in the chop. It was the last thing we needed after a four-day sail-tearing passage, but the visibility was too poor to navigate around the many uncharted coral bommies to a better anchoring position inside the reef.

When the weather settled, we moved across the inner lagoon. We anchored next to half a dozen other cruising sailboats tucked in behind a motu, a small island created where a portion of the atoll was high enough above sea level to sustain plant life. We were an instant community, this wee group of boats. Dried palm fronds, coconut husks, and driftwood were collected by day and ablaze by evening. By sundown there was a circle of glowing faces around the beach bonfire: one couple cooking dinner on a grill, a guitar player singing, others roasting marshmallows on sticks, while hermit crabs scrawled their zig-zag paths through the sand – these were the kind of nights that, to me, were exactly what cruising was all about.

There were no houses, no stores, no shopping, nothing to be done. Each day was about snorkelling expeditions, bocce ball tournaments, Frisbee, beachcombing, shell collecting, and the hope of laying eyes on the elusive coconut crab. At night it was simple – we returned to the fire.

We took some time to lick our wounds, removing the torn genoa and replacing it with the higher-cut Yankee we had stored under the V-berth bed. We also removed not only the staysail, but the entire self-tacking boom apparatus to give us more space on our foredeck for dinghy storage.

This was such a beautiful place and a restful stop that it wasn't easy to leave, literally and figuratively. Everyone had trouble getting anchors up off the bottom when it came time to go. In the shifting winds our chain had wrapped itself in a complex pattern around old coral heads in thirty feet of water. To pull the anchor up, Nik stood on the bow and shouted directions to me at the helm while I drove the slalom course forward in an effort to retrieve our ground tackle from the rocky bottom. It didn't work.

Nik jumped in with mask and snorkel to take a good look at what was going on. He dived down and found that our chain had slipped into a coral crevasse so narrow it was as though we'd threaded a coral needle with our anchor chain. We enlisted the help of our neighbour, Gord on *Elakha*, to be our go-between. Nik dived thirty feet to the bottom to pull our chain free from the narrow trap. Gord watched from the surface to tell me exactly when I could activate the windlass on the bow. We couldn't have done it without two in the water.

From Makemo, we sailed overnight to Fakarava. Here, we enjoyed one of our most remarkable experiences ever – drift snorkelling in an atoll pass. By timing the tides to ensure we had an onshore current, we picked our time of day. On the flood tide, we took our dinghy out the atoll pass, jumped in the water, then held onto the dinghy handholds for the ride. The pass at Fakarava was deep but the slopes were lined with a craggy coral forest and crowded with more fish than I'd ever seen. The several-knot flood current whisked us into the lagoon along the navigable pass. We floated, drifted, and soon flew into the anchorage, past a huge Napolean fish and countless groupers with their khaki camouflage scales. Moray eels protruded from holes in the reef and swayed sinisterly in the current. Marauding blacktip reef sharks passed below us, while sleek barracuda hunted their prey. Gliding over that underwater world, whisked along by the strong current, I felt like Superman. It was better than a ride at Disney World. No tickets, no crowds, no waiting. We did it again and again and again.

With only four hundred gallons in our tanks and no watermaker, after two weeks in the Tuamotus, our low water supply forced us to move on. I didn't want to leave Fakarava, but I was also glad to be going. I've always believed that it's better to leave when you long to stay than to stay 'til you can't wait to go. If you stay anywhere until you're pining to leave, a negativity develops that forever taints your memory. For me, the bittersweet taste of a too-soon departure pins a deeply satisfied positive memory to an experience. I relish the longing to return. We left the Tuamotus when I hated to go and the barren, wild, untouched Tuamotus remain one of my favourite places.

✸

Our three-day, two-night trip to the island of Tahiti was wonderfully boring. We were plagued by light air and ended up motoring most of the way.

We arrived in the Society Islands unprepared for the culture shock of Papeete. We hadn't been on an island with a population of more than twenty-four hundred people in three months. We hadn't seen fresh milk or done our laundry by machine in that time period either. Tahiti, with a population then of about 150,000 (half in Papeete), not only had fresh milk and launderettes, it had two McDonald's restaurants, an international airport, and gorgeous grocery stores. We were wowed by rush hour, dazzled by the crowds downtown, and thrilled by the five different kinds of lettuce in the Continent grocery store. I laughed at my Canadian tendency, taking items off the shelves in order to turn them around to read the English side of the label. Of course, both sides were in French, but otherwise it was no different from shopping at a grocery store back home, but better – the food was French.

We worked hard for a week hoping to restock, repair, and be ready for fun before a Vancouver friend arrived for a visit. We ordered the new forestay and roller furling, and booked a rigger and dock space for the installation. We took our staysail in for repair and threw out the shredded genoa.

Cockroaches still danced "La Cucaracha" across our countertops each night. Shopping for insecticide, we asked a local man in a hardware store what could be done.

"What do you mean?" he asked. "There is nothing to be done about cockroaches. They do what they do, you do what you do, that is all."

We couldn't embrace his charitable nature toward our little Mexican friends and so we prepared for war, filling our shopping basket with sprays and bombs and mysterious white powder. None of them worked.

When our friend Scott arrived, we set sail for Bora Bora, the perfect distraction for our guest and ourselves while we waited for our new Profurl system to be delivered from France.

After regaling Scott with tales of our high seas adventures, the trip to Bora Bora was boring boring. There was no wind, not a breath. No waves, not a one. Not even a ripple. No fish. No squalls. After all our storytelling, our friend caught a thirty-hour ride on a pond-like Pacific by way of the iron genny.

If the Inuit language has twenty-six different words for snow, surely the Polynesian language must have as many for the shades of blue in the lagoon of Bora Bora. The island was too perfect to be real, as though it was the Hollywood creation of a South Pacific paradise. We rounded the lagoon with *Green Ghost*, anchoring off Motu Piti Aau where we ate BBQ dinners, snorkelled with graceful manta rays, and studied poisonous lionfish from a distance. We rented scooters and circled the island's single road. We read books on the beach and soaked in the turquoise water. Toward the end of our stay we visited Marama, the master tattooist on Matira Point for a group ink outing. In three consecutive appointments, Nik's arm, Scott's leg, and my mastoid (behind the ear) were permanently decorated with some Polynesian art. After all, tattoos are like potato chips – you can never have just one.

When Scott flew out of Bora Bora we found ourselves experiencing our usual post-guest melancholy. Guests distracted us and enforced a play time that might otherwise have evaporated in days of boat chores. They reminded us to be tourists and enjoy the moment, to step out of the endless get ready mindset. They also gave us a break from one another and introduced a fresh dynamic on board. After our personal failures on the long crossing, I'd worried that Nik and I had become so insular, we'd lost our ability to socialize. Scott's visit relieved us. We'd learned our lesson. For us, entertaining guests in port was good fun; entertaining guests offshore was not a good idea.

⚓

We'd sent messages home raving about the Society Islands and beckoning family to join us there. I didn't think anyone would come – we hadn't given them enough time. Much to my surprise, with less than two weeks' notice, my mom booked a ticket, packed a bag, and jumped on a plane to make the twenty-seven-hour journey. I was thrilled, if a little taken aback, that my never-travelled-alone-before, seventy-year-old mom would embark on such an adventure. Then again, maybe it runs in the family. We sailed back to Tahiti via Mo'orea to pick her up.

Not only was Mom on the scene but our roller furling had finally arrived. For installation, we traded our Maeva Beach anchorage view of moonsets over Mo'orea for sunsets over fuel tanks at the Nautisport dock on the more industrial side of town.

Green Ghost was soon whole again with her full complement of sails repaired and functioning properly. After sailing to Mo'orea and back for some fun with my mom, it was time to check out of French Polynesia. Ahead was the longest offshore leg we would have in the islands and we'd be doing it alone.

On our way out of the island group, we stopped again at Bora Bora. On our final night, we treated ourselves to dinner on shore and we fell into deep discussion about our future.

We'd set out with the goal to cross the Pacific, to get to Australia in a single season. But now that we were underway, we realized very few other boats had that plan. Friends in the fleet planned to go as far as Tonga before heading south to New Zealand for the antipodean summer where they would enjoy the off-season in safe waters, below the cyclone belt. They planned a second season of sailing the southwest Pacific through Fiji, Vanuatu, and New Caledonia before crossing the Coral Sea to Australia the following year. It made us wonder – was there a way for us to do that too?

What we were doing no longer felt like a single expedition. Nearly twelve months in, it had begun to feel like a lifestyle. We felt we'd discovered a secret world, a magical life that was there for the taking. We knew two things for sure: the cruising life was fantastic and we weren't ready for an ending. We decided to make it our goal to extend our time in the Pacific. There had to be a way to sail on.

CHAPTER 11

West and South

(September – November 2001)

We flew out of French Polynesia on a brisk beam reach rushing westward toward Suwarrow atoll in the northern Cook Islands. The seas slammed us down thirty-five degrees to starboard and with each passing trough we rolled back fifteen degrees to port. The motion was relentless and it made for an uncomfortable ride.

Nik was seasick on the first night out. At this point he was so practiced at the art that he could vomit into his mouth while he lay in his bunk and hold it there until he made it to the stern rail where he spewed into the sea. By the second night out, despite being medicated, we were shoulder to shoulder at the stern rail. It was distressing. We were not getting better at overcoming seasickness. I settled into my mantra: *This won't last, this won't last, this won't last* while Nik visualized La-Z-Boy chairs in suburban living rooms. Finally, we got used to the motion after about four days. Too bad it was only a six-day trip.

At Suwarrow we anchored with six other sailboats behind Shelter Island. We went ashore by dinghy and stepped onto the makeshift wharf. On shore, still in use were the cabins built by the famous Tom Neale, a New Zealander and author who lived alone (by choice) at Suwarrow over three periods totalling sixteen years, between 1952 until his death from cancer in 1977. It felt like a castaways' island – a swing dangled from a leaning palm, several large hammocks fashioned from old fishing nets were slung between the trees, and a conference of makeshift benches encircled a fire pit.

We met the locals, all two of them. They were the marine preserve caretakers, John and Tom, each in his seventies, and both excellent hosts. They had a Panga-style open boat with a twenty-five-horsepower outboard that they used to entertain cruisers. Sailors who chipped in fuel were taken fishing in the pass. The day we arrived they had reeled in mahi-mahi, barracuda, and a whopping yellowfin tuna. Another day, an outing for shellfish produced a catch of over a dozen huge lobster. The caretakers hosted a potluck dinner every night featuring the day's catch and whatever other delights cruisers brought to shore. In this way, John and Tom ensured they had variety in their diet and augmented their small supply of stores.

Our enjoyment of the castaway's life was cut short when the weather changed three days after our arrival. Three days of reinforced trade winds meant Shelter Island wouldn't be much of a shelter anymore. The increased winds would sweep across 11 NM of open water inside the atoll, straight into the anchorage. Upon hearing the evening forecast, we planned to move to a safer anchorage the following day, but the stronger winds came early.

Before morning a significant wind chop had developed in the lagoon. Our bow was jerking wildly and we woke to the sound of a loud snap. Our anchor bridle had broken and the line and hook sank to the bottom. Nik quickly fashioned another bridle out of our dock lines and went forward. He could see from the bow that the violent motion on the *Ghost* was the result of shortened scope. The wind direction had shifted in the night and *Green Ghost* rotated ninety degrees in the anchorage, hooking a deep coral head in the process. Instead of being held by the length of chain attached to the anchor on the bottom, we were on a short leash, held instead by a short length of chain wrapped on a coral head off our bow.

In daylight, we turned the engine on and tried to better our position. But attempts to untangle our chain from the coral were fruitless. Even with Nik in the water, shouting instructions to me at the helm it couldn't be done. Our only solution was to let more chain out, to increase our scope and lengthen the catenary, creating more elasticity in our ground tackle.

Only one boat in the anchorage had managed to get their anchor up and move across the inner lagoon before the wind picked up. The remaining five were pinned in the uncomfortable anchorage like we were.

As the day wore on, the chop got steeper and our bow bounced more wildly. The pitching was so furious that we were taking water over the bow. We kept a close watch for chafe on the bridle. We didn't dare leave the boat. All day we sat aboard our bucking bronco hoping everything would hold. Even if we could have gotten our anchor up, it was no time to be moving around in the coral-studded lagoon. Visibility was poor in the white-capped waters.

We listened to anxious discussions on the VHF radio. Other boats were experiencing similar difficulties. One sailor reported he was going through bridles every couple of hours and he worried he would run out of spare line.

The reinforced trade winds did not let up. Of our six days at Suwarrow, three of them were spent confined to the boat on a stressful anchor watch. It was worse than being at sea. We endured three nights of interrupted sleep in our sea berths, we were tired and out of sorts, but we had to leave on the next offshore passage. It was time for us to head for the Kingdom of Tonga. Once again, we had company coming.

All sailors tell potential guests the same thing – that we may or may not make it to the rendezvous location on time. You tell yourself that you won't allow prior plans to alter your thinking, but they do. Sailing to a schedule can cause you to make poor choices: to sail in weather you wouldn't normally sail in, to go to sea with equipment not operating at 100 percent, or to set out on a journey when you aren't physically ready. Normally we wouldn't leave on an offshore passage as exhausted as we were leaving Suwarrow, but we felt that we couldn't turn up in Tonga days late with the excuse that we'd been sleeping. To meet with our next rendezvous on time, we had to go.

After a boisterous 723 NM passage making better than 140 NM per day, we arrived in Tonga five days later, a record time for our heavy-hulled home.

Landfall in Neiafu harbour was a treat. The Tongan islands of the Vava'u Group reminded us of the Gulf Islands off Vancouver. We felt like we were home again, only in a tropical setting. Thinking ourselves quite smart for arriving on Sunday, a full twenty-four hours before our friend was due to fly in, we were startled to find Gwil standing on the wharf as we pulled into the customs dock. It wasn't Sunday. It was Monday. We'd failed to notice that in sailing from the Cook Islands to Tonga we'd crossed the International Date Line.

The Pacific fleet had spread out since leaving French Polynesia. There had been many routes to take – north to Samoa, south to the Cook Islands, over to Niue, or straight across as we did. Neiafu was a reunion of all the yachties we'd met in the Pacific, resulting in one of the greatest pressures (and pleasures) of the cruising life, a very hectic social schedule among the sixty-odd boats in the bay.

Our time in Tonga was full of fun. Explorations took us into swallows' caves where the late afternoon sun sent shafts of light to the bottom sixty feet below us. Above, great stalactites hung from the darkness. We allowed our dinghy to drift while we jumped in to snorkel. Swimming inside the cave in the clear water I had the sensation I was flying, soaring through a sapphire blue sky over the pinnacles and spires of a stalagmite city below. We visited another location where we dived down eight feet and swam fourteen feet in through a black hole in a vertical coral wall. We surfaced inside spacious Mariner's Cave, an opening in the limestone completely sealed off from the outside air, the only light coming in through the watery entry. Inside I kept trying to de-fog my mask until I realized the fog was on the outside, not the inside of my goggles. Even in a light swell, water pulsing into the cave compressed the atmosphere within. When the sea receded, the moisture in the air condensed into a heavy fog, the result of the water vapour cooling as it expands. As each swell entered, our ears popped and the air cleared. Then our ears cleared and the heavy fog reappeared as the next swell receded.

Island walks and beachcombing complemented the beautiful snorkelling. It was in Tonga that my passion for shell collecting began. Up until then I'd resisted collecting things to store in our tiny living space but the beachcombing in Tonga was so rewarding it became impossible for me not to pick things up. The abundance of stunning shells amazed me, each one a work of natural art.

Tongan time flew by and, after our leisurely cruise through the Vava'u group with Gwil, we looped our way back to the main town of Neiafu. I had a special event to look forward to. It was my thirty-ninth birthday and I wanted to celebrate in style. Weeks before arriving in Tonga I'd spread the word by radio and e-mail, asking many of our friends on other cruising boats to join us at the Mermaid Grill for a birthday party. I was honoured as friends sailed in from other countries specifically to be in Tonga for that date. International well-wishers spoiled me throughout the day with three birthday cakes, handmade cards and gifts, a paper birthday crown, fireworks, sparklers, and bubbles. A large group of sailors enjoyed dinner at the restaurant, cold Ikale (beer), and colourful Jell-O shots. With music and dancing, surrounded by friends I had a fantastic birthday party, one I will never forget and certainly one I hoped to repeat, as I planned on turning thirty-nine a few times.

At times Tonga's similarity to the Gulf Islands went a little too far. The weather became most Pacific Northwest – overcast, windy, and varying from drizzle to an entire day of downpour. The unfavourable weather delayed our departure from the Vava'u Group for a full week.

Once underway, we enjoyed anchoring off the beautiful uninhabited islands in the gorgeous Ha'apai Group as we day-sailed south to Nomuka. From there we made our final 60 NM dash to the capital of the Kingdom, Nuku'alofa on Tongatapu, the stepping-off point for the passage to New Zealand.

✵

We departed Nuku'alofa for North Minerva Reef. This is such a simple sentence that it can't possibly impart the weight of this decision. No other crossing on the Pacific was more talked about than this one. We'd been sailing in the trade wind belt plus or minus twenty degrees off the equator for the better part of the year. The thought of sailing into the higher latitudes was unappealing not only because of the cooler weather we would experience, but also because of the low pressure systems we were bound to meet en route. As many a passage planner has written, it isn't a matter of *if* you are going to get hammered on the way to New Zealand, it's a matter of *when*.

The atmosphere in the fleet reminded me of exam time. There was an undercurrent of both group panic and quiet brooding. When you crossed paths with other sailors at the market or the fuel pump, the usually loud jovial cruisers were speaking in hushed conspiratorial tones. "Did you get the latest weatherfax? What do you think? When are you going?" It was just like university days, predicting what would be on the final exam. Concerns, weatherfaxes, and e-mails were shared among the fleet of boats hovering in Nuku'alofa. We religiously tuned into the radio broadcast weather forecasts several times a day. We all wanted to pass the test, the crossing to New Zealand.

Low-pressure systems are bred somewhere over Australia and traverse the Tasman Sea and the northern part of New Zealand before moving east across the southern Pacific. New systems pop up and pass through about once a week. The general strategy is to leave Tonga as a low-pressure system passes over the northern tip of New Zealand and hope to make it safely into a New Zealand harbour before the next low comes along.

With almost 800 NM between Minerva Reefs and Opua, New Zealand, you must make at least 100 NM per day to make landfall before the next system passes over. If you don't make it in the weather window between fronts, you risk getting caught in a nasty low-pressure system off the north cape of New Zealand, a situation that has caused more than a few shipwrecks in recent history.

The trouble is that when there is a low over northern New Zealand, there may be a high over southern Tonga and that means you may depart on a windless sea. And because you needed to be making your mileage, smart use of your engine and your fuel was a major part of the passage strategy. *Green Ghost* carries 120 gallons of diesel in two fibreglass fuel tanks and we had no qualms about using it.

We had a great start out of Nuku'alofa on our trip south to Minerva Reef, enjoying a perfect fifteen-knot wind on the beam, flat seas, and incredibly beautiful sailing for our first twenty-four hours. The following day the wind became light and the sea, flat. On our second night at sea the only ripple on the ocean was the wake behind *Green Ghost*. It was eerie to see the ocean that lifeless. It was as though somebody had turned the lights out and the wind off, as though the whole world had stopped and we were the only thing in motion. We motored through calms for thirty hours in order to get into the shelter of Minerva Reef by the afternoon of the third day.

As we approached the co-ordinates for North Minerva, it appeared to be no different than every other middle-of-nowhere patch of water on the Pacific except that we counted more than twenty masts sticking up out of the ocean. They were all anchored within the protected waters of the lagoon. At high tide, a ring of breakers could be seen around the reef. At low tide, the reef was exposed, allowing long walks on the coral ring. Spear-fishers in the fleet had a heyday collecting lobsters and hunting the huge fish that call Minerva home.

Within forty-eight hours we were motoring out of the pass, leaving a single boat behind. Armed with the same weather forecast we could all see that it was the right time to go. We had our weather window for the 785 NM dash to New Zealand.

☸

I awoke from my off-watch sleep and glanced at my watch. I was early. I wasn't on for an hour, but I felt well rested and decided to get up. I stumbled into the galley to put the kettle on, then I glanced into the cockpit to see how Nik was doing, but I didn't see him there. He must have woken me up as he came below to use the head, I figured. So I went forward and looked in the head. He wasn't there. Hopefully, I moved the shower curtain. He wasn't there either. Hmm, he must be on deck, I thought, starting to feel a little worried. Maybe he woke me up stomping around overhead. With rising concern, I walked aft again, climbed the companionway stairs, stepped out into the cockpit, and turned around to look forward. I looked toward the bow through the dodger. I didn't see him. He wasn't there. I leaned over to the starboard side, to look around the dodger and see forward around the mast. There was nobody on deck.

"*Niiiik!*" I screamed, terror-stricken. I'd been asleep for three hours. When had he fallen overboard? I thought I was going to vomit. Nik was gone.

"Jeez, what's your problem, I'm right here," his voice came back.

"Oh my God," I said with my hands on my heart. My knees buckled and I sat heavily on the cockpit seat. "Oh my God," I repeated as my eyes filled with tears. "I thought ... I thought you were ... gone."

"I'm right here."

"But I thought ... you'd ... gone ... overboard." I was breathless.

"I climbed up the rat lines to have a look. I thought I saw a whale."

Nik had climbed about eight feet up the rope ladder I'd made in our portside rigging. When I looked for him, it hadn't occurred to me to look up.

"Don't ever do that again," I scolded him.

"Ah, you love me!" he joked and embraced me when he returned to the cockpit. "Settle down! I didn't fall off. It's okay." Then he gently turned me to look forward again. "Keep your eyes peeled," he said, pointing. "At about eleven o'clock, I think you'll see a whale spouting ..."

For Nik, it was business as usual, but my heart was still beating rapidly. I'd just experienced my worst two minutes of the whole trip.

☸

Despite all the hype about weather, and that frightful two minutes aside, our trip to New Zealand was one of our best voyages. We had a little bit of everything wind-wise, but overall, uncommonly flat seas. We had twenty-four hours of beating into a southwesterly for our final day, but on the last day at sea before a beautiful landfall, a bit of work to weather was tolerable because we knew the torture wouldn't last.

We were nostalgic as we closed in on Opua. So much had happened in the fifteen months since our departure from Vancouver. On our journey south and west, we'd sailed into a different world. The seasons had changed inside out. It was November and it was spring. The Southern Cross appeared in the night sky and slowly lay down on its side; a rising Scorpius now took a dip beyond the horizon every night.

Before our departure from Canada, I'd worried that nights at sea would be frightening but by the time we were sailing into New Zealand I'd fallen in love with the starry night sky. It was dawn that was the nuisance. I'd come to realize that the sun was just one more star rising and when it did, it ruined my view of all the rest.

We arrived in Opua, New Zealand, in late November 2001. We tied up in a slip at the Opua Marina and walked up the ramp toward shore. A pace before the threshold Nik stopped me.

"Wait," he said. He took my hand. "We should do this together."

Hand in hand we jumped from the floating dock onto terra firma where we high-fived one another, wide grins on our faces. We had done it. We had crossed the Pacific Ocean.

CHAPTER 12

New Zealand

(November 2001 – May 2003)

Our tans began fading and our feet blistered when we crammed them into long-lost shoes, but we didn't care. We smiled non-stop for days as we settled into beautiful New Zealand. We were overjoyed to be there, overwhelmed with the self-satisfaction of having the Pacific in our wake, and relaxed by the thought of having offshore passages behind us for a time.

After exploring the Bay of Islands area, we sailed down the east coast of the North Island and arrived in Auckland just before Christmas. We tied up at the Bayswater Marina on Auckland's North Shore and we didn't move for months. It was cruising downtime.

While life was easy tied to a dock in a first-world English-speaking country, there was still much to get used to. We had the usual complications with understanding the Kiwi accent. In New Zealand, yis is yes, tin is ten, and sux is six, but six is sex; you pronounce the letters "wh" (and sometimes "th") with an "ff" sound; and don't pronounce "r's" at all, unless there are two of them. We bought a used cah (car) that had a boot and a bonnet. We pushed a trundler around the grocery store. We ate fush and chups at the seaside. We often heard that something was "sweet as" but nobody seemed to know sweet as what. Hanging similes were everywhere. "Cool as," "strong as," and "sick as" were common expressions, but, again, as what exactly? We never knew.

In New Zealand eggs came in sizes of six, seven, and eight, whole chickens came in twelves and fourteens. My bra size dropped to a twelve and my shoe size grew to a thirty-seven. Hokey Pokey was a flavour of ice cream, not a dance. It was fifteen degrees Celsius in the dead of winter and no matter what the weather, every Kiwi's comment on it was, "It's not usually like this." The water swirled down the drain the other way, the cold winds came from the south, and summer came in January. Our world was upside-down.

We'd come to New Zealand to extend our cruising time in the Pacific and to make some money. Our decision was made when, still in the islands, Nik's former Vancouver employer responded to an e-mail proposal and agreed that Nik should work a short contract for them, testing their product in the New Zealand market.

Nik's pre-arranged work set him up nicely. But what was I to do? With fifteen years of geology and mining on my résumé, looking for work in a country where I had no work permit and they had no mining industry wasn't going to be easy.

Nik's six-month contract began in March and that meant that we couldn't leave New Zealand at the end of the cyclone season in May 2002. It would be eighteen months before we could depart for the southwest Pacific and resume cruising in May 2003. Our decision to sail south was no small pit stop.

I felt a loss at letting go of the cruising life and fell into a grief of sorts. I mourned the freedom of being out there exploring the world and pined for the wonders of the previous year. I worried that we would grow roots or not grow at all. Mostly I worried that we would not *go* at all. I wanted to live as frugally as possible, to preserve every dollar toward more cruising.

Nik, on the other hand, felt it was time to let loose. Soon he'd be busy during business hours and we'd have money coming in. In Nik's mind our interminable privation was finally over, so why not live it up a little? Within a week of being tied to the Bayswater dock, Nik had bought a flat screen TV. He waited slightly longer for a new surfboard, a board bag, and a roof rack – perfect accessories for our new used car. Once the landline and the high-speed Internet connection were installed directly

to our berth on E-dock, all was well in Nik's universe. If only a
La-Z-Boy recliner would've fit in our salon.

Nik was not the only one. The landlubber came out in
everyone.

Excluding boats with paid crew, the cruising world is a
relatively level playing field. Sure, some folks have fancier boats,
more gadgets or better toys; some folks go out for dinner more
often, or pay for more touristy outings, but when you're cruising offshore, it doesn't matter how much money you have. Your
head still clogs, your engine oil still has to be changed, and
your sails tear like everyone else's. Out there, on the big blue,
we shared a waterfront view with our fellow sailors. We all lived
in the same neighbourhood. We all had the same address: *Boat
Name*, blue ocean, no fixed address. We'd all stepped away from
our familiar social circles. We'd all left our comfort zones behind.
We'd had to make new friends and new fun and we did. The best
times were the games nights and snorkelling outings, the potluck dinners and birthday parties where everyone hand-made
a gift or a card or a cake.

When we arrived in Auckland everything changed. The
used-car purchases said it all. Our friends purchased flashy
red sports cars, his and hers BMWs, and kitted-out camper
vans. At the other end of the spectrum, some bought decade-
old cars with mismatched doors and jammed locks. We were
somewhere in the middle, settling on an inexpensive Honda
Accord at an auction. The cruising community of the Pacific
Ocean had not emphasized financial status, but life on land
did.

Suddenly being out with the gang meant taking part in
costly outings. Restaurant dinners, movies, rock concerts,
go-cart racing, glow-in-the-dark bowling ... "We're going this
weekend – you should come!"

The instant lifestyle change put stress on our relationship.
Nik loved to be at the centre of whatever was going on and was
inclined to say yes to everything. But the consumption caused
me concern. I didn't want to spend money on glow-in-the-dark

bowling. I wanted only to go cruising again. As a result, I became the restraint – the boring voice of reason.

I found it difficult to abandon the finely tuned focus we'd had on cruising while Nik embraced everything about stopping. He wanted to enjoy the time before his contract began while I saw my future – an expanse of days with nothing to do – as a slow form of torture for my goal-oriented, A-type personality.

A mail packet received from our P.O. box manager in Vancouver exacerbated my funk. In it, there was a letter from a Vancouver adoption agency about the closing of our file. It re-opened a wound and stirred a sadness within me. When we'd made our decisions back in B.C., we'd had cruising to look forward to, but now, I was tied to a dock in Auckland with what felt like an uncertain future. I struggled with my identity. The letter was a reminder that I would never be a mother. I was not a sailor anymore. I was unemployed. I felt like I was nothing and I was miserable.

I took it out on the cockroaches, waging war and winning with copious amounts of boric acid sprinkled liberally throughout the galley.

Meanwhile Nik was loving New Zealand. Before starting his contract work he reacquainted himself with surfing, a sport he had learned in his childhood on his many Florida vacations. He surfed as often as possible, checking out Raglan, Muriwai, Bethells, Pakiri, Mangawhai Heads, and Piha, his favourite haunt. He couldn't get enough.

He constantly tried to reassure me that we would go sailing again and that I shouldn't fret.

"Enjoy what we're doing here and now," he advised me. "We'll sail out of here eventually, we'll get to Australia, don't worry!" A habitual optimist and a natural bohemian, he was good at enjoying the moment. But despite his assurances, I remained low in spirit and I didn't enjoy our break in Auckland the way I should have.

In the end, my job hunt was fruitless and when Nik's

contract work was over, our goals were unified again as we set to work on *Green Ghost*.

The paint that had begun peeling off the hull on the first leg of our Pacific crossing continued to sheer off on each successive passage. The topsides looked battered, the bottom side needed attention, and while we were at it, we decided to replace the standing rigging. Of major concern was our compression post, a stainless-steel post that sits atop the keel and supports our deck-stepped mast. It was undersized and it had bowed. It needed replacement. We spent a great deal of time visiting potential boatyards, talking to professionals, lining up contractors and searching the chandleries for equipment and supplies before moving to a haul-out facility to begin our work.

The move from the Bayswater Marina, Devonport, to the boatyard in Half Moon Bay, Pakuranga, should have been a simple 10 NM trip, but it turned into a morning of drama. Conditions weren't great on our morning of departure, but we were impatient to get started on our maintenance work and, although it was challenging in the twenty-five knot winds, we backed out of our slip anyway, setting off together with our friend Ian, who had joined us to help out.

"Something doesn't feel right – it's pretty sluggish," Nik said, handing me the helm outside the marina.

At three knots, we were making only half our usual speed. We weren't too surprised as we suspected the hull was covered with marine growth – one of the reasons we were hauling out. We couldn't make use of the wind because we'd removed all our sails in preparation for pulling our mast in the boatyard. So we motored along, fretting, because we realized our slow speed meant we would miss the end of the flood tide and have an ebb current against us as we turned up the Tamaki River. We were going to be late for our haul-out time.

After a long slow crawl, within a half-mile of the marina entrance, *Green Ghost* struggled to make headway. With only one final marker to round before entering the marina we found ourselves in strong current with thirty knots of wind right on our nose. I watched the knot meter go from two knots to one knot to zero.

"Zero velocity, we're not making way!" I yelled from the helm.

In seconds the wind pushed us back, blowing us sideways down the narrow channel. I kept us in forward at full throttle, hoping to regain control of the bow with some forward momentum in the direction of deep water. But the wind and current were too strong, and very quickly we were blown backwards, out of the channel and into the shallow water of the lee shore.

"Get the anchor down as fast as you can!" I shouted to Nik. If I could not control the boat, at the very least we had to stop it.

As Nik rushed forward to lower the anchor, we were drifting backwards toward a minefield of small boats on moorings along the rocky shoreline of Bucklands Beach. I glanced over my shoulder, then grabbed a dock line, planning to tie onto whichever one we hit first. The depth sounder flashed ever smaller numbers – the bottom was rapidly shoaling, when finally, the anchor bit. With the first of the moored boats only ten feet off our stern, *Green Ghost* came to a stop.

"I think we should motor forward, pick up the anchor, and get into some deeper water. We've got to get away from these moored boats," Nik said.

"That's not going to work," I said, "because we're at max rpms right now." We lay at anchor with full forward throttle and we were still being driven back by the wind with our anchor chain pulled taut. I had tears in my eyes. After making it all the way to New Zealand, I thought we were going to lose the boat right there in Half Moon Bay.

Fortunately, help was at hand. We radioed the marina and got towed in for the price of a case of beer. The marina had already cancelled the crane that was to pull our mast and cancelled our haul-out too. Conditions were too windy. It was a harsh lesson in impatience.

Later, relaxing over Chinese food and cold beer, we laughed and congratulated ourselves that during the whole episode no one had lost their cool. We each admitted that in the direst moment, as we drifted toward the rocky shore, none of us had been afraid for our own physical safety. Instead we'd all been silently making a plan for how we would step off *Green Ghost* and wade ashore without even getting our hair wet.

The next day upon haul-out we discovered a large colony of fist-sized mussels growing on our propeller, the main reason for the boat's lack of performance. The ordeal was also a lesson in local knowledge. Not appreciating how the wind conditions behaved around local landforms, not realizing how quickly the tide turned to a strong ebb current in the channel, and not knowing the biology of the marine environment at Bayswater Marina had all contributed to our harrowing experience. Next time, we promised ourselves, we'd dive our hull, or pay a commercial diver to dive the hull when we'd been sitting in foreign water for over a year.

And so began our time at the Half Moon Bay haul-out facility. For ten weeks from September to November 2002, we lived aboard high and dry, up on the hardstand in the boatyard. Our lives became all about carbide pull scrapers and sandpaper, orbital sanders, earplugs, dust masks and safety glasses, two-part epoxy fillers, and more sandpaper, micro-balloons, masking tape, fibreglass, epoxy primers and more sandpaper, undercoats, topcoats, brushes and rollers, more masking tape, and even more sandpaper. It went on and on, but the end result was a gleaming jade mist green topcoat, a stunning white boot strip, and an epoxy-barrier-coated bottom with bright red antifouling paint. Except for the undercoat and green top coat which were professionally sprayed, we did all the work ourselves. In the end, *Green Ghost* looked sweet as.

☸

With the maintenance done, but still a few months to wait out the cyclone season, we took the opportunity to fly back to Canada for a visit. I spent time with my family while Nik attended a dinner party at his sister's Toronto home. The story of our sailing lifestyle preceded him and many of the guests at the party asked questions with interest. Not one to shy away from the spotlight, Nik amused enthusiastic listeners with a few salty tales over drinks and appetizers. Later, seated at the long dining table, a bejewelled woman beside him leaned over.

"I want your life!" she announced in that exaggerated dinner party manner.

"Well, it's not all Hendrick's and hammocks," Nik replied. "I mean, it is fantastic, we love it, but there's some hard work involved, and the living conditions, well, it wouldn't be for everyone, that's for sure. It's a lot like camping ... on a roller coaster."

"Oh, come on, it's fabulous, it *must* be *fabulous*!" she said, unconvinced. "I want your life! I do!" she repeated, poking the air with her manicured nail for emphasis.

With the gold-rimmed crystal wine glasses and sterling silver cutlery gleaming at every place, Nik thought the setting too elegant to explain what ten weeks in a boatyard was like, peeing in a bucket in the middle of the night because you had no saltwater for flushing the toilet when you were up high and dry on the hardstand, lugging the bucket down a twelve-foot ladder each morning to dump it in the public loo. The maintenance and repairs, the day-to-day boat work, the provisioning and planning, the physical demands of offshore – it was hard to describe that to landlubbers. From a distance, from the outside, I suppose cruising a boat to Fiji did sound simply "*fabulous!*"

⚓

The early months of 2003 passed quickly. Since our time on the hardstand, we'd had several more visitors pass through. We enjoyed hiking and surfing through another New Zealand summer and we thrilled to the America's Cup racing in the harbour, but before we knew it we had only thirty days left in the country. Through April we wore ourselves ragged with the preparations for departure. It was just like the fall of 2000 when we left Vancouver, only this time we knew the hard work would be worth it.

This time we wanted to capture it. Unable to afford the digital cameras that were being introduced to the market when our journey began, we'd been shooting slide film in 35mm cameras, making our photographs inaccessible, even to us. Realizing how profoundly special our experiences had been, we wanted to record our Coral Sea adventures in the most modern way possible, in a way that was easy to share.

Before leaving New Zealand, we splurged extravagantly on a state-of-the-art digital camera. The Nikon Coolpix 5700 captured five megapixel images and had an eight-times zoom. At C$2,000, it was considered the top digital camera on the market. It was an enormous price tag for us at the time.

After all our hard work in New Zealand, *Green Ghost* was ready to go. I was happy again – happy to have a direction and a role to play, happy to be moving on to Australia in our steamer trunk with a mast.

CHAPTER 13

The Gouda Cruise to Fiji

(May – August 2003)

Once again, we'd reached escape velocity. We left behind the convenience of a car, the normality of a mailing address, the comfort of a social circle. We disconnected the phone, the TV, the Internet, and we did it all on schedule. Departing takes enormous energy and considerable faith. There are few sailors who fail at cruising, but there are plenty who fail to ever leave the dock. If letting go of all you know was easy, everyone would be doing it.

On May 1, 2003, we began with a short trip out to New Zealand's Great Barrier Island and the Coromandel Peninsula as a shake-down cruise. Our first few days went like this: the first afternoon was okay, the second day it was blowing thirty knots and the chop was so terrible that I burped spring garden soup all afternoon. I never want to taste that soup again. The third day we spent at anchor, rained in all day. The fourth day we stayed put with settled weather, except for a two-hour pulse of high wind that slammed our cozy little anchorage with thirty-five-knot gusts. A mere two hours of high winds may not sound like much of a hardship but you're probably picturing a windy afternoon. When you're cruising, the shit hits the fan in the dark.

Nik awoke from a deep sleep at midnight.

"I think we're dragging anchor," he said as he climbed over me to get out of bed. "I can hear it rumbling over the bottom."

"Shit," I answered, getting up too.

Nik looked around outside and confirmed that our position relative to the shoreline had changed. We were dragging into shallow water.

I turned the battery switch to the start position and Nik turned the ignition key in the cockpit. Our Isuzu diesel engine rumbled to life. It was a relief to know that we still had anchoring down to an art form. As Nik went forward to the bow, I manned the helm. With arm gestures Nik indicated where the anchor lay and I drove the boat forward at low speed while he operated the electric windlass to bring in the chain.

"We're up!" he yelled back when he saw the anchor at the surface.

I repositioned the boat, bringing it to a standstill with the bow pointed directly into the wind.

"Ten feet below the keel!" I called forward, giving Nik the depth of the water so that he would let out the appropriate amount of chain as the boat drifted back. Nik then attached the anchor bridle, two strong lines that took the strain of the anchor chain off the windlass and transferred it to the deck cleats on either side of the bow.

"Okay!" Nik called back, as he signalled to put the boat in reverse. I backed up slowly, setting the anchor, then revved up to 1,500 rpms just to be sure we had a good hold on the bottom.

Even though we were pretty good at it, re-anchoring at midnight never made for a good night's sleep. On our fifth day, we were tired, the weather was poor, and we didn't move.

A friend wrote an e-mail from Canada: *So, you're back to not having a care in the world. Is cruising better than you remembered it?* In my journal, I answered her question: *It's all coming back to me now – I remember cruising, first some bullshit, then some more.*

We tried to settle into it, sailing through waters alive with tiny blue penguins bobbing at the surface, dodging water spouts, and reacquainting ourselves with the frustrations of too much wind, not enough wind, and just the right amount of wind but from the wrong direction. We struggled to hit our stride.

At least one thing was good. Considering our eighteen-month hiatus of dockside living, Nik's stomach was doing well. He wasn't experiencing any seasickness. I figured that meant he was feeling pretty relaxed until the incident in the bilges one morning.

Thinking he smelled diesel and fearing a leak in one of our fuel tanks, Nik opened the floorboard over the engine room, lay down on the floor and leaned his whole torso into the hole, lowering his head and shoulders deep into the bilge. Then I heard a muffled yell.

"Uh-oh. My head's stuck, my head is stuck!"

In a cramped space in the bilge he had his head tightly wedged between the engine and the fibreglass hull.

"I can't get my head out!" he bellowed, more panicky now, his face down in the bilge.

"Calm down. There has to be a way to get it out if you got it in there in the first place," I said, aware that he was becoming more alarmed with every passing second.

I offered some suggestions regarding which way to move and he managed to wriggle out without tearing his ears off. His panic seemed a massive overreaction until I realized that his tension sprang from his pent-up anxiety about the 1,200 NM journey ahead. Nik liked everything about cruising, except going to sea.

⎈

By mid-May we'd sailed to Opua, the jumping-off point for most cruisers heading north to the islands of the southwest Pacific. We had a rendezvous with Vancouver friends in Fiji and we were pressed for time – the worst way to go to sea. We chose our weather window and two days after departure, we found ourselves close-reaching, pounding into three-metre seas with twenty-five knots of wind gusting to thirty-five. We hadn't chosen well. Our pending rendezvous had clouded our judgement and we were paying for our haste.

Conditions were unpleasant. Huge sprays of cold seawater launched from the bow flew back on the wind to dump heavily on the dodger and sometimes fly right over it, drenching the cockpit and anyone who sat in it.

The motion was dreadful. Duped by the pleasant coastal cruising before departure, Nik had decided not to take medication, an unfortunate gamble. In the rough offshore conditions, he applied a scopolamine patch, but it was already too late. He became seasick, throwing up every time he moved. When I came to wake him for his four-hour watch, I removed the bucket wedged into his bunk beside him. He sat up and retched; he swung his feet to the floor and heaved again; he stood up, convulsing. It was terrible to see him so seasick, but I'd been on for four hours myself and I had to sleep, so he had to go on watch.

On the off watch, I lay in my bunk and listened to every sound. The dominos shifted noisily in their tin box in a starboard locker. The forks were leaping in the cutlery drawer. The chain in the anchor locker was rising up – *chink, chink* – and settling back down again – *calunk*. I could hear a spoon repeatedly tracing an arc around the rim of a coffee cup in the galley sink: *zink* around, *zunk* back again. Now and then, over the cacophony below deck, I could hear the sound of Nik's stomach turning itself inside out in the cockpit.

As usual, my sense of smell was hyper activated. I smelled everything and everything smelled terrible. We were hot bunking. Beating into the weather as we were, heeled over, there was only one good spot to sleep. Lying on the leeward bunk, I could tell that Nik had eaten peanut butter on his previous shift. I could smell it on the pillow. I could smell the galley sink too. On a starboard tack our sinks did not drain well, causing the dregs from the latest dishwater to sit and rot in the drainpipe until the boat levelled out again. We'd been heeled over for days and the pounding of the seas pushed pulses of stink into the air, a fishy reek like tinned cat food.

Nothing tasted good. I couldn't drink coffee. I couldn't drink tea. Not even water appealed to me. I couldn't eat anything that was the slightest bit distasteful. The last bites of an apple near the core made me gag. The crusts of a sandwich turned me off.

Off watch I slept and dreamed of land, the earthy, smoky smell of it. I drooled on my pillow. Upon waking I experienced a strange phenomenon, a moment of remarkable calm. Deaf to all around me, I had a few seconds of delight when it seemed that all was quiet and motionless. Then full consciousness hit. In an instant the noise, the smell, the motion – I was awake and back in it, back in that place of nightless sleeps and sleepless nights.

By day four we couldn't take it anymore. It wasn't that we were afraid, we were just miserable. We decided to stop the boat and wait for better conditions. We hove to, setting our sails to go nowhere. It's the sailing equivalent to pulling over on the shoulder of the road, but not nearly as comfortable. That said, it was far more comfortable than the beating we were taking trying to sail to weather. Once we backed the foresail and locked the helm hard over, it was amazing how much the motion calmed down. Everything got quieter. The boat was flat. The forks stopped leaping. The dominoes settled in their tin. We could hear ourselves think, and better yet, we could hear our radar alarm.

On the radar, we set a range ring around the boat so that an alarm would sound should another vessel come within 3 NM of us. This allowed the two of us to rest together, something we'd never done before on an offshore passage. We'd always kept a human watch, switching places every four hours, but now, hove to with the radar alarm set, we both climbed into our bunks. Not well enough to read, we lay there and waited for the wind to abate.

Through the day we lost gear. It got blown off, washed off, or chafed off the boat. It was like letting fifty-dollar bills go in the wind. *Whoosh!* The life ring was torn from the stern rail and swept off the boat by a huge swell. *Whoosh!* One of our large docking fenders suffered the same fate. *Whoosh!* The BBQ cover was blown off in the wind. We rushed to tie the lid down before the grills were tossed into the sea.

In daylight, the conditions were bad. Then, darkness

brought a drama of its own. A sickening crashing sound, a sudden *bang-smash-clang* had us both bolt to attention just before midnight. The primary anchor tied down at the bow that had never *ever* budged before suddenly came loose and started swinging around on a few feet of chain. It flailed wildly, all sixty-five pounds of it, hitting the bow on the port side, then starboard, smashing against our newly painted hull of gleaming green perfection.

We both went out into the darkness. I watched from the cockpit as Nik bravely clipped his harness to the jacklines and crawled forward along the salty decks to wrestle in the flailing anchor and secure it once again. He couldn't see the damage in the darkness, but we both knew it was there. I could have cried at the thought of it. All that time we'd spent in the Half Moon Bay boatyard. Ten weeks of scraping, filling and fairing, sanding and priming and painting. I thought of the brand-new white vinyl lettering proclaiming our moniker on the bows. All that time and money and tender loving care to make *Green Ghost* beautiful again and now this. For all we knew, we'd pull into Fiji in a boat named, *Green ho*. The insult of the punishing weather was bad enough, but the injury to our pristine paint job by that flailing anchor was heartbreaking.

With the anchor wrestled in we both went below, stripped off our salty wet gear, and slumped back into our bunks. We'd been hove to for thirty-three hours and the bad weather was predicted to continue for another twenty-four. An endurance test, that's what it was – and it was wearing me down. I was in a strangely incongruous mental state, both maudlin and giddy. I turned in my bunk to face Nik.

"I want your life," I said sarcastically and we both burst out laughing.

Luckily the weather abated sooner than expected and in the end, we were hove to for only thirty-six hours before resuming our course. On the upside, we were well-rested and acclimatized, Nik's seasickness was over. While hove to, we were blown back, losing 60 NM of northing. Between the downtime and the lost miles, we'd added two days to our trip, but there was nothing to be done about it. Set the sails and carry on. That was all we could do. So we did.

After a week at sea, conditions improved as the wind veered south. The boat had become so salt encrusted during the rough weather that we were happy when a day of pouring rain cleaned up the decks and the cockpit. The interior was another matter. We'd sailed out of the temperate climes into the tropics. It was suffocating and stuffy below deck. Between the seas spraying over us and the rain pouring from the skies, every hatch and porthole had been sealed up tight for days. Our small 12-volt fans weren't helping much. There was a horrendous cheesy smell, an old towel smell. You know that smell – that damp dishcloth that never got rinsed out and sat wet-in-a-corner-for-way-too-long smell? Our boat, our beds, for all we knew, even our bodies smelled like that. For the aromatic nature of the passage, we dubbed it "The Gouda Cruise."

Flying fish welcomed us back into tropical waters. The days became gorgeously hot, the nights star filled and wondrous, and the sea mirrored the night sky with stellar flashes of phosphorescent light dancing in our wake. The weather became so benign we had to start the engine. In the calm conditions Nik put a line in the water and filled what little room was left in our freezer with mahi-mahi and wahoo.

On our fourteenth day, in time for our rendezvous, we glided through the mooring field at Savusavu, Fiji, the forty-third boat to arrive that season.

"Ahoy, *Green Ghost!*" someone shouted across the anchorage.

How wonderful it was to hear salutations called out by the familiar voices of our sailing friends. How thrilling it was to have found Fiji. To have set out from New Zealand and charted our course, to have earned every mile all on our own – it was a satisfaction so deep it felt bottomless. Our hearts swelled in the rush of accomplishment. How proud we were to arrive safe and sound, and well, okay, a little bit cheesy.

Our arrival called for celebration, but upon making our landfall, we couldn't enjoy a night out on dry land because the customs office closed at five p.m. and it was ten minutes after. Our check-in with the officials would have to wait for the following morning. But that didn't matter. We tied up to a mooring ball in the peaceful anchorage and in our stock-still, flat-floored floating home we poured ourselves strong G&Ts, turned up the music, and danced like fools in our tiny salon.

☸

Our high spirits continued through two weeks of entertaining guests. Having guests aboard always put us in a festive frame of mind. Our Vancouver friends, Brenda and Scott, came and went. In the void of their departure we fell into a familiar funk. By this time, we had a name for it – PGD, Post-Guest Depression. In the wake of guest departures, it was back to the work of cruising: tidy up, top up, and move on.

Our initial movements among the islands proved to us the size of the Fijian archipelago. With more than three hundred islands in the nation, there were thousands of anchorages. After leaving Savusavu, we visited some less-travelled isles and found ourselves completely alone. The privacy and seclusion was unparalleled, but the lonely anchorages gave way to a cheerless feeling of isolation. Then we went to Musket Cove.

At Malolo Lailai Island, just over 10 NM from Nadi off the west coast of Viti Levu, over forty boats idled at anchor in turquoise water off the cruiser-friendly four-star island resort. Peopled and touristy with bead-your-hair kiosks, pedicures, and back massages, it was most definitely not the real Fiji but it was what we needed – company and fun. It may have also been the reason the rest of Fiji felt empty. Everybody was at Musket Cove.

Offering a laundry facility, hot water showers, garbage disposal, a dinghy dock, fresh water, a small grocery store, telephones, beach BBQs, and a Three Dollar Bar, Musket Cove was a little slice of heaven. Wherever we go in the world, the place that makes all these things available to yachties is the place where we find all the boats. It was not a cultural immersion, but it was a vacation from our vacation and a distraction from the fact that our New Zealand-repaired alternator had gone on the fritz.

While I was elated by the access to a washing machine, Nik thrilled to the surfing charters. He was taken out to the reef breaks by a well-powered boat and enjoyed the best spots with other surfers. With so many things to spend money on, there was a daily flight of fifties from our hands. I suppose it was not surprising that in my role as the voice of reason, the expensive resort life began to wear on me. To give our wallet a rest, we sailed west to Waya Island in the Mamanucas and then on to the Yasawas, made famous by the movie *The Blue Lagoon*.

While the cost of fun wore me down, the gear breakages were wearing down Nik. The alternator was repaired after two ferry trips to Nadi, but then the outboard engine began acting up. These mechanical failures sent the captain into violent spasms. He had little patience for it. While Nik had learned a great deal since our early sailing days, I remained next to useless as an apprentice to the mechanical/electrical workings of our boat. If he couldn't fix it, I certainly couldn't. Although I felt concern or disappointment when breakdowns occurred, Nik was apoplectic. I suppose I never felt like I should be able to fix it; I didn't know how and I didn't care that I didn't know. It wasn't a reflection on me as a person. I figured, if you don't know how, you find someone who does. Nik, I suppose, felt the shame of inadequacy. Perhaps he felt emasculated when he didn't have a manly quick fix for all things greasy and mechanical. Systems failures themselves didn't upset me much, but the explosive fury of the captain, when inanimate objects failed to function, did.

"What's wrong now?" were frequent words from my lips. I urged the captain to keep it all in perspective, imploring him to see that despite all the work of it, despite the gear failures and breakdowns, overall, cruising was a good life. But my entreaties were often met with a stream of profanity, not at me, but at the inanimate object that failed to co-operate.

There was no doubt that we hadn't hit our stride in Fiji. I strived to make the best of it, to live in the moment. After all, it would soon be over. Our unplanned future loomed on the western horizon. At the end of the season we would arrive in Australia, the end of the road for us. I harboured hope for a cruising life beyond Australia, but the captain's reaction to breakages threatened that dream. In a reversal of the roles we'd played in New Zealand, what I worked to cherish, he began to loath, often expressing a general negativity about any future cruising.

The recent trip up from New Zealand hadn't helped. Nik's propensity for seasickness wasn't getting better and his dislike of offshore passages was growing. As we sailed west, with the Pacific behind us and the Coral Sea slowly disappearing in our wake, I began to despair. I began to think Nik would never sail past Australia and I didn't want our trip to end there.

☸

It always seemed a pity that our last few days in every country were spent frantically running around an urban area searching out customs offices, immigration officials, parts, charts, and grocery carts. We left the stunning waters of the Yasawa Islands for the crowded man-made marina basin at Vuda Point Marina near Lautoka. There, we fell into the usual frenzied preparations for the next offshore leg to Vanuatu.

As always, we were so busy upon departure that we had no time to pause and reflect on our time in Fiji. It was only when we put to sea and looked back at the mountainous horizon line fading in our wake that we contemplated the laughter and the smiles we were leaving behind. As we sailed west for the sunset, although we'd struggled to find our groove in Fiji, we smiled at our memories of the many anchorages where the giggles of the women and children drifted from the beach out across the water and filled our cockpit with delight.

CHAPTER 14

Tanna and New Caledonia

(August – October 2003)

After four and a half days at sea, Tanna, an island in southern Vanuatu, rose up on the western horizon as beautiful and welcome as a landfall can be. On a Thursday morning, we motorsailed into Port Resolution filled with a sense of discovery. Here, there were no resort hotels, no motorized vehicles, and no electricity. We imagined it looked much the same as it did for Captain Cook who had arrived just like we had, 229 years and nine days before.

At nearly every destination so far, Nik had gone ashore, looked around, taken a deep breath, and confidently exhaled the affirmative, "I could live here!"

"You *are* living here," was always my reply.

In Tanna, it was my turn to make that pronouncement. Port Resolution is stunning. We glided through sapphire water over soft coral forests swaying in the current, past a surf beach to our port side and hot springs steaming in rocky pools at the water's edge to starboard. Cliffs of buff-coloured ash strata and a white sand beach marked the entrance to the harbour, while inside, a black rocky shoreline gave way to a jet sand beach at the head of the bay. Tropical emerald jungle tumbled over itself, nearly spilling into the sea. A local man paddled across the bay in a primitive dugout canoe balanced by a crude outrigger lashed together with bits of twine. A mountainous horizon line crowned the scene. The active volcano, Mount Yasur, was spewing ash and steam into the sky. No wonder there were twenty-seven cruising boats in the anchorage; this was the most beautiful place on earth.

Ashore we found the Port Resolution Yacht Club, an open-air meeting house that had once been a church. Nearby was a tap with fresh water, a place to do laundry by hand, a shower, a tidy garbage drop, and a fire pit. Various national flags and ensigns hung from the yacht club ceiling, most of them wind-worn and frayed, left behind by cruisers who likely looked much the same. Stanley, a young Melanesian man neatly dressed in western clothing, greeted us. Over a hundred languages are spoken in the Vanuatu archipelago, but English, French, and Bislama (English-based creole) are the official languages and Stanley spoke English very well. He told us about check-in procedures on the far side of the island and offered to make arrangements to get us there by truck. He took groups of cruisers across every few days, so we signed up for the next trip to check in. In the meantime, Stanley told us, we were welcome to come ashore to the yacht club or to visit the village.

Taking a short walk about the village, we were immediately struck by the difference in the standard of living compared to Fiji. There was not nearly as much corrugated iron and cinderblock housing in Port Resolution. The village was traditional with most of the homes being thatched huts with low entranceways. The plumbing was entirely outdoors in neatly thatched outhouses with palm frond doors. The boats were all dugouts. There were no outboards here.

The pathways in the village were lined with white stones and landscaped with colourful plants, the kind that grow in corporate offices back home. Flowering fragrant brugmansia hung overhead, dangling their peach-coloured trumpet-shaped blooms. Every yard was neatly swept, every garden perfectly tended. A professional landscape architect couldn't have planned a more appealing setting. I thought we'd sailed into a fairy tale.

Getting lost on our walk through the village, we came upon a graveyard. There was a perimeter of plants around the cemetery. Each grave was neatly outlined with small stones and crowned with a jar of red, yellow, and green leaves. The dirt between the graves had been meticulously swept, leaving a bristle broom pattern like a vacuum cleaner pattern in deep pile carpet. There was not a footprint anywhere. It was spotless, weedless, and perfectly heart-breaking. There were so many tiny graves. I wondered who they cried with – all the mothers who lost their children here. I wondered how they healed their heartache. A familiar sadness swept over me and grief tightened my throat – not a fairy tale after all.

⚓

Stanley arranged a Mount Yasur tour for a group of cruisers. Nik and I could scarcely believe it. In our geology student days, this was an adventure we'd never dreamed we'd have.

At dusk, our group tumbled into the back of pickup trucks and set off for the national park in great anticipation. The road ended in a parking area on a small plateau. This was the closest tourists were allowed to get to the volcano during active periods. Lucky for us, the volcano was relatively inactive at the time and we were allowed to proceed to the rim on foot.

We hiked up a worn path of black sand. I took a pinch of it and noted it was angular and gritty between my fingertips. I thought back to Dr. Plach, my third-year professor of Igneous Petrology, and I knew because he'd taught me, this wasn't sand – it was ash. As we ascended the final ten metres, there was a deep rumbling, like the throaty roar of a wild cat. Thunder, but not from the sky. It rumbled up through my legs, right up out of Mother Earth herself. At the rim of the crater, we could hear the volcano's respiration, hissing and wheezing, breathing and spitting. Yasur was alive – alive and a little bit testy. We stood in the sulphurous atmosphere, mesmerized while molten red bombs of lava flew high into the air. A live volcano, actively erupting only three hundred metres from us! How thrilling it was to witness the very thing we'd studied in school. As dusk gave way to darkness, the contrast grew and an ever more impressive light show emerged – fierce red fireworks, Gaia's violent blazing blood arced across the black night sky.

All around us the ash slopes were covered in solidified bombs that had been shot out of the volcano during periods of higher activity. The newly formed rock varied from fist-sized chunks to blobs the size of Volkswagens. I looked around the edges of the larger bombs half expecting to see a melted video camera and the charred arm of a tourist sticking out. It was more than a little unnerving standing among the boulders and contemplating the fact that they had all rained down from the sky.

We stood on the rim of the crater, awestruck by the processes of our magnificent planet, full of wonder at our dynamic Earth. There was nothing about Tanna that was familiar. It was as though we'd arrived on an entirely different planet, where we were challenged by the extraordinary at every turn. It was hard to believe Tanna could get even better, yet it did.

⚓

We'd heard from the local people that there would soon be days of celebration at the Nekiowar Festival. They said it would begin with the Toka ceremony.

"What is this festival for?" we asked Stanley. "Do you have it every year?"

"It is a meeting of the tribes. There is feasting and dancing and gifts are exchanged. Usually we have it between August and November, but sometimes we don't have it," he answered in his usual way, both exacting and vague.

We'd heard that the Toka ceremony would begin on a Friday, but a chicken changed everything. Someone at the host village had gutted a chicken and it was seen that its organs were reversed – the heart was on the right. This was deemed a bad omen by the Chief and the festival was delayed for four days.

When the Toka began, we were convinced to rise at 3:45 a.m. to pile into the back of pickup trucks by 4:30 a.m. to ride across the island, past the steaming Mount Yasur, over the ash plateau to the first village on the right beyond the dried river-bed. With the early start, we hoped to catch the Napen-Napen, the women's dance in the darkness, followed by the start of the men's ceremony at sunrise.

Hopping out of the back of the trucks, we could hear and feel a tribal beat above a chorus of male voices more than one hundred strong. Like the subterranean rumble of Mount Yasur itself, a rhythmic pounding vibrated up from the earth, through our legs, into our bodies. We looked at one another in disbelief. We were immediately collectively swept up in it – whatever *it* was.

The thumping sound drew us in and we ran toward the source. We dashed down a grass path and as we crested a small rise we saw them: a thousand or more Tannese people gathered in a large clearing. The dancers, in golden grass skirts, stomped their feet in unison and sang in a low throaty harmony. With the sun rising over the hill behind us, the first rays of dawn shot glittering shafts of light through the dust kicked up at their feet.

We'd missed the women's dance but they were still in at-tendance, still in full dress from their nocturnal performance, wearing costumes of brilliantly dyed grass skirts. Their faces were brightly painted and they had vibrantly coloured foot-long feathers sticking out of their hair. Colourful adornment abound-ed. Red, blue, green, and gold tinsel garlands – the kind we put on Christmas trees – were wrapped around heads and necks and chests.

The local people cleared a path for us to get to the front of the crowd to take photographs. We stood with our jaws hanging open and our eyes wide. Our throats were tight – speechless. The hair on my neck stood on end. Tears welled up in my eyes. The energy of that spiritual frenzy awakened a kindred primeval connection, a sense of unity I'd never felt before.

When the dancing ceased late in the morning, the pig-slaughtering ceremony began. Groups of men and boys arrived in a procession, each group carrying aloft a live pig tied on a bamboo palette. The pig was straddled by a man or a boy who held the ears of the pig high. The group sang in unison, and circled the area, displaying their offering for the feast. Finally, the palette was laid down and the pig was given one quick blow to the head, dying instantly.

By mid-day there were a dozen hogs lying out on the grounds ready to be dressed for the feasting. Tired and dirty, covered in the dust kicked up by the dancers, we headed back to the anchorage in the early afternoon, leaving the Tannese to the feasting of the Nekiowar Festival. As the truck bumped along the dirt road back toward Port Resolution, Nik and I agreed that Tanna was the most remarkable place we'd seen yet. Tanna reminded us of why we set sail in the first place, to seek the magic and find the treasures life holds.

⚓

Rather than sail north to other islands in Vanuatu we chose to move on to Nouméa, the capital city of the French territory of New Caledonia. Same planet, different worlds; from the land of dugout canoes, thatched huts, and outhouses we stepped into the happening, high-end super-styling French culture of Nouméa, the Paris of the South Pacific.

We pulled into the marina at Port Moselle where customs, immigration, and quarantine officials came to the boat in an orderly and timely fashion. When the paperwork was done, there was no need to move from the dockside. We'd been given one free night's stay at the dock and a voucher for a free beer at the nearby pub. How very civilized. The French appreciate the sailor.

We'd been told that New Caledonia was extraordinarily expensive and it was, but we fell in love with the place the moment we went ashore. Everything was posh – lovely shops, gorgeous clothing, beautiful art, and great groceries. Less than five minutes' walk from the docks the public market teamed with fresh fish, fragrant baked goods, and perfect produce. The handcrafted art was an explosion of colour, with tables full of the beautiful products of people's imagination. Beads abounded and shells and polished serpentinite were incorporated into everything you could think of. Bamboo carvings, ceramics, and beautiful fabrics were also for sale.

Beyond the market, in town, we noted how different Nouméa was. New Zealand had been a bit too carbon copy of North America with their Body Shops, Starbucks, and Chapters bookstores. Nouméa was refreshing, not yet franchised North American-style and nearly all the shops were new to us. We spent time in fancy kitchen shops and restaurant supply stores, ogling the cookware. At the supermarket, we behaved like kids in a candy shop. Everything was imported directly from France. Soon we were gorging on baguettes, Brie cheese, blue cheese, Emmental, olive herb bread, dry cured salami, and wine. In Nouméa we centred our lives on the culinary delights, working our day around morning chocolate éclairs and afternoon café stops for espresso.

We soon made a break from the city life and enjoyed a downwind southbound run to Île des Pins where we revelled in the delights of the island. We snorkelled through fantastic sea fans and collected flour-fine white sand from the beach. We walked through the ruins of an old prison, read tombstones in a cemetery for deportees, and hiked the 262 metres up to Pic N'Ga, the highest point on the island. As in Bora Bora, the hues in the lagoon were unbelievable. Even as we stood there taking in the view, we both declared that it couldn't be real, it was too blue.

After weeks away from the Port Moselle market, our fridge was bare, the water and fuel tanks were low, and the laundry hamper was overflowing. There were many chores to address before departing New Caledonia, so we decided to get back to town early, with plenty of time before our month-long visa ran out. For once, we'd have a leisurely departure.

Back in Port Moselle, hoping to send some images home by e-mail from an Internet cafe, Nik downloaded photos from our new digital camera. Placing it on the navigation table, he inadvertently set the camera down on the safety string for the lens cap. When he turned the camera on, the zoom lens was prevented from extending by the trapped string. The lens jammed, resulting in a persistant error message on the camera's visual display. The manual indicated that the only way to correct this was to take the camera to a qualified representative for service.

I was annoyed. The camera had been so expensive. We'd owned it for only eight months and we had the rest of the magnificent islands of Vanuatu to photograph before the season was out.

In moments like this the best thing is to get far, far away from one's spouse before you start asking stupid questions like, What did you do that for? and Why can't you be more careful? In normal life, I would've called my sisters to let off some steam, or met with a girlfriend and whined into my latte about the broken camera. But I couldn't do either of these things. The only person I knew in Nouméa was Nik and I was stuck in a forty-two-foot space with him. I knew it was best to keep quiet, so I went out the next day and had my jaw wired shut. Ha. I'm kidding, of course. Instead, I pulled myself together. It was an accident pure and simple and such a ridiculous design-flaw in an expensive camera. There was nothing to be done but add *camera repair shop* to our long list of things to do before departure. Thank goodness, we'd given ourselves a little extra time.

Late on Thursday morning, we dropped by the immigration office to make sure we knew the process for our Monday checkout.

"We've come to check your office hours for our Monday departure," we announced.

"You will not be seeing me on Monday, you will be seeing me tomorrow," the officer replied sternly as he reviewed our passports.

"But we have a month-long visa," we claimed, knowing we'd arrived on August 29.

"No," the officer said, "you have a thirty-day visa. Sunday is the 28th so you must check out on Friday."

He was right and we were frantic. So much for our leisurely departure.

We set to our errands in high gear, hitting the market, the souvenir shops, the grocery stores, and a couple of camera repair shops. We sent rushed e-mails at the Internet café and found a phone booth for phone calls home. By Friday, the last of our laundry was done, our water tanks were full, and our camera was being looked at by a shop that would have an answer for us at the close of business. If we got lucky, perhaps a repair could be completed by Monday. We taxied to immigration and customs where we unabashedly begged both offices for an extension of our stay until Monday. They took pity on us – tourists with a broken camera – allowing a Monday morning checkout.

In the end, all was for nothing because our camera could not be repaired in Nouméa. On Monday morning, we packed it up, went to the FedEx office, paid for insurance, and sent it by courier to Australia for repair. We hoped it could be fixed and return shipped to Port Vila, Vanuatu, our next destination.

By the time we'd checked out with the customs officials and fuelled up duty-free, it was too late in the day for an offshore departure. As the sun went down, we made our way 20 NM south, where we set our anchor for the night. We needed a night's rest before tackling open water.

That night as I lay in bed seeking the peace of sleep, I thought back to the FedEx office. All day I'd been thinking that the insurance we'd purchased was so reasonable. I did the mental math again, thinking through the currency conversions. My eyes flew open. Staring up through the hatch at the starry night sky, I suddenly realized that we'd insured our expensive camera at one-tenth its original cost.

CHAPTER 15

Vanuatu, The Northern Islands

(October – November 2003)

We sailed out of New Caledonia on flat seas and gentle breezes, which freed up time I normally spent thinking about weather and allowed me to worry about our camera all the way to our next destination. On our final day of sailing toward Port Vila, the capital of Vanuatu on the island of Efate, we realized our timing was poor. Our GPS indicated an arrival time of ten p.m. A nighttime arrival into an unknown harbour was against our better judgement, but the thought of standing off the island until daylight was equally unappealing, particularly because the conditions were building with every passing hour.

We knew some friends were already at anchor in the port so we called them on the VHF radio for advice on the harbour. Learning that the entrance was well marked we decided to proceed. We sailed into the harbour effortlessly, anchored next to our friends, and settled in for a comfortable night's sleep, every second of it relished all the more for not being at sea.

In Port Vila, we spent the usual half-day doing the quarantine, customs, and immigration dance and then roamed the streets of town to see what was on offer. I liked Port Vila. It was not nearly as flashy as Nouméa, but it had a pleasant vibe, the right combination of off-the-beaten-track third-worldliness and sushi bars.

We made efficient use of a few days of adverse weather tackling some must-dos. The most pressing item was to secure entry into the next country on our planned route and that meant a stop at the Australian Consulate to apply for visitors' visas.

Next, we searched out the FedEx office in the hope that the camera-fixers in Australia might have come through. No luck. This left us with a tough choice. When weather conditions became favourable, we weren't sure whether we should wait or move on. We discussed the matter with friends over the radio.

Here's something you might not know. Cruisers are a nosey bunch. Most everyone leaves their VHF radio either on Channel 16 or on the local working channel so that they can get in touch with their friends on other boats about trips ashore, cocktail hour, and other plans or problems. It's like a party telephone line – for everyone. When one boat calls another you better believe half the anchorage is listening. This eavesdropping on other people's conversations is called "lurking." Myself, I wasn't much for it. I felt it put me in an awkward position. I never knew if I should act as if I did know or pretend as though I didn't know everyone's personal business the next time I saw them on shore. Bolder lurkers didn't give a damn – they listened and they let you know it.

Shortly after our chat on the radio, Nik jumped in the dinghy to do an errand on shore. A neighbouring boat waved him over. We'd met the owner only once. Norbert was a mammoth German man. He had shoulder-length blond hair, a missing thumb, and a belly scar that looked like a gunshot wound. With his barrel-chested six-foot-four stature, he looked more Viking than German.

As Nik pulled alongside his boat, Norbert bent over the lifelines, booming in his German accent: "I'm going to give you some advice. Don't vait for zee camera." This man was clearly a bold lurker. "You know vy? I'll tell you vy. Because I vill swim with zee dugong tree times, I vill catch four tunas, and I vill scuba dive zee *Coolidge* twice, and vare vill you be? You vill be stuck in zis shithole vaiting for your camera, dat is vare you vill be."

We took his point and left Port Vila the following day without the camera. We departed on an overnight sail to the island of Epi hoping to swim with a relatively tame dugong, a relative of the manatee, that was known to frequent the anchorage there. As we approached the island the following morning, we downloaded our Sailmail and received a message from Australia that read: Your camera has been repaired and is ready for shipment.

Damn.

At Epi, we watched and waited for four days, but we never did see the dugong. Perhaps he only came out for people who had cameras.

A forecast for poor weather hurried us on to the large island of Malekula where we sought shelter in Port Sandwich, anchoring off a farm, before the skies opened up and unleashed a torrent of rain upon us.

The weather cleared by morning and as we sat in the cockpit enjoying our first cup of coffee, a man in a dugout canoe startled us when he called out in broken English.

"Hello, my name is Ezekiel!" he shouted. "Always nice to say hello!"

We returned his greeting and soon he was alongside, and despite his proximity, still shouting.

"My name is bible name! Ezekiel!"

We quickly realized he was quite deaf and shouted just to hear himself speak. Ezekiel invited us and the other boat in the anchorage to visit his home later that day. When we did, he showed us his photo albums that were bursting with boat cards and photographs, mementos from other cruisers. After some interesting discussion about his family, his farm, his religion, and the local politics, he presented us with gifts. Neatly arranged on two woven mats stood two huge piles of fruit and vegetables. We were taken aback by his generosity and although we were inclined to refuse some of the bounty on the grounds that we couldn't possibly consume it all, we felt that might be rude, so we accepted every coconut, papaya, lemon, lime, hot pepper, and spring onion with gratitude. We too left our boat cards, and when we eventually made it to Australia, I shipped him a new photo album to continue his collection.

※

"This place is fantastic," Nik said, sipping strong brew from a new French espresso cup. "I am loving Vanuatu."

"It's two o'clock on Tuesday. What would you be doing if you were back at work right now?" I asked him.

"Preparing a sales forecast for a Friday deadline," he said.

"And where would you rather be?"

We were both loving Vanuatu. It was so different from any where we'd ever been.

We were gliding along in perfect conditions on an inter-island afternoon sail. Nik's attitude toward cruising had improved steadily after leaving Fiji. I wanted to believe we'd become more relaxed, more accepting of the unpredictability of the cruising life, but in reality, I think it was just that *Green Ghost* had settled in too. In Fiji, there'd been maintenance issues with the outboard and the alternator that detracted from fun. New Caledonia had recharged us, and Vanuatu was smooth sailing, both literally and figuratively. We were finally hitting our stride.

"Well, that's a no-brainer. I'd rather be here, obviously."

"We can't afford to forget this, you know – this feeling right now," I said.

"I won't forget Vanuatu," he answered.

"I won't forget Vanuatu either," I said, "but that's not what I mean. I want us to remember how good this is. When we go home and get jobs and get caught up in the rat race again, I'm afraid we'll forget what freedom tastes like. I'm afraid we'll forget this feeling of wonder. I'm afraid we'll forget to come back."

※

Farther north along the east coast of Malekula, in Banam Bay, there was a village known for its dance performances.

"Kastam Dancing," it was called in the local Bislama language, meaning a dance according to their original customs. We had no difficulty searching it out. Within half an hour of setting our anchor, John Eddy, the son of the chief, had paddled out to us in his dugout canoe. He was the local Kastam Dance booking agent and he asked us whether we would like to come ashore for a dance performance planned in four hours' time.

The men and the women danced in separate performances. The men wore the traditional "nambas," a long leaf wrapped in a spiral fashion around the penis, sheathing it from base to tip. The end of the leaf was then tucked into a belt that was worn around the waist. In this way, the penis is held up and out from the body in an erect position while the scrotum is left hanging. The men's performance was musical and rhythmic and the dancers appeared to enjoy their performance as much as we did.

The women were less enthusiastic. Bare-breasted and in grass-skirts they danced in a less demonstrative way. They seemed disconcerted by our audience and their disinterest made me feel uncomfortable. It was work. It was a tourist show. It brought income to the village, but it did not exude the raw energy of the Toka ceremony on Tanna where the people danced in the joy of celebration oblivious to our presence.

We stayed on at Banam Bay and hired Dixon, a local guide, to take us on a jungle walk to some caves high on the volcanic slopes on land belonging to a man named Carl. Dixon and Carl showed us the easiest route to walk, right up the middle of a jungle stream, leeches and all. Later, ankle deep in bat shit, we viewed the promised cave and, looking up at the noisy colony, promptly lost our footing. I caught myself and regained my balance, but Nik and the rest of our party found themselves either knee down or hand down in six inches of guano.

After a swim in a freshwater pond, we lunched by a rushing river, sharing our picnic with the two men. They asked if we would like to see another cave and we eagerly agreed. They confessed that they had never taken tourists there and that was obvious from the not-so-obvious path.

At first look, it wasn't much of a cave; it was more of a corridor in the rock. It was dry at the opening but the deeper you went inside the more water was underfoot. Forty metres in it became so dark that we couldn't see. Just when it seemed too dark to go on a faint light glowed ahead. We kept going. I assumed we'd step out into daylight at the other end, but what we came upon was far more fantastic. The narrow passageway opened up into a huge cathedral-like room. Shafts of jungle-green light shot through a hole in the top of the vaulted ceiling, lighting the cave floor. A spring-fed creek flowed into the cave and formed a large pond within it.

As we leapt over the water to gain entry, we were startled by an EOUS – an eel of unusual size. It was like something right out of *The Princess Bride*. Its head was huge, its body thick, long and tapering. We were fascinated by what seemed a magic creature, a mighty eel emperor patrolling his cave kingdom in the highlands of Vanuatu. But Dixon called for a machete. He raised a steady hand high and struck a blow with considerable force. The machete walloped the surface and water sprayed everywhere, but the eel was gone. Horrified, I asked him why he wanted to kill it.

"To eat," he said.

Of course, I thought. How ignorant I was. Where I saw a magnificent eel, a precious creature, he saw protein. As we hiked back down to sea level, my happiness that the eel had survived was tempered by my concern over what Dixon would have for supper.

The volcanic island of Ambrym is known for its wood and stone carvers. Ashore in Ranon Bay we spoke with a local man, Jeffrey, and told him that we were interested in trading goods for carvings. He suggested we return to our boat and bring our trade goods to shore, and in the meantime he would have some carvings lined up for us to browse.

Back on *Green Ghost* we got ruthless. What T-shirts could go? Did we have extra food we could unload? Tools? Rope? We took a smattering of things to shore in a bag and hoped to find a carving we liked, planning to offer one or more of our goods in trade. On our return to the village Jeffrey informed us that this was not how it worked. We were told to lay out everything we'd brought and let the men from the village take a look. We weren't shopping. They were. I found the situation awkward. Fortunately, my input didn't seem to matter. On the island of Ambrym business transactions such as these were the man's job, and Nik took the lead.

We'd brought a large coil of yacht braid rope to shore. It was an old halyard, three-eighths of an inch thick and well over a hundred feet long. This was a desirable item and the men pounced upon it. Unfortunately for us, there were few carvings on offer and the ones that had been coughed up were not of particularly good quality. We couldn't part with the line for any of the items we'd seen at our first stop in the village, so we asked Jeffrey if we could take the rope to the central carving "warehouse" in the middle of the village and see if anyone there was willing to trade.

There, among a small group of men, was a very elderly man with beautifully carved pieces. We fell into negotiations with him using Jeffrey as translator. We chose his walking stick and one of his war clubs and produced the length of line and several other items for trade. The old carver's eyes got big and round. He folded his arms. He unfolded his arms. He put his hands together and pressed his fingertips to his lips. All the other men began talking. A few more men came around to see what was going on, and soon there was a small crowd gathered around the rope. The old carver stood there with his hands cupped around his face – what to do, what to do, he seemed to be thinking. His cronies shouted instructions at him as if it was a game show.

"Choose the yacht braid!"

"Ask for cash!"

"Ask for both!" they might have been saying.

The poor old carver was hard pressed. His hands moved again, now one on the hip, one over the eyes, then both over the eyes, then both hands through his hair, then back to his face. Either he was deftly working this bartering scene or it was a big decision, maybe both. He wanted the rope, that was obvious, but he needed cash as well. We produced the 2,000 vatu that we had in our pockets and asked if he would consider taking the money, the rope, and all the other items we had with us for the two carvings. Deep breaths were taken, mental calculations were made. Finally, he nodded his head, "Yes."

The small crowd erupted in approval, big smiles all around. The local men nearly knocked the old carver over with all the backslapping that followed. The halyard was then passed around the gathering, which produced more affirmative nodding among the men. Yes! Yes! It was a good deal.

✵

We'd idled away a month in the northern islands of Vanuatu and we would've stayed longer, but cyclone season was approaching. On this northbound journey, we'd found ourselves in the company of a dwindling number of other yachts. The local radio nets had quieted while the long-distance cruising nets were abuzz with communications from boats already en route to Australia.

At the island of Espiritu Santo, we pulled into Luganville among half a dozen other boats and took the last mooring buoy off the resort on Aore Island across from town. Paying for a mooring ball allowed us free use of the resort facilities. We tied up to the float, jumped in the dinghy, and hit the swimming pool to do some research. A group of our cruising friends were already there and twelve of us soaked in the warm water, enjoying cold beer delivered poolside by the charming hotel staff.

Despite the idyllic setting it was tough to relax. Every boat at Aore was waiting for weather to voyage west to Australia before cyclonic activity developed in the southwestern Pacific.

The usual pre-crossing group hype was ramping up among the sailors and the conversation turned to who was already out there getting beat up in heavy weather. On the threshold of a significant passage, it was always a bit of a trick to insulate ourselves from the edginess of other cruisers and remain immune to their tension while remaining open to information they might provide. Talking to the folks who had been holed up at Aore for a week waiting for the perfect weather system, we learned everything we needed to know – how best to get to town, the ferry schedule, the location of customs and immigration, where the market was, and how to get fuel, water, and groceries.

In all we were in Luganville for only four days, a record for us for preparing for an ocean passage. It was the same thing every time: paperwork with the officials, food at the market, fuel and water, then wait for the weather, then go.

We opted to water-up by jerry jug using the water available from a hose at the resort's small dinghy dock. We borrowed empty jugs from other people and used every water carrier we had to speed the process by minimizing our dinghy trips. *Green Ghost* carries eight hundred litres of water and though we could live on less, we always filled the water tanks before a big ocean passage, just in case. We'd done two trips in the dinghy carting about 150 litres per load and we were back for our third run. I filled one of our white buckets when Nik stopped me.

"Wait. What's that in the water?" he said.

I stopped the water flow and hopped down into the dinghy to take a look. Through the clear water in the bottom of a white bucket we could see reddish-brown five-millimetre thread-like *worms*! We'd half-filled our on-board water tanks with worm-water. With all the boats moored off the hotel and all the water usage, the reservoir on shore had been drained very low. The draw pipe was accessing the sludgy bottom and the scummy top of the remaining water supply. We stopped filling up, gave our tanks a double-dose of bleach, and purchased carboys of bottled water for drinking. Getting water anywhere else was not an option. We had to live with worm-water – all the way to Australia.

Our route took us across the top of New Caledonia and Chesterfield Reefs then bent southwest toward Bundaberg, Queensland. In consistently strong twenty- to twenty-five-knot trade winds, it was our fastest passage yet. We covered the nearly 1,000 NM to Australia in seven days and three hours, averaging six and a half knots.

The passage was a triumph not only because of our respectable speed, but because it was the first open-water passage in a long time that had not made Nik sick. He felt good. Even when the forks were leaping in the drawer, he didn't barf once, in no small part because he was back on the patch.

Nearing the coast, full of anticipation, we searched the blue scalloped horizon for hours. With only 20 NM to go, there was no hint of a continental landmass. No wonder it took early explorers so long to find Australia. It's practically invisible from the sea. Finally, the thin brown smudge of Bundaberg appeared on the horizon.

"Land, ho! Hello, Australia!" Nik called out.

I thought of Ezekiel. He was right. It's always nice to say hello.

CHAPTER 16

Toronto

(November 2003 – November 2008)

By late November 2003, we'd sailed into Australia and land-ed in reality. We'd reached our destination and had come face to face with the "figuring it out when we get there" part of our plan that long ago had seemed so very far away. There were many possible endings to a Pacific odyssey; you could keep sailing north then west, up and over Australia then on through Asia to continue a circumnavigation, or you could head for the North Pacific to circle back toward North America in a circum-Pacific route. Some sailors were happy with their one ocean adventure and sold their boats in New Zealand or Australia. Some stayed put and worked on their immigration status. Others paid to have their boats shipped home by freighter. But we weren't looking for an ending. Our hearts whispered, "Further" – we wanted *more* but our bank account cried out much louder for the same. We were the only couple in the fleet who packed up our boat for long-term storage in Scarborough, Queensland. We weren't saying goodbye to *Green Ghost*. We were only saying, "See ya laytah, mate."

In Australia, we crossed paths with Norbert.

"*Green Ghost*, vat is zee plan now?" he asked us.

He laughed when he told us we'd only just been re-united with our repaired camera. (It had finally been couriered to us upon our arrival in Australia.) But he grew more serious when we told him our longer-term plan – that we would store our boat for two or three years while we went back to Canada to make some money.

"No," he told us flatly. "You vill not be two or zree years, you vill take longer. Ven you vork you vill have to pay for zee haircut and you vill have to pay for zee cloze. You vill be spending so much money to make money. You cannot save. You vill be gone longer zan two years, longer zan zree. I know, I have just done it."

It was advice we didn't want to hear.

✹

Packing up *Green Ghost* was a sweaty, back-breaking process in the Australian heat. Cleaned of all grime, unloaded of all food, and packed up with all the sails and deck gear stored below decks, she was hauled out and moved to the long-term storage yard at Scarborough Marina. In the barbed wire enclosure, she was protected by security cameras in daylight and by guard dogs at night. Out of the cyclone belt she was safe and sound.

I expected a maudlin mood to settle upon me on our day of departure. After all, *Green Ghost* had been our home for eight years – four and a half years in Vancouver prior to cruising, and three and a half years of grand adventure. She had facilitated our dream and carried us safely across the Pacific. On our last day, we swung the chain-link gate closed behind us and fastened the lock. Lugging our bags down the road to catch a bus to Brisbane, exhausted by the heat and the process, I was so completely spent I didn't even look back.

In late March 2004, it was time for us to return to Canada to work. I suggested we fly to Ontario – not an easy sell to the captain, who, through most of his adult life, has habitually run fast and far from Toronto. But, at this time, Toronto made sense. All our immediate family members lived within an hour of the city's centre. Nik's eldest sister was unwell; my father had been hospitalized with early onset Alzheimer's disease. I knew my mom would welcome some support. Nik's parents were elderly and still living in the split-level family home. They'd asked us to help them move to a condo. My nieces were six and seven years old; we'd been missing their childhood. I argued that for all these reasons, it was the right time to be living near family.

There were other pluses to Toronto that worked well for us too. We could live in the basement of Nik's parents' home for a while. They had two cars and allowed us to use one of them. The job market was large. As far as an easy re-entry plan went, all things pointed to Ontario.

When we turned up in Toronto many assumed we were back for a visit. At a party at my sister's house my uncle greeted us enthusiastically.

"Good to see you guys. How long are you visiting?"

"We're not visiting. We're back," I answered.

"Back? You can't be back," was his astonished reply.

"We are back. We've left our boat in long-term storage on the hardstand in Queensland, Australia, and we've come back to Canada to work."

"You're not allowed to be *back*. You're what we live for. You're living the dream. We wait in rapt anticipation of your news. Your e-mails keep us going. What are we supposed to do now? Don't tell me you have a fixed address. Back? Bah! You can't be *back*." Then he turned and walked away, leaving us standing there with our drinks.

It suddenly dawned on me that we weren't us anymore. We'd become mascots. Turning up at a Toronto cocktail party was like being caught out of costume. We'd been unaware of our own transformation, but in our absence, we'd been completely redefined.

We soon settled into our fixed address – a small one-bedroom apartment in Bloor West Village. Compared to boat living, it felt palatial, all 650 square feet of it. We revelled in the luxury of a rectangular bed and long hot showers – to have great volumes of fresh water pour down upon you for as long as you liked every single day seemed nothing short of a miracle. We bought an old car from my cousin. We shipped possessions left in storage in Vancouver to our new Toronto address.

I wish I could boast that we smartly planned our return to the corporate world by studying world economics and graphing stock market movements, but the truth is our timing was pure luck. After years in the on-again/off-again mining business, we arrived in Toronto in the midst of the most impressive rise in metal prices that had occurred in our lifetime. The mining industry was booming. Job prospects were good.

We worried that the three-and-a-half-year gap on our résumés would be a concern for future employers so we confronted it head on, boldly stating our recent experience at the top of the page: *Co-Captain aboard Green Ghost ...* Remarkably the downtime on our résumés did not discount us; instead it drew people in. One company interviewed Nik for four hours over two sessions before admitting that they didn't have a role to fill; they just wanted to meet him.

But the transition from the cruising life to the city life was not easy. We found the city unfriendly and demanding. There was so much don't-cut-me-off, I'm-not-letting-you-in, get-out-of-my-way mindset. Even the squirrels in the courtyard seemed to have a what-have-you-done-for-me-lately attitude. We didn't know anyone in our apartment building. No one spoke to each other in the elevator. In the cruising world, no occasion was ever needed for an impromptu cocktail party on a beach. But we were sure we'd be met with suspicion if we knocked on neighbours' doors and invited them in for drinks. There was no doubt about it – we'd left the cruising world far behind.

We both got work within a couple of months and we were back on a mission. We focused on the plan – to make enough money to go cruising again. Two to three years, that's what we told ourselves, that's what we told everybody, but four and a half years later we were still in Toronto. Norbert-the-wise was right again.

On our break from cruising we got some things right and we got some things wrong.

In a booming industry, we found ourselves in ambitious and professionally satisfying roles. Nik worked in sales as an Account

Manager for a well-known mining software company. I worked as
a VP of Corporate Development involved in financing, mergers,
and acquisitions for a uranium mining company. For two years, I
averaged one out of every four nights in a hotel room somewhere,
travelling in the U.S. and Europe to fulfill the company's aggres-
sive growth plans.

We were smart to rent a one-bedroom apartment, a space
that felt like a great indulgence at first, but soon felt like a tiny
home. Our restraint on square footage enforced a restraint on
the accumulation of things. We saved one paycheque and lived
on the other, often saving some of that too. For the first two
years, we doggedly built up our bank balance.

We were right to be near family. A couple of months after
our arrival, Nik's sister succumbed to her battle with cancer. A
year later, my father passed away. My mom and Nik's parents
were glad to have us home.

We adapted to the city life: the subway crush, expensive
lattes, pressed shirts, take-home food, and weekends that were
much too short. With family, friends, demanding jobs, and happy pastimes, our lives were full. We'd made a comfortable space
for ourselves in Toronto, so what did we get wrong?

We didn't give ourselves a goal or a deadline. As we worked
and saved our bank balance grew, but how much was enough?
Nik frequently spoke of wanting more of a cushion. He hadn't
liked the precarious feeling of low bank balances when we returned from the Pacific. He often said he didn't want to feel that
poor again.

On our first foray in the cruising world we'd picked a number, a savings threshold that would prompt departure. During
our cruising hiatus, we failed to do the same. Without a goal, we
were blindly moving forward. Two years went by in a flash, then,
three. Making money felt good. Saving money felt good. Watching our bank account rise was the reason we were in Toronto.
Meanwhile the feel-goods of the cruising life faded in our minds
just as I'd feared they would.

Australian Customs wouldn't allow us to keep our boat in

the country indefinitely. We were initially granted a six-month Temporary Import Permit and had to apply for extensions biannually. The maximum allowable stay was three years. While in Toronto we routinely submitted our request for extension on a timely basis, but eventually we bumped up against the three-year mark. We had two choices: pay 15 percent duty or get the boat out of the country. After so many months on the hardstand, we knew much maintenance would be required to sail *Green Ghost* out of Australia. The mining industry continued to thrive. It made sense to keep making hay while the sun was shining. We paid Australian Customs and worked on.

While this allowed us to continue to enjoy our careers in the buoyant mining market, it removed the one and only deadline we had. The date to restart our cruising life remained uncertain.

In our fourth year of work, we bought a new car – a brand-new car. I was spending hundreds of dollars on suit jackets and shopping for jewelry. Nik indulged in a radio-controlled airplane hobby which transformed into the pursuit of a pilot's license – an actual pilot's license. We'd saved enough money to go cruising but we'd lost our focus. To keep ourselves entertained while we lived the busy urban professional life, we were blowing money on distractions and things. Of course, if that makes you happy, then why not? If you can afford nice things or a wonderful experience, then why not go for it? But clothes and jewelry had never made me happy. We had a dream, a big, grand dream, and we were distracting ourselves from achieving it with trinkets and baubles. Something was wrong with our plan.

I began to get restless. In the ever-merging company I worked for my job unwound before me. My title was re-jigged and I was slowly elbowed out of my role, constructively dismissed. I sat in my office with nothing to do. It was no wonder that a return to cruising grew ever larger in my mind.

More than four years had gone by since we left *Green Ghost* high and dry in Queensland. We owned a boat in Australia. If we weren't planning on returning to it, then what *were* we doing?

If we weren't going back, the boat should be sold. If we were going back, what was stopping us?

Nik was stopping us. He was reluctant to let go. His role as top salesperson filled him with a sense of achievement unparalleled in his career. At odds with one another, in an incredibly lucky turn of events we were able to find a compromise. In November 2008, Nik was promoted to the role of Sales Director for East Asia, a position that required a move. His new role was in Brisbane, Australia, thirty-six kilometres from *Green Ghost*. It wasn't a return to cruising, but it was the next best thing.

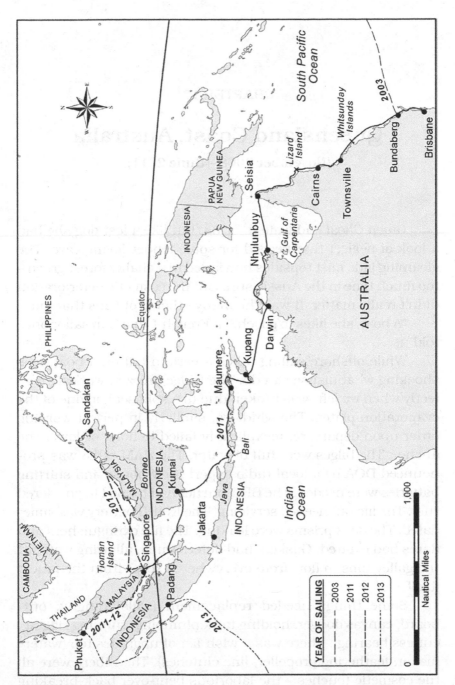

Figure 2. Asia Route Map

CHAPTER 17

Queensland Coast, Australia

(November 2008 – June 2011)

Green Ghost had waited for us, but like a lost dog she had a look of neglect that begged for some tender loving care. The gleaming jade mist topsides had faded to a chalky forest green – too much time in the Aussie sun. But the cosmetic deterioration didn't really matter. It was the many other problems that did.

"A boat, she likes to go, eh?" a French-Canadian sailor once told us.

While offshore sailing takes a certain toll on a boat, it is shocking what disuse can do. The fridge/freezer, working perfectly when we left, was broken due to a split seal on one of the evaporation plates. The windlass, similarly in perfect working order upon departure, inexplicably failed to hoist or lower the anchor. The bilges were full of water. The HAM radio was pronounced DOA by a local radio expert. New house and starting batteries were needed. The BBQ burner had turned to powdered rust. The life raft needed servicing. The EPIRB battery was stale-dated. The deck prisms were leaking. The fire extinguishers and flares had expired. Gaskets had deteriorated, allowing water at the galley taps to flow from everywhere except from the faucet itself.

Some things needed replacement (sails, dinghy, outboard, canvas dodger, holding tank plumbing, running rigging, cutless bearing). There was a wish list of upgrades too (watermaker, feathering propeller, line clutches). Then there were all the cosmetic touches – the laborious bent-over back-breaking make-it-look-pretty work. The brightwork all had to be sanded back to bare wood and revarnished. The stainless steel was in a sorry rust-spotted state. The teak decks were filthy.

While Nik settled into his new role in Brisbane and laboured for pay, I settled in to commuting to Scarborough where I laboured for love. On weekends, we jointly tackled the larger projects and Nik turned his attention to the mechanical and electrical work that was not my forte. There was much to do, but there wasn't anything that time and money couldn't fix.

After eighteen months in Brisbane, Nik resigned from his position and we extracted ourselves from the fixed address life once again. In June 2010, at the age of forty-eight, we began our second installment of retirement, part two of our sailing adventure.

For our first season, we decided to keep it simple and stick to coastal cruising with a relatively short trip to the Whitsunday Islands and a plan to return south to the Mooloolaba Marina before the threat of cyclone season.

With southeasterly winds at our backs, the 600 NM trip north to the Whitsundays proved a good reintroduction to cruising. Friends from Vancouver, Toronto, and Brisbane flew in to enjoy that world-renowned sailing destination with us. We were energized by the islands and chuffed with how well *Green Ghost* had done.

In our fifteen-week round trip up the coast, we noticed a few things that had changed in the decade since our previous cruising adventure. New technologies made some things easier. Older joints made some things harder. Older parents made us worry just a little more about the happenings back home. As it turned out our concerns were justified. On our southbound journey, we panicked when we got the news that Nik's mom had had a mild stroke and we scrambled to get to Mooloolaba so that Nik could make an emergency trip home.

In 2011, we registered for the Sail Indonesia Rally, a gathering of cruising boats that would sail out of Darwin in late July and, in a loosely defined fleet, cruise the waters of Indonesia all the way to Singapore. From Mooloolaba it was a 2,000 NM journey to the Darwin starting line. For the first time, we were sailing to a deadline in a flotilla with other boats.

Much like the first time we went cruising, before our departure from Mooloolaba, we made one last trip home to Canada to visit family. Nik's mom was recovering well. Upon our return, we again performed that immutable act and severed our connection to the land life – we sold our car. It was late April when we set off up the Queensland coast. We were already behind schedule.

The northbound trip was challenging. Long distances between safe anchorages required twelve- to fourteen-hour sailing days. Rising as early as four a.m., once the kettle had boiled and coffees were poured, we weighed anchor and departed under a starry scattering of white diamonds on a black velvet sky. It was cold, only 14°C (57°F) and the chill, exacerbated by the fifteen-knot wind, was too much for our summer-thin Queensland blood. There was something terribly incongruous about wearing long underwear as we rounded Cape Capricorn, so named because of its position on the Tropic. I winced as I bent over to stuff my legs into my long johns. After all our preparations before departure, an old herniated disc injury in my lower back was acting up. I found it dreadful to be up so early, to be braced against pain and hunched against the chill air. I was a bundle of clenched muscles and, despite the cold, my back was on fire.

Starry nights gave way to blue-sky days. We warmed ourselves with hot breakfasts and eased into sunny afternoons. *Green Ghost* was happy to have water flying past her keel again, but conditions were poor and the long days were tiring. We experienced tremendous southeasterly winds as we moved through Broad Sound and Shoalwater Bay. We slept poorly in rolly conditions, only to rise still fatigued to sail on.

"You know what my friends back home are saying?" I complained to Nik one night. "They're saying, 'I know this woman, she and her husband they're sailing around the world! They're living the dream!'" I wasn't feeling it. "It's at times like this, right now, when I just think, Bah – what are we doing this for anyway?"

Obviously, I needed a break. And I got it. We ducked out of the big seas and spent a couple of days at the lovely Scawfell Island where dolphins were arcing about the anchorage and turtles swam by our hull. It was a much-needed rest and welcome respite.

☸

On our journey north from Mooloolaba, we'd met very few boats heading to Darwin for the rally. Our late departure had put us at the back of the fleet. In Cairns, we finally caught up to the others. How exciting it was to be in the midst of long-distance voyagers again. There were Americans, French, Swedes, Germans, Britons, South Africans, Kiwis, Brazilians, and of course plenty of Aussies too. Nearly every yachtie we met was registered for the rally. We immediately felt part of something. From Cairns, north and west to Darwin, we felt sure there would be more fun in store, more social time with fellow sailors. We were certain we'd never be far from one of the hundred other rally boats.

After celebrating Nik's forty-ninth birthday with a A$10 steak and mash special, we pulled out of Cairns for far northern Queensland (FNQ). The next phase of our journey was a six-week voyage that would take us to Cape York. From there we'd turn left and sail west to Darwin. We were venturing into the wilder, more far-flung parts of Australia. Happy to be back on schedule, we allowed ourselves to take our foot off the gas pedal and enjoy ourselves a little more through the northern section of the coast.

✸

We made a stop in historic Cooktown, and when I say a stop I mean it.

Cooktown is the very place Captain Cook came in for repairs in June of 1770 after running his ship *Endeavour* aground in an attempt to get out to sea through the Great Barrier Reef. We arrived at low tide late in the day and in a salute to the famous sea captain we came into the small crowded anchorage and immediately ran aground ourselves. It was only the third time we'd ever made that mistake. Fortunately, it was a low-speed grounding, such a soft touch that Nik, who was on the bow readying the anchor for deployment, didn't even feel it.

"I think you need to head over there," he called back to me at the helm.

As I watched the depth sounder zero out I replied, "Well, maybe later. For now, I think we're going to have to enjoy this spot right here."

We tried reversing out. No luck. We launched the tender then lowered our anchor off the bow into the dinghy. Nik drove the dinghy over to deeper water and chucked the anchor in. Using the winch to pull against the anchor, an action called "kedging," didn't work for us either. We had a two-hour wait before we would float off on the rising tide, so we made the most of it. Nik was already in the dinghy, it was getting late, we were both hungry, and the smell of fried food wafting out from shore was too tempting. There was only one thing to do: buy take-away fish and chips and wait for high water.

✸

Our sail to Cape Flattery and on to Lizard Island was pure pleasure in perfect conditions. We were enjoying some of the best sailing we'd ever had. Along this section of the coast, the Great Barrier Reef blocks the ocean swell and with the genoa poled out, *Green Ghost* cruised downwind with good speed on flat seas. All the way to Cape York we had day after day of down-wind runs with my favourite soundtrack playing – the most mellifluous sound in my ears, that gentle gurgle and swish of a following sea.

At long last we reached Lizard Island, a much more beautiful place than its moniker suggests. Well offshore and unlikely to be croc infested, we could finally get in the water. We'd read that Lizard Island is the site of one of the few remaining giant clam beds in the world. When it came to snorkelling, we were getting pretty hard to impress – we'd seen plenty of giant clams before. Nonetheless, we had to take a look and we were mightily impressed when we did. The clams in Watson's Bay were truly giant-sized with gorgeous jewel-toned mantels. Like something right out of a *Flintstones* cartoon, they were large enough to contain my entire torso. They were the largest clams we'd ever seen and there were so many of them it was impossible not to be wowed.

At that time of year there are few boats that go north of Lizard Island that are planning to return south. In June, if you were up there, it was because you were headed north and west. During our stay, the anchorage population varied from eight to eighteen boats from nearly a dozen different countries. As in Cairns, it was an international crowd of long-distance cruisers. Most were on their way to Darwin for the rally and everyone was in a companionable frame of mind. The announcement of sundowners on the beach one night resulted in sixteen dinghies lined up on shore and about fifty people mingling in an impromptu cocktail party.

After six days of fun we departed Lizard Island at 4:30 a.m. and picked our way through the anchored boats in the dark. As we exited the bay we viewed a partial eclipse of the full moon. The sunrise enhanced the lighting – the bottom sliver of moon, the only segment visible in the dark, glowed with amber light. It was an effect similar to a person in total darkness holding a flashlight up against their chin, the light causing all their features to become intensely highlighted. I was awestruck.

I'd never seen the moon more spherical, more heavenly, more unforgettably beautiful.

We were surrounded by nature: emu tracks on long lovely stretches of sand, sightings of dugong, dolphins at the bow, evening walks on ribbon-like sand cays exposed at low tide. The sailing was fantastic, the environment was stunning, but there was no denying that the trip up the Queensland coast was a forced march with brief rests in what felt like an endless series of anchorages.

Some would argue that you could never consider yourself on a forced march if the fishing was good – and the fishing *was* good. We caught a bonito, a shark, and a barracuda, but a good edible fish was eluding us and Nik started to worry about running out of food.

Normally I'm confident about what's in the pantry, but there in FNQ, Nik's panic undermined me. I began counting days. It had been thirteen days since we were in a grocery store. We had about another twenty days before the next one. With a refrigerator less than four and a half cubic feet, five weeks was a long time to go between shops. We had little in the way of fresh produce left. We had to rely on canned provisions to carry us through the longer stretches. Fortunately, our reasonably large freezer (two and a half cubic feet) helped us to store protein and keep meals interesting.

I discreetly made a menu plan for every lunch and dinner for the next twenty days based on the existing food stores. The exercise alleviated my fear. We would make it to Darwin, even if we didn't catch an edible fish. To our delight we soon landed a large wahoo, adding eight meals for two to the freezer and doubling our meat supply in a single catch.

⚓

A strong high-pressure system developing in south central Australia was beginning to kick up the winds on the Queensland coast. Blustery conditions and rambunctious sailing came about as we were nearing the top of the country where there is little barrier reef protection from the offshore swell. The forecast was predicting strengthening winds and some nasty weather as we approached Cape York. With only 25 NM to go to the tip of the continent we decided to duck out for a day or two and hole up in what was for us the aptly named Escape River.

The wind was ripping through the broad low-lying area at the mouth. It was a hairy ride going in over the bar at low tide. Seeing two metres under our keel in a couple of spots, I was holding my breath that we didn't go aground in that lonely unfamiliar place. We soon saw that it wasn't completely uninhabited – there was a pearl farm at the river's mouth that wasn't much to see. The floats in the water marking the man-made pearl oyster beds kept us on our toes at the helm, but there was no sign of life whatsoever around the half-dozen small structures on shore. Without a trace of movement and no sign of human inhabitants, there was an apocalyptic feel to the place.

Although the wind was blowing hard just off the coast, the anchorage upstream was so settled our wind generator blades ceased spinning completely. There was only one other boat in the anchorage, and when they departed the following morning we had the place to ourselves except for the crocodiles basking on the muddy shoreline.

After one day of rest we hoped to move on but the strong wind warning continued. It was hard to believe that the weather was raging while we sat in the quiet calm of the upriver anchorage. We decided to go out to the river mouth and review the conditions ourselves. As we approached the open water the wind was howling at thirty knots, a squall was coming through, we were pelted with rain, and visibility was obliterated. We got our answer – it was not a day to move on. We turned *Green Ghost* around and went back to anchor. Down went the anchor and before the silt had settled around it we were below with a bowl of buttered popcorn and a game of *Scrabble* on the go.

In the afternoon, we heard the sound of an engine – the pearl farm was inhabited after all. The farmers came zotting over in their tinny. They had seen us do the about-face at the river bar earlier in the day, and concerned that we didn't have access to a long-range weather forecast, they very kindly came out to us with information. In that remote and wild place, they hand-delivered a weather report printed from the Internet which they had sheathed in a professional-looking plastic sleeve to save it from getting wet en route. After a brief exchange, they handed over the weather report and left us with a bit of advice.

"Looks like the weatha might keep you in a coupla days, mate. Don't get in the watah – plenny a crocs 'round heah!"

And with that they were gone, buzzing back to the pearl farm where they'd lived for twenty years.

We spent two nights alone in Escape River, leaving us to wonder where all the other boats had gone. We'd repeatedly seen the same boats since leaving Lizard Island. *Felix, Fantasia, Boomerang, Pegasus*, and *Invictus Reward* were in each of the anchorages on our route north, but none of them stopped at Escape River. We headed for Mount Adolphus Island feeling sure we would once again catch up with everyone, but there was not a single other boat in that anchorage either. Either we'd been left in the dust again, or no one else was moving in the still boisterous weather.

The high-pressure system that gave rise to the wind warning up and down the Queensland coast continued to generate twenty to thirty knots of wind. The seas inside the reef were two to three metres high; our flat-water sailing days were over. We sailed the short hop from Mount Adolphus Island to the anchorage at Cape York, for the first time in six weeks heading west rather than north. At the Cape, once again there were no other boats. We were beginning to wonder if we'd sailed into some parallel universe. Where was everyone?

Since Cairns, we'd developed a herd mentality. In crowded anchorages we wished the herd away, longing for the privilege to have an anchorage to ourselves, but as soon as we found ourselves alone we experienced a growing anxiety – had we been left behind? Where was the herd?

Herdless, we set anchor and put the dinghy in the water to go and set foot on the Cape itself. As far as destinations go, that pointy bit at the top did not disappoint. I spent the day wearing out superlatives; it was beautiful, it was stunning, it was gorgeous! The gently rolling green landscape, white beaches, and emerald water made for jaw-dropping views. I'd hoped for something dramatic at Cape York, but I'd no idea it would be as impressive as it was.

We walked up the crest of the rise to the cairn on the Cape, adding a rock to the pile on our way by. We took pictures of the touristy sign that read, "This is the most northerly point on the continent of Australia." While up there, we looked out at the breathtaking scenery that stretched down Australia's east coast behind us and across Australia's north coast to the west. As we did, we watched a few other sailboats round the cape. My heart leapt.

"There they are! The herd!" I said excitedly.

All but one of the boats sailed past. Only a catamaran came into the anchorage and pulled to a stop right next to *Green Ghost*. As we descended the promontory and crossed the sand beach, the catamaran's dinghy was unloading on the beach.

"There they are!" I heard the occupants say.

Friends from the Mooloolaba Marina who we'd not seen once on our thousand-mile journey stood on the beach before us. It was wonderful to see some familiar faces and share hugs all around. Our chance rendezvous eased our herd anxiety; we'd not entirely lost the flock.

We were also pleased to learn a welcome piece of news: there was a small settlement called Seisia on the west side of the Cape and apparently there was a grocery store there. We hoped for apples, a head of lettuce, anything that might crunch when you bit it. There wasn't a single piece of fresh food left on *Green Ghost*.

Not only was the grocery store a great find, there was also a trailer marked "BIN" at the wharf. We were thrilled to be able to take our garbage ashore and deposit it in a proper receptacle. It may sound crazy but one of the things we really dislike is carting our garbage around with us for weeks on end. For both of us, finding an appropriate place to drop garbage is nearly as exciting as finding a grocery store.

After the thrill of the garbage drop, we drooled around the fresh food section of the small shop and loaded up on fruit, vegetables, and dairy. We didn't need meat with all the fish we had in the freezer. We had a brief exchange with the checkout girl before heading back to the boat. The conversation was notable only in hindsight because it was our last human interaction for a rather long time.

It was the end of June and there was still another 750 NM to get to Darwin. The Gulf of Carpentaria was before us. There was no more behind-the-reef sailing. The next leg was the real deal, back out on open water.

The first step was a 350 NM trip across the Gulf. We expected it would take us about sixty hours to get to an anchorage on the other side. Three nights and two days to cross the Gulf – how bad could it be?

Green Ghost under sail entering Indonesian waters. Photo credit: Jim and Barbara Wallace of s/v *Contrails*.

Green Ghost crosses Singapore Strait, the busiest shipping lane in the world. Photo credit: Robert Ayotte of s/v *Caminata*.

Nik by the navigation station below deck as *Green Ghost* heels under sail in steady trade winds. Photo credit: Jennifer M. Smith.

Jennifer with a nurse shark, Warderick Wells Cay, Bahamas. Photo credit: Alex Nikolajevich.

Nik with a giant tortoise, Francois Leguat Giant Tortoise and Cave Reserve, island of Rodrigues, Indian Ocean. Photo credit: Jennifer M. Smith.

Jennifer and Nik visiting Angkor Wat temple in Siem Reap, Cambodia. Photo credit: Alex Nikolajevich, self-portrait with a tripod.

Dancers at the Toka Festival, island of Tanna, Vanuatu. Photo credit: Jennifer M. Smith.

CHAPTER 18

Across the Top

(June – July 2011)

How bad could it be? Sixty-four hours of hell on keel, that's how bad it could be.

We set out from Queensland hoping to make landfall in the Northern Territory's picturesque Wessel Islands. We ended up on the Gove Peninsula, in Nhulunbuy, a bauxite mining town with a processing plant and an industrial deep-sea loading facility. Upon our arrival Nik announced that he'd never been so happy to lay eyes on a smelter.

We were foolish. On our trip up the Queensland coast we'd sailed many smooth-water days with only the foresail in use. In the flat waters behind the Great Barrier Reef we didn't need the mainsail for stability. Sailing downwind, the genoa pulled us along nicely day after day on the flat slab of sea. In the habit of leaving the mainsail down and poling out the genny, we departed Seisia in the same fashion. What were we thinking?

The Gulf is a large shallow basin notorious for the uncomfortable wave patterns it can produce. The waves were short steep pointy bastards that were organized in two distinct sets, one set wind driven and another set refracted from the shores of Hades. The sea state was profoundly disproportionate to the wind strength and the pyramidal form of the waves made us feel like we were sailing in a washing machine.

On the first night, I barely slept at all. The motion on board was violent. Curled up in my sea berth, I was being thrown from side to side with such force that I was shaken awake every few minutes. It was not just the motion that was unsettling – it was the sound. *Green Ghost* was being picked up and slammed down repeatedly in the short period waves. Every few seconds there was a deafening *BAM!* Every item on board was being beaten against the inside of the lockers. I felt like I was a gerbil in a plastic ball falling down an endless staircase, or a cat in a pillowcase tormented by children.

In the light of the following day we pulled ourselves together and rearranged the sail plan. It was too late – by then both of us were suffering, me from sleep deprivation and queasiness and Nik from all-out seasickness. Nik stopped eating.

Thirty-six hours in and the wind had cranked up to twenty-five knots and the nasty seas picked up too. We crept through the second day, the two of us trading shifts every two hours. Neither one of us could manage our usual four-hour shifts. Nik was trying a new prescription-strength antiemetic but it wasn't doing anything for him. There was a lot of dry heaving and moaning going on.

At last the final night was upon us. When I went off watch at midnight, my vision went as I crawled into my bunk. Pixels shimmered before me. Everything looked like an unfinished jigsaw puzzle. In an instant, I was on my feet with my head over the galley sink just in time to throw up the four crackers and the half cup of water consumed on my watch. I ran water into the sink then flicked on a light. To my disgust, the sink had the plug in it. As I reached in and pulled it out, I mused over the metaphor – if only I could pull the plug on the bilious trip itself.

I was back on watch at two a.m. A deep-sea commercial port, Gove was well-lit with navigation markers, an easy place to approach in the dark. The light. Go to the light. I was managing now but still desperate for the trip to be over. By 5:30 a.m. I turned on the engine to assist us against a land breeze that was developing right on our nose. Nik joined me in the cockpit for the final two-and-a-half-hour push. By eight a.m. the hook was down, the boat was at rest, and so were we after sixty-four hours of torture.

Despite the relief of arrival, we remained shell-shocked. Oh, the thoughts that go through your mind in a small boat on a terrible sea! It was the first time I'd become so miserable that I'd decided we should sell the boat. Land travel seemed an excellent idea. We could backpack Southeast Asia; there was no need to sail there. We would find a broker, sell the boat, and ship our possessions home. We could move back to Canada, buy real estate, and tell stories of our sailing days. We always said we would keep going until it wasn't fun anymore and the Gulf of Barfentaria wasn't fun at all.

☸

We didn't go ashore in Gove. We spoke to no one else. We laid low for twenty-four hours, resting up, rehydrating, and confessing our boat-for-sale-fantasies. Nik, of course, had been having similar thoughts. In the morning, we were up and underway. Under sunny skies we headed west to Elisabeth Bay. How quickly we forget.

Beyond the Wessels lay the Arafura Sea, a vast wasteland with few sheltered anchorages. We considered coast hopping to avoid an overnighter but there were too many holes in the charts, large sections that were poorly surveyed or not surveyed at all. It was too risky.

We decided to make a straight shot across the stunning aqua-emerald-coloured seas of the north coast. We passed one other motor yacht on our journey, but otherwise we'd not seen a single other vessel at sea since leaving Seisia nearly a week earlier. It was a desolate, human-less coastline.

Once again, the Australian Bureau of Meteorology issued a strong wind warning. Gale-force winds set in, gusting to over fifty knots on our port quarter, but the skies remained sunny and the air, warm. The seas were a most remarkable aqua-green, frothing white as they tumbled over themselves at our stern. Over land we noticed that the stark sky took on a mauve light from the reflection of the red earth on blue. The sea and sky were remarkably beautiful, but the smudge of landscape between them was not. Low flat scraggy bush, some exposed stratigraphy, reddish shorelines of alternating rock or sand beach, dull green vegetation. Flat, flat, flat – everything around us was a horizontal line.

The insignificant elevation of the coastline offered little protection. The strong southeast winds blasted across the continent and ripped across the open shallow bays, creating whitecaps on waves that formed not far from the shore. The only way to get protection from the chop was to press in as close to shore as possible, carefully picking our way into shallow water and anchoring with as little as four feet under our keel. Close to shore, out of the chop, the wind still hummed through the blades of our wind generator. Dinghy down and dinghy up again was abandoned in favour of bum down, feet up and once anchored we both ducked below to get out of the elements for the day. With not another soul in sight and a vast expanse of sea and sky to the north and west behind us, we settled into these lonely spots with a slip of low-lying dry land for our pillow.

One evening as I put dinner together in the galley, Nik grabbed both my hands and began a silly dance to the music he'd queued up on the stereo.

"I'm trying to make dinner. Quit bugging me!" I laughed.

"I have to bug you! I have nobody else to bug!"

"You're losing it," I said.

"It's true," he said. "I'm not playing with all my marbles."

"Cards," I said.

"What?"

"Cards – you're not playing with a full deck of cards or you've lost your marbles," I said.

"Whatever," Nik said. "You know what I mean."

We were going a little stir crazy on this lonely coast. Our last major social interaction had been twenty-four days earlier, when fifty people had gathered on the beach at Lizard Island. We'd been isolated in one another's company for a little too long.

Ten days after leaving Seisia we curved into Alcaro Bay. We were looking forward to taking a day off in this marine park. A dinghy ride and a walk on the beach were in order. Feeling worn out by the heavy weather and a bit dejected by our lonely coastal run, we were pleased to find one other sailboat at anchor in the bay. We called them on the VHF radio.

First let me explain, I am not good at tempering the in-flows of human interaction. I'm easily influenced by the comments and moods of other people. Everything gets in. Much gets taken to heart. Negativity, even a tinge of it, can affect me quickly. I'm equally likely to be overwhelmed by the ultra-positive. Perhaps this is why I often feel the need to take myself away from the crowd. When you have no intake filter, people are an exhausting proposition. And, at this point, my limited abilities were rusty from disuse.

Over the radio our neighbour proceeded to tell us about their "fabulous outback experience" and their "most wonderful time" at the Coral Bay resort, a bay we'd sailed past earlier in the day. How had we missed it? They described their trip across the top as "exhilarating."

The thrill of having neighbours evaporated. I hung up the mic in a bit of a funk. Somehow, we'd missed "fabulous" and "wonderful." "Exhilarating" didn't fit how I was feeling. Had we blown it as travellers across this godforsaken stretch of barren coastline?

I consoled myself with the prospect of a walk on shore in the morning, but just as I cheered, our neighbours called us back to warn us of a large crocodile in the area and to urge us to exercise extreme caution on the beach. After "fabulous, wonderful and exhilarating," they rained on what was left of my parade. Human interaction. Bah! Humbug!

As usual, Nik had not been affected one bit by the ups and downs of the news from the neighbouring boat. All he heard was, "Blah, blah, blah large croc on shore." While I went to bed thinking the beach walk was off, he was packing his camera bag for the morning.

We did walk the beach the following day and we did see the very large crocodile basking in the sun on the shore of the back-beach lagoon. Nik was in ecstasies filming the Attenborough moment. We returned to the boat to enjoy a peaceful evening. Our neighbours had left. The howling winds had eased through the afternoon. By sundown, the anchorage was quiet and glassy and we spun on the hook to gentle land breezes and shifts of the tide.

☸

West around Cape Don and on toward Cape Hotham, we put our final day of sailing in and arrived in Darwin, our final port in Australia. We'd been on the move for forty-six of the previous sixty-five days. We'd had fifteen days at rest at anchor, only four of those days near communities, the rest in outlying empty places. We'd had the luxury of four nights in marinas: one in Airlie Beach and three in Cairns. Up the east coast, around the corner, and across the top, it had been a long lonely journey.

As we pulled into Fannie Bay, Darwin, and set the hook among dozens of other sailing yachts, we looked forward to a more social scene and an Indonesian adventure.

CHAPTER 19

Indonesia

(July – October 2011)

The Timor Sea was kind to us. Light winds and calm seas made for an easy 450 NM crossing that restored our faith in our abilities. No drama. Just the way we liked it.

It had been a long time coming. *Green Ghost* had not been in a new country for eight years, and it felt good. We arrived in the land of Islamic calls to prayer, corrugated iron roofing, multi-passenger motorbikes, tear-inducing spices, sleepy dogs, smiling people, and shouted greetings of "Hello, mister!" everywhere we went. Kupang, West Timor, was a loud alarm clock, awakening senses still drowsy from their long nap in stable, comfortable Australia.

We tidied up the boat, took showers, and dressed ourselves decently while we motored up the calm waters of Selat Semau. Over eighty boats had arrived in Kupang in a twenty-four-hour period and the local officials were hopping. When the anchor was down and the quarantine flag was up, signalling our arrival to the officials, *seven* officers clambered aboard for the check-in procedure. Representatives from quarantine, customs, immigration, and the police barrelled down the companionway and packed in around the salon table. The body heat coupled with the Indonesian heat created a sweaty, sauna-like atmosphere.

The paper started to fly. Copies of the boat registration, copies of our passports, copies of our CAIT (Clearance Approval for Indonesian Territory), our exit paperwork from Australia, arrival cards for immigration, and the crew list, all were requested in duplicate. Indonesians like their paperwork.

The quarantine officer cornered me. With his pen and clipboard poised, he asked, "Do you have fresh food on board?"

"Yes."

"Don't bring to shore. Bad for us."

"Okay," I responded.

He placed a check on his form and asked, "Do you have medicine?"

"Yes. Would you like a list of the prescription drugs we have on board?"

"No." Check.

"Have you had vaccinations?"

"Yes. Would you like to see the records?"

"No." Check.

"Are you sick now?"

"No. We are healthy."

"Healthy, good." Check.

Meanwhile Nik was interrogated by the customs officer.

"*Hantu Ijau*," he said. Nik looked at him quizzically, not understanding this phrase. "*Hantu Ijau*," he repeated. "Your boat name, in Indonesian Bahasa (language) *Green Ghost* is *Hantu Ijau.*"

"Oh!" Nik said, smiling, but the chit-chat was over.

"Do you have guns?" he asked sternly.

"No."

"Good. Do you have whiskey? Wine?"

"Yes."

Eyes lit up all around. Now that we were talking about alcohol, three officers began speaking at once.

"How many bottles?"

"Show me the whiskey."

"Show me the wine," they insisted.

Suddenly, fourteen hands got busy. Every cupboard door, every drawer, every floorboard on *Green Ghost* fastens with a positive click. Each cleverly engineered fastener is carefully and aesthetically installed and each custom closure opens in a very specific way. I winced at the thought of which latch would be broken first.

"*Hati! Hati!*" I said, telling them to be careful in one of the few phrases I'd practised in Bahasa.

There was nothing systematic about the search, but at last they found it – in the liquor cabinet.

"This bottle for me?" one of them asked.

"No," Nik said.

"I want a bottle of whiskey."

"No." Nik held firm. "The whiskey must remain on the boat."

They moved on from requests for full bottles to requests for drinks. We poured Coke over ice and water for those who preferred it. Some were satisfied, but others remained fixated on beer, whiskey, and rum.

At first, we'd been taken aback by their determination, but we finally came to realize that it was all a bit of a game. It was more about the fun of asking for a drink than it was a threatening demand for goods. Nik was the first to catch on. He realized that they didn't *all* want to drink; what they wanted was to see *someone* drinking. Nik agreed to pour a shot of rum for anyone who wanted it. One of the older and wiser men requested a small pour into his glass of Coke. Three others pointed excitedly at one of the youngest officers. They wanted to see him drink a proper shot straight up. The young officer held the shooter glass with apprehension, psyching up while his buddies egged him on. He downed the shot with an undisguised grimace. A cheer went up from the others. This bit of bravado settled the crowd; they laughed heartily at their friend, the designated drinker. They clapped him on the back, welcomed us to Indonesia, and disembarked, official duties done.

⚓

We did not stay long in Kupang. A nation of more than 17,500 islands stretched out before us over five thousand kilometres along the equator. No two boats would have the same voyage through Indonesia – there was no way to see it all. From the first port of entry a crew had to start making choices. Like most of the boats in the rally, we chose the western route to Singapore. Unlike most of the boats in the rally, we chose to start by heading south to Rote Island.

Rote was a 60 NM journey in a slightly backtracking direction. The island has a world-class surf break off a little village called Nembrala and Nik had his heart set on surfing it.

The break was like nothing I'd ever seen before. Here, long wavelength swells push in from the Indian Ocean, rising up as they meet the reef where they become huge left-hand breakers. The strong southeast trade winds roaring over the topographically low limestone island made for a constant offshore wind, blowing the tops off the breaking waves and sending the spindrift up into the air and out to sea. The spray over each successive wave formed a rainbow in the sunlight, which disappeared with each passing trough, then reformed as the next crest was atomized by the trade winds. The surf was both daunting and beautiful.

The thought of Nik on these powerful waves frightened me, but there were a dozen other surfers in the water and I knew there was no stopping him. He left me alone on board at anchor and went off in the dinghy, anchoring just beyond the break to paddle in. He caught the ride of his life on those sizeable waves, and better yet he caught it all on his new GoPro camera. He contemplated being satisfied with his one spectacular ride, but his surfer's heart got the better of him, begging just one more.

Back in the break he paddled hard to catch another but his timing was off. He couldn't drop in on it and missed the ride. In his attempt, he'd been pushed fifty metres inshore toward the reef. He turned to paddle back out only to see a huge set approaching, larger waves that would break in deeper water. He was exactly where he didn't want to be, caught on the inside. He was hammered by the surf, relentlessly tumbled and held down by the weight of the water pounding down upon him.

His leash snapped. His board was gone. In that frothing low-density whitewater he was sinking – without his board he had nothing for flotation. His lungs were burning as his head broke the surface. He sucked in some air and was hammered down again.

After being repeatedly slammed down and held under by the force of the breaking waves for what felt like eternity, he found himself at the surface again, this time yelling for help. But of course, there wasn't any. He gulped some air and floated on his back, pushed ever closer to the reef by the onslaught of the surf. Finally, he was able to put his feet down on the bottom. His board had snapped in two. The back end of it was tangled in the seaweed beds near shore, but the nose of the board was gone with the camera and the footage of the ride of his life.

Back on board, I sat in rapt silence as he relayed the details of his misadventure to me. Before he could finish his story, a dinghy approached *Green Ghost*. Another surfer was driving it and, reaching into the bottom of his boat, he yelled out, "Is this yours?"

Unbelievably he had found the nose of Nik's surfboard. The camera was still on it, and it was still filming! Over the next couple of days, Nik's longboard was expertly repaired ashore. His Rote adventure had a happy ending after all.

⎈

The Sail Indonesia Rally organization had planned cultural events on many of the islands the fleet visited. In Larantuka on the northeast coast of the island of Flores we found a waterfront that was the local garbage dump but we gladly stepped over it to engage in the festive reception awaiting us on the wharf.

Drummers, dancers, and greeters treated us like visiting royalty, crowning us with palm frond headbands as we came ashore. We were handed mock weapons and encouraged to join in a ceremonial battle dance. As the drums beat out a rhythm, the dance became a parade and we were swept up the street, our headbands bob-bobbing in step, the mock swords in our hands chop-chopping the air. We hopped and whooped our way the two or three blocks to the Regent's house where a welcome ceremony of traditional dance and a buffet gala dinner of traditional dishes was presented to us by the Regent, Vice-Regent, and local government officials of the East Flores Regency.

☸

We sailed west along the north coast of Flores and anchored off a resort called Sea World, not far from Maumere, the largest town on the island. It was the best place to access Kelimutu, the volcano famous for its tri-colour lakes. Our arrival in the anchorage was perfectly timed for happy hour. At four p.m. thirty yachties stormed the beach and drank the bar out of cold Bintang beer in less than two hours. Even so it was a productive time. We caught up with other sailors we hadn't seen in a while, hearing stories of one another's travels, discussing future plans, and complaining of the poor anchoring conditions in the steep-bottomed bay. We learned that earlier in the week three boats had dragged their anchors after a change in wind direction. We compared notes on weather forecasts and teamed up on plans for shore excursions the following day. Shared taxis were discussed, groups were formed, and phone calls were made. By the end of happy hour, we'd organized a dozen people for a four a.m. wake-up call and five a.m. departure for an all-day tour to Kelimutu.

Our day trip was an eleven-hour commitment and I was hoping there would be some eyes left in the anchorage to watch the boats while we were away. With the anchor-dragging stories in the back of my mind I asked around to see who planned to stay in the anchorage, but my attempts at locating a boat baby-sitter were fruitless. Many of the boats had already been there for a couple of days and planned to move on. The remaining boats were newcomers like us with plans to see Kelimutu.

We'd arrived in what was an unusual onshore breeze, albeit a light one. As a result, in order to anchor we had to point our bow out to sea and back down on our anchor with our stern towards shore, setting our anchor uphill on the steeply sloping bottom. As a result, we weren't completely confident that we'd set the anchor well and knowing that a moderate offshore breeze was the norm in this anchorage, we were particularly concerned about what a 180-degree wind shift would mean for our ground tackle.

In the morning, we did something we'd rarely done before. We left the keys in the ignition. We closed hatches and portholes and doors, but we left the boat unlocked. We wrote on a sheet of paper our cell phone number followed by step-by-step instructions on how to start the engine, how to turn on the navigation equipment, and how to operate the windlass. We taped the note to the binnacle and left *Green Ghost* for our day trip.

Our four-car convoy took in the countryside between the anchorage and the crater lakes as the sun came up. At the top of Kelimutu, we marvelled at the tri-colour lakes and rejoiced in a nearly forgotten sensation – although we sat at the hearth of the planet, we were wonderfully *cold.*

We returned at day's end to find that there were no dramas in the anchorage while we were away. My concerns were for nothing. *Green Ghost* waited patiently for us in the now offshore breeze.

The following day we went to the town of Maumere to do some shopping. It was rumoured that a store in town called Roxy stocked dairy products, such as long-life milk and canned butter. Oh, for whole milk on our cereal and buttered popcorn on the afternoon watch! It was a twenty-minute drive. To get there we could hire a private taxi (Rp50,000, about C$6), get on a local minibus (Rp3,000, cheap at about C$0.35), or wait for a local to stop and offer us a ride.

Motorcyclists, seeing a tourist on the road, were very likely to stop and let you hop on the back for a price even lower than bus fare. You may think I'm adventurous crossing oceans on a small boat, but hopping helmet-less on the back of a motorcycle driven by a total stranger weaving through traffic in a foreign town did not appeal to me at all – a girl has her limits. I voted for the minibus. At thirty-five cents, I argued we could afford it.

On the path up to the main road, some young English-speaking resort employees offered us advice about the owner-operated minivans, locally called "Beemos." They kindly helped us flag one down, translating for us, explaining to the driver that we were headed for Roxy.

Content we'd be dropped at the store, we sat back to enjoy the ride, crammed in with local passengers in the back of the pimped-up vehicle. An extended rap version of "Brown Girl in the Ring" thumped over the stereo system, threatening permanent hearing loss. Conversation wasn't an option. Zoned out in the onslaught of music, we were slow to realize that the shopping district had come and gone and we were driving through a suburban no man's land.

"Roxy?" Nik yelled forward.

In the rearview mirror, we saw eyebrows shoot up and an *Oh, shit* expression cross the driver's face. He indicated with a twirl of his index finger that we should stay on board until he completed his loop through suburbia and circled back into town. Finally, the Beemo jerked to a stop, the driver called, "Roxy!" We piled out and he peeled away.

The large store was across the street from the bus stop. We approached expectantly only to find it dark, the door locked. CLOSED. Although every local we'd spoken to had provided us with assistance on how to find Roxy, not one person mentioned that the shop was closed on a Sunday afternoon. This was so very Indonesian; always very helpful, never wanting to disappoint, not one kind person dared to burst our bubble.

We decided to make the most of our excursion and find a place to have lunch. We spied a squeaky clean, air-conditioned fast-food joint hilariously named Amazy Chicken, marketed as The Most Wanted Crispy. It was the Indo equivalent to KFC.

We were finger lickin' after our Combo #3s when Nik's cell phone rang.

"Is this a joke?" he asked. "Come on. Are you kidding me?" he continued, not giving me a clue as to who was calling or what they were calling about. "No. Seriously? Shit! Thanks!" Looking slightly panicked Nik blurted out, "We're adrift! We've gotta go!"

Mike and Kim on *Cheetah II* were underway along the coast and overheard some chatter on the VHF radio. They'd called to tell us that *Green Ghost* had dragged anchor and was drifting out to sea. We ran out of the restaurant onto the street, finding a mass of parked motorcycles and a couple of Beemos with their side doors open. Nik ran to a minibus and asked the driver, "How much to go to Sea World, straight there, very fast?"

Seeing that the van was crammed with people and picturing an endless series of stops and starts, I blurted out, "No! Nik! Not a bus! It'll take too long!"

We must have looked pretty desperate because within seconds we had three men around us, each astride a motorcycle with a vacant seat on the back.

"Two people, how much to Sea World?" Nik asked them.

"10,000 Rupiah," a driver answered.

"Too much," replied Nik.

"Seriously, you're haggling?" I said.

"Oh, right," Nik came to his senses, "10,000 Rupiah. Okay! Let's go!"

How quickly my concerns about motorcycles evaporated. Faster than you can say *hati hati*, we were each on the back of a stranger's motorcycle, our thoughts racing and weaving like the motorbikes themselves as we flew through traffic out of town. My thoughts vacillated; in one moment, I feared for my safety, in the next moment I revelled in the beauty of it all, speeding down a tropic road, warm air rushing past, my hair flying, a volcano in the distance. Flores was a beautiful island. I both believed and disbelieved, hoping the *Ghost* was okay, convinced there had to be some mistake. The song from the blaring Beemo continued to play in my mind, taunting me with switched-up lyrics, "*Green Ghost* on the run, tra-la-la-la-la ..."

I snapped out of the earworm and willed the driver to go faster, to get there in time. In the next moment, I wished he'd slow down – I wasn't wearing a helmet. My thoughts went 'round and 'round, flying past like the scenery, a blurred rush. It was farther than I remembered – a long ride for a buck twenty. Nik was bartering! What the hell? Was the *Ghost* okay? Be there. Please, be there when we get back. I willed everything to turn out all right. Hurry! Faster, I thought, as we peeled down a straight stretch. Then on a corner – My God! Slow down!

Upon arrival at Sea World we had no small bills to pay our drivers. With repeated thanks, we handed over twice the expected amount, leaving two confused but happy looking men in our dust as we ran between the palm trees, frantic, to the beach.

And there she was. *Green Ghost* was right there, right where we'd left her. Well, not quite where we'd left her. There were two dinghies alongside our boat, a woman in each one. There were three men on the foredeck. We slid our dinghy into the water and zotted out to the *Ghost* to find the crews of *Gryphon II* and *Amaryllis* on board, concluding the reanchoring exercise.

It was true. *Hantu Ijau* had made a bid for freedom while we dined out on chicken. Amazy. That had never happened before. How lucky we were that our neighbours had noticed and sprang into action when they realized *Green Ghost* was adrift. She was half a mile out to sea by the time her rescuers scrambled on board. Without our good neighbours, *Green Ghost* could've disappeared over the horizon, taking everything we owned with her.

☸

The island of Flores had been a delight and Labuan Bajo on the western coast was as gorgeous as the rest of it. Wheat-coloured golden hills dotted with dark green trees met a sea of unparalleled clarity. From a distance, it was beautiful but sadly, as in so many other places, there was an endless stream of plastic refuse drifting by our hull in the anchorage. The shoreline was equally polluted with plastics piled high at the tide line. World-class scuba diving and the famous Komodo dragons bring many tourists to Labuan Bajo, resulting in a slightly more upscale vibe in town. Great pizza served to diners lounging in a bean-bag-strewn loft provided a decidedly western bar experience, but the littered shore, goats tethered to sticks, and roaming roosters left us in no doubt that we were still in Indonesia.

As good as the cold beer and hot pizza was it wasn't the onshore tourist scene that impressed us – it was Komodo National Park. From the ranger-guided walks among the dragons, to the scuba diving in sapphire waters with manta rays, dugong, whitetip reef sharks, and fabulous coral reefs, we were impressed by each adventure.

⚓

Certain places were a vacation from the cruising life and Komodo had been one of them. Not having to make miles every day, we'd idly moved from one lovely anchorage to the next. Spending a week in the remote outer islands, we enjoyed impromptu cocktail parties on pink sand beaches, we snorkelled through massive schools of fish that darted about like a subaqueous murmuration of starlings, we hiked up arid headlands where our views took in manta rays gliding through the crystal-clear waters below. Each day we were delighted with some natural wonder – Komodo was a remarkable place. With no signal on our cell phone we were completely off the grid. Even for cruisers who seem so disconnected from the real world already, these small escapes from the distraction of the digital world were a welcome retreat.

In early September, we set sail for an overnight trip to skip across the north shore of the island of Sumbawa and head straight to the island of Lombok where we had some sea-to-sky adventures planned. Nik wanted to surf at Ekas Bay and I was interested in climbing Mount Rinjani, at least as far as the crater lakes, if not to the summit itself. On our first day out, we sailed past the shipbuilding village of Wepa and within range of the village's cell phone tower. Nik used our iPhone as a hot spot and e-mails from the past week piled up in our inbox.

In preparation for night watches I was having a mid-morning sleep on the settee when Nik woke me.

"Jenn," he said. "My dad died."

We had to get home.

CHAPTER 20

Kalimantan, Singapore, and Malacca

(October – November 2011)

Vladimir Nikolajevich passed away at the age of ninety-three. His death was sudden and unexpected. Vlad Daddy-O, as we liked to call him, had few health issues. From his seniors' residence, he was admitted to hospital on a Friday afternoon with a diagnosis of pneumonia. Three days later he died. Out of cell phone range in Komodo National Park, we didn't even know he was ill. As we sailed past the cell phone tower in Wepa, Sumbawa, we got the news of his passing within six hours of his death.

We knew what we had to do. Our first priority was to find somewhere safe to leave the boat. We made a series of quick decisions. There would be no surfing at Ekas, no views from Mount Rinjani. Instead of our overnight sail to Lombok, we sailed on, continuing west for fifty hours, heading for Bali with heavy hearts. Each time we passed a cell phone tower we were able to make a few more arrangements. The Sail Indonesia Rally organizers assisted us by booking a berth at the Bali Marina and ensuring that our visas would allow a re-entry into Indonesia. Our niece, a travel agent, looked into flights and began planning a memorial service.

On that first night at sea after learning of Vlad's passing I sat alone in the cockpit on my watch. Memories of my father-in-law filled my mind. I pictured his hands in his habit of repeatedly successively tapping each fingertip to his thumb. I could hear his sing-song voice declaring, "I am a doctor!"

Like his hands, his mind was always in motion, his head often bent in concentration over the latest medical journal. Yet his intellect was an enigma; while he'd delivered hundreds of babies in his long career as a GP, he was entirely useless in the kitchen. Unable to feed himself he was known to beg, "Jenny! Make me the coffee!" I smiled when I thought of his advice. "Kids" (he always called us), "take care of your mother and always remember to have fun." When the swoop of a shadow flew through my peripheral vision, I looked up to see a seabird circling the boat in the dark. *You found us*, I thought. *We will, I promise you*, I answered him. I had the overwhelming sense that Vlad's spirit had circled the earth to find us.

It was a long, convoluted trip home: fifty hours of sailing to get to Bali, a two-day wait for a berth at the marina, a flight from Bali to Singapore, then a twenty-four-hour layover, a flight to Seoul, another to San Francisco, a nine-hour layover, and finally a red-eye flight to Toronto. My sister met us at the airport at 5:30 a.m. with two Tim Hortons coffees in the cup holders of her minivan.

The memorial service was a cheerful tribute to Vlad's life and an uplifting experience for my mother-in-law, Olga, which was what we'd hoped it would be. As we walked the three blocks from the funeral home, pushing Olga in her wheelchair before us, we saw a commotion outside the entrance to the seniors' residence. Again, a bird. Drivers were impatiently sounding their horns at a beautiful swan standing in the middle of the road. The swan stopped traffic in both directions until we got Olga settled back in her room. When the three of us peered out her window onto the street below, the swan flew off, perhaps content that we were together and Olga was safely home.

But Nik was distraught at the loss of his father and full of regret for not being there when his dad had needed him most. Our short stay in Canada distressed him too. It was a difficult goodbye, leaving his mother, Olga, alone in the seniors' residence, grieving her husband of over fifty years.

We arrived back at the Bali Marina to find *Green Ghost*

dirty but otherwise fine. Shell-shocked by the previous two and a half weeks, it was hard to get back into the swing of things. There was jet lag of course, as well as a surprising difficulty in readjusting to the heat and humidity, but mostly we were suffering from depressed spirits. It's not easy losing a parent. We didn't feel like having fun and we didn't feel like hearing other people tell us about all the fun they'd been having either.

We had a tough time wrapping our minds around what was next. Stopping on a dime and disengaging from cruising was challenging, but re-engaging was harder. You can't parachute back in to where you left off. It doesn't work that way. Nearly every other boat we knew had moved on. The deadline on our Indonesian cruising permit stared back at us. As the crow flies, we were a thousand miles from Singapore. Once again, we were at the back of the pack feeling like we needed to catch up. Rather than pursue touristy things in Bali, three days after getting back, we left the marina to head north and west.

We set out at noon for a twenty-two-hour sail to Lovina on the north coast of Bali where we stopped for thirty hours. From Lovina we did a fifteen-hour overnight trip to the island of Raas, just off Java. We enjoyed a twenty-hour rest stop there then embarked on a twenty-eight-hour sail to the island of Bawean where we had a sixteen-hour rest stop at anchor, rising at four a.m. to sail thirty-six hours to Kalimantan, the Indonesian state on the island of Borneo.

Being jet-lagged at the outset was no hindrance. Our state of exhaustion probably helped. There were so many days of disrupted sleep patterns, it was easy to sleep on the off watch no matter the time of day or night. Even so, it was a demanding stretch.

As *Green Ghost* weaved between the dozens of sailboats anchored off the town of Kumai looking for a spot to anchor, our recognizable dark green hull invited many calls of sympathy over our VHF radio. We were buoyed up and moved by the care and kindness of all our fellow cruisers. It felt good to be back in our neighbourhood. We were home.

We were soon enthralled by another experience – a two-day one-night journey up the Sekonyer River to the orangutan sanctuary ("Camp Leakey") in Tanjung Puting National Park.

For a change, we were not in control of the vessel. All we had to do was sit back and be taken on a magical ride, putt-putting along in a klotok, a traditional wooden shallow-draft riverboat. We sat in chairs on the breezy upper deck while the captain, his wife, and their small boy remained on the lower deck tending to the vessel's navigation and our needs. Our guide, Kres, a handsome and charismatic young Indonesian man who spoke excellent English, hovered between the two decks, sometimes sitting to chat with us, sometimes serving meals, and never missing an opportunity to point out a kingfisher among the low branches at the shoreline or a monkey high in the trees. Upriver, the orangutans were impressive and the other wildlife was equally entertaining; proboscis monkeys, long-tailed macaques, red monkeys, and tropical birds delighted us.

Kres was light-hearted and fun, but he took his job very seriously, whispering gentle reprimands if we did too much chatting and not enough watching the wildlife. He was passionate about the natural world and the experience in the moment. He charmed me by referring to me as Princess Jennifer but he endlessly teased Nik, finding all his picture-taking and videotaping a bit much. Nik was forever adding voice-over narration in a very serious tone while he shot footage. This made Kres laugh – he didn't see the next David Attenborough, he saw some white guy talking endlessly into his microphone. While I enjoyed a royal title, Kres referred to Nik as Mr. Blah-blah-blah.

Most of the fleet congregated in Belitung for the Sail Indonesia Rally Closing Ceremony and Gala Dinner in mid-October. Our experience in Indonesia had been enhanced one hundred-fold by having been a part of it.

From Belitung, all the boats fanned out according to their northern destinations. Whether headed for Danga Bay or Puteri Harbour in Malaysia, or to one of the marinas available in Singapore, we were all in the final few hundred miles.

From Bangksa to Lingga, we sailed in a shrinking flotilla, as other boats went their way. On our final night in Indonesia, we anchored off the tiny island of Kentar with only three other boats, remarkably all Canadian. *Green Ghost* was back in the northern hemisphere for the first time in a decade. We were ready to wave wonderful Indonesia goodbye, to cross the busiest shipping lanes in the world, and to pounce on the first-world delights of Singapore.

⚓

In the Customs and Immigration basin we made contact by radio. The customs boat pulled alongside and held a fish net across the gap between us. We giggled as we placed our passports and boat paperwork in it, it seemed so unofficial. The officer hauled it in, taking our papers inside the vessel. We hovered in the basin. They hovered in the basin. Questions were answered over the VHF. Once cleared in, our paperwork was handed back to us in the fish net and we were free to enter the country. It was a no-nonsense neat and tidy process, just like the island country itself.

We pulled into the luxurious One°15 Marina in Sentosa Cove, Singapore, so called for its position at one degree and fifteen minutes of latitude north of the equator. Friends who had stayed there years earlier had told us it was a don't-miss location, so we'd booked ourselves a three-week stay believing they were right. With its beautiful modern docks, infinity pool, weight room, and air-conditioned Internet lounge complete with coffee bar and barista ready to serve up a latte, we'd landed in the lap of luxury. It felt like a different planet compared to the relative poverty of Indonesia just a day's sail to the south.

During our first week in Singapore we were sightseeing by day and not sleeping at night. At the dock, in the confined marina basin there was no breeze. It was impossibly hot. We didn't want the expense or complication of figuring out how to air-condition our boat, but two weeks in, exhausted and cranky from our sticky restless nights, we caved. We bought a portable household unit, measured carefully to ensure it would store in a hanging locker when at sea or at anchor. It saved us – an air conditioner was the only way to tolerate a live-aboard life in Singapore.

☸

In mid-November, we departed northbound up the Straits of Malacca to cruise the Malaysian peninsula's west coast en route to Phuket, Thailand, for Christmas.

Since arriving in equatorial waters we'd been experiencing thunderstorms, intense tropical downpours accompanied by plenty of lightning nearly every afternoon. Singapore has one of the highest rates of lightning activity in the world and daily light shows persisted as we rounded the corner to transit the strait between the Indonesian island of Sumatra and the Malay Peninsula, dodging great rafts of garbage on our route. Sadly, the area appeared to have one of the highest pollution levels as well – it was the most garbage-strewn stretch of water we'd ever seen.

The usual atmospheric rumblings were going on when we pulled into the Admiral Marina in Port Dickson, about 170 NM north of Singapore. Being among the forest of masts in the marina made Nik nervous. Were we better off isolated at anchor somewhere or being one of many metal objects sticking up into the electrically charged sky? It was tough to say.

"Give me your laptop," Nik said.

"Why?"

"Because I'm going to put it in the oven before we head up to the bar."

"A Faraday cage?" I asked, thinking back to my university physics courses.

"Yeah," he responded. "It might work. If the boat got struck by lightning, the stainless steel stove would conduct the current around the outside of the oven and prevent the current from passing through the interior, wouldn't it?" He busily filled our tiny oven with his laptop, my laptop, and the GPS chartplotter from the binnacle. Then looking at me smugly, with his finger in the air, suggesting even more great ideas, he grabbed the HF radio and the mic, the handheld VHF and the handheld GPS and stuffed them in as well. "In for a penny, in for the rest," he said.

"A pound," I came back.

"What?"

"A pound," I said. "In for a penny in for a pound."

"Whatever," he said, his usual retort.

It was hot as Hades in the late afternoon. We sealed up the boat to the pending storm then dashed up the dock before the rain began. It was easy to rationalize not cooking at home and treating ourselves to dinner in the air-conditioned bar while our air conditioner brought the temperature down on board.

We dined with Toni and Peter from the catamaran *Tigger*, friends we'd made in Singapore and with friends of theirs, Diane and Alan of *Moonfleet*. We shared information and stories, hearing of *Tigger*'s experience with a lightning strike near Borneo and laughing about the time we stood talking on the docks in Singapore, when we suddenly noticed that our hair was standing on end in the electrified air.

Our goal at Port Dickson was to arrange a short land trip to the city of Malacca, a UNESCO World Heritage Site, that had once been the capital of a Malay kingdom and was subsequently ruled by the Portuguese, the Dutch, and the British. Taking a bus trip south to the city to stay in a bed and breakfast was a decadent little getaway from cruising – a few delicious nights off the boat. The Peranakan culture of the area was fascinating and the Chinese-Javanese-Sumatran fusion with the added European influences made for unique architecture and some unforgettable dining.

I enjoyed our break in Malacca but back at the boat in the swank Port Dickson marina I put on my accounting hat again. I was tallying up our expenses and voiced my concerns about our over-spending on marina fees and dinners out.

"We've got to get back out to anchor, and we've got to stop eating out," I told the captain in my voice-of-reason tone.

"Yeah, I know," he agreed.

At that very moment, there was a knock on the hull. It was *Tigger* telling us that a bunch of sailors were meeting for happy hour at the bar and we must come out to play.

"Sounds good, what time?" Nik asked. He never wanted to miss out on fun.

The following night I put my foot down. "Tonight, we're eating in!" I said, as I pulled tomato sauce out of the freezer. I put water on to boil, pulled out the spaghetti, and turned on the oven to heat up some garlic bread.

A minute or two went by.

"What's that smell?"

"What smell?" Nik replied.

"Ho-lee shit!" I gasped as I launched myself across the galley, turning the heat off and yanking open the oven door in one swift movement.

Tucked in four days earlier, our electronics were still inside, safe from electrical storms maybe, but certainly not safe from me.

CHAPTER 21

A Year in Asia

(November 2011 – September 2012)

Friends met us for Christmas in Thailand and the four of us cruised around Phang Nga Bay, enjoying the dramatic scenery of limestone karst towers in the blue-green sea and cave explorations ashore. Fortunately, we hadn't had to replace our electronics. The cremation damage was minimal – a melted welt across the plastic cover of the chartplotter GPS and some slight damage to the cord for the HF radio mic (fixed with a little electrical tape).

By now, we had years of experience and yet we could still come up with new ways to make mistakes. Further use of our oven as a Faraday cage involved an added safety measure – removing all the knobs from the control panel when items were put inside.

Even though we were spared an expensive electrical refit, typical of most cruising sailors, the moment we found ourselves in an area of the world where getting boat work done was relatively easy, we pounced on the opportunity to make a couple of upgrades to *Green Ghost*. We'd seen the sailboat *Dionysus* sparkling in the sunshine in the anchorage at Krabi. After speaking with the owners, we learned of the massive refit they'd undertaken, including beautifully installed new teak decks.

It was the one thing *Green Ghost* had that we hadn't wanted when we bought her: teak decks. We knew that someday we'd have to replace them, or tear the teak off and redo the decks in fibreglass. Our thirty-year-old decks were looking their age and we worried about the expense of replacement. But the yard that had done the work on *Dionysus* gave us a quote that was so reasonable, we couldn't afford not to take advantage of it, so we settled in at the dock at Yacht Haven Marina for the many weeks of work that lay ahead.

We weren't the only ones. For many, Phuket was the first stop since Trinidad, South America, or New Zealand, where major boat maintenance could be accomplished at a reasonable price. For circumnavigators, it was the last stop before the long Indian Ocean crossing – a good place to get things done.

There is a "while we're at it" thing that happens when you begin a big project on a boat. We're at the dock for a month anyway, so while we're at it, let's get davits made too. And since the deck is being removed, while we're at it, let's get new stanchion bases, and new deck cleats, and let's change the location of the radar post. There are always a dozen smaller projects you can do while you're at the big one.

On some boats, we saw this cause trouble when the male on board was ankle deep in power tools, tinkering with his toy – in some cases loving it, in other cases not, but doing it anyway. The female on board may have been up for the idea at first, but quickly became disenchanted, losing interest not just in the work at hand, but in the boat and the lifestyle, and finally in cruising itself. I wondered why more skippers didn't see it coming. When you kill your partner with project fatigue you may kill the cruising dream too and find yourself alone on a smart-looking boat.

But in Thailand, lonely Caucasian men didn't have too much trouble finding a first mate as Nik found out for himself.

In the new year, we'd run out of tonic, which was far worse than running out of gin. Gin you could buy cheaply anywhere, but tonic was expensive and harder to find. When we heard that tonic was available at a small grocery store on a resort property a short drive north, Nik rented a scooter.

At the destination, a lovely young Thai woman engaged him in conversation.

"You American?" she asked as he dismounted the motorbike.

"Canadian," he answered.

"Oh, Canadian, very nice," she replied with a high-pitched nasal twang on her English. "You live here?" she asked. Judging from Nik's tan, it was a reasonable question.

"No, just visiting. I'm here on a boat," he answered.

"Very niice," she replied. "You want to meet Thai girl? Thai girl very niice."

"Oh no, no thank you," Nik replied, flattered. "I'm married."

"You marry Thai girl?" she asked hopefully.

"No, no, I'm married to a Canadian girl," he explained. "My wife sailed here with me."

"Why you not marry Thai girl? Thai girl very niice!" she scolded him, disappointed in his choice of spouse.

He was still chuckling about it when he returned with the tonic and a slightly inflated ego – chuffed in part for being mistaken for an exotic expat, but more so for being approached by a gorgeous young Thai.

⎈

While the teak deck work carried on, we took inexpensive Air Asia flights to Kuala Lumpur in Malaysia for some sightseeing and to renew our Thai visas. The boat could stay in Thailand a while, but we needed new stamps in our passports.

We were enjoying our time in Asia – the food, the culture, the inexpensive air travel to locations far from the boat. We were in no hurry to leave. It was the northeast monsoon season from November to February, and despite being considered the cool time of year and a good time for cruising in relatively dry conditions, we were glad to be at a dock and plugged into air conditioning. March would bring the wet southwest monsoon – a period of heavy storms beginning in April, lasting until October, and hitting the Andaman Coast of the southern peninsula harder than anywhere else in the country.

Come March, it would be a good time to move from the western side of Southeast Asia toward the east, to cruise Malaysian Borneo.

Besides, we'd heard you could sail 40 NM up a river called the Kinabatangan on the northeast coast of Borneo. And we'd heard you might see elephants up that river – you might even have them swim right out in front of your boat and that was reason enough to go.

⚓

With our boat work completed we departed Yacht Haven Marina both pleased and displeased. I loved the teak work – we were looking like a mini mega yacht with our gorgeous new decks – but I was unimpressed with the davits that we'd added on our stern. Nik had always wanted an alternative to stowing the dinghy on the foredeck or towing it behind. He'd pined for davits for years. The stainless steel contraptions gave him a place to store his surf boards, thrilling him, but upsetting me by ruining the aesthetic line of the boat. With beautiful decks and ugly davits, we left Thailand and headed for Tioman Island on the southeast coast of Malaysia, reportedly the spot depicted as Bali Ha'i in the 1958 film *South Pacific*.

Southbound in Malacca Strait we made a stop in Kuah on the island of Langkawi. There wasn't much to see in Kuah. It was a murky-water port busy with Malaysian tourists disembarking from the ferries that brought them from the mainland. Vacationers came to the duty-free island for the luxurious resorts and the pristine beaches located on the north shore. We came for the temple.

It was a short taxi ride out of town. Picture a post-apocalypse Costco full of alcohol. The place was massive – you could back a truck in through the front door. Despite the wide opening, it was dark inside the cavernous warehouse, dark and hot. Near the front was a large desk, piled with stacks of papers, some of which had toppled over, spilling onto the floor. On a decrepit wheelie chair sat the manager, a thin-haired Chinese man, bare-chested, pot-bellied, wearing only a pair of slippers and some dirty shorts. He sat hunched over and sweating, a cigarette dangling from his lower lip, a long length of paper spooling from his adding machine and coiling at his feet. Not your average liquor store. Not your average cashier either.

Booze was piled everywhere – down every aisle there was shelving filled with every kind of alcohol imaginable. Palettes sat helter-skelter on the floor – here a shipment of apple cider from South Africa, there dusty water-damaged cases of Bénédictine D.O.M piled high. We trolled the aisles, entertained by the selection, amazed at the quantity, and bug-eyed at the prices. A litre of Bombay Sapphire Gin was C$13.

A separate temperature controlled room housed the wine inventory. Entering, we realized that the warehouse was the picture of tidiness by comparison. Cases of wine were stacked willy-nilly – some cases torn open, a couple of bottles removed, some toppled over, some looking like they'd been recovered from shipwrecks in the harbour a decade earlier. Selecting anything was pure guesswork, but we did our best in The Temple of Booze.

☸

With the bar well stocked we carried on, south through Malacca Strait, around Singapore, and up to Tioman, positioning ourselves to cross the South China Sea to the city of Kuching, in Sarawak, one of two Malaysian states on the island of Borneo. The South China Sea worried us. We were concerned about pirates.

Nik often checked the International Chamber of Commerce Commercial Crime Services website to read up on acts of piracy. Just a few months earlier, a disturbing story had been reported from the very area we intended to cross. A tug and barge had been boarded by pirates, the seven-man crew set adrift in a small boat. The barge turned up in the Philippines; the stolen tug was never found. Fortunately for the crew, they were rescued off the coast of Vietnam six days later.

We decided to cross from Tioman to Kuching, sailing closely with another vessel. Greg and Sylvia, Australians aboard *Escapades*, were keen to mitigate their risk as well. Sailing together would be easy, as their boat was a sister-ship to ours, another Vancouver 42.

Our trip was uneventful until we sailed within view of the Riau Islands on our second day out.

"A boat appeared on the horizon from the southwest about half an hour ago," Nik reported to me as I made my breakfast in the galley, preparing for the eight a.m. watch change. "Looks like an Indonesian boat. They don't look like they're fishing. I'm not sure what they're up to. Maybe they'll just cross our stern, maybe they're just headed to the Riaus."

We changed over in the cockpit and Nik went below to take a shower and ready himself for his off-watch. I kept my eye on the foreign boat while I ate my cereal.

"They've turned a little and they've fallen in behind us. They're about a quarter mile off," I called below to Nik.

Being intercepted by pirates seemed so positively unlikely, I thought. Then again if it did happen, we were in big trouble.

I radioed *Escapades*, a mile or so behind us on our port quarter. "What do you think of this vessel?" I asked.

"I don't think it's a problem," Greg answered.

Ha! I thought, Of course he didn't think it was a problem – they were following us, not them. Although I had to agree, it wasn't the type of boat I would've expected for pirates. Pirates were more likely to be in a high-speed, highly maneuverable vessel. Pirates might have already given us a show of force, but this vessel, which appeared to be more of a cargo vessel, was just plodding along. Still, it was bigger than we were, it carried several men, it was catching up, and I didn't like it.

"Can you put on some different clothes, then come back up here?" I called down to Nik.

"Okay, sure, but why?" Nik answered.

"I read that if you think you're being approached by pirates you should make it appear that there are more people on board than there really are."

He'd been bare-chested in surf shorts and reappeared on deck in camo shorts and an army-green shirt. He even had a camo ball cap on.

"Impressive," I said, admiring his effort.

He took the paddle end from one of our sectional stand-up paddleboard paddles from a cockpit locker. Nik held it across his body like a firearm and started parading around the deck. From a distance, it probably looked pretty convincing. The dark orange paddle might have looked like a butt, the black shaft like a barrel.

"Maybe they're just curious," I said hopefully.

"Maybe," Nik said, "but I wish they'd go away."

Nik presented the onlookers with a good frontal view. Then he raised the paddle to his shoulder and took aim, sighting down the shaft. Right after he did that, the boat turned away and continued its easterly course.

Was it a risky, escalating move on our part? Maybe. Were they thwarted by Nik's antics? We'll never know. For all we know they were laughing at the funny white guy aiming a paddle at them from his puny boat. Either way, we were happy for the outcome, glad to be left alone to sail on to beautiful Borneo in peace.

⚓

After resting up at anchor in the lee of Tanjung Datu National Park, the northwestern point of Sarawak, we sailed on to the turtle sanctuary at Pulau Telang Besar. The view was stunning – a beautiful blue sky with towering white cumulus clouds forming over Borneo's tropical topography, and in the foreground, turquoise waters lapping at black rocks on a white sand beach. Walking on the hard sand below the high-tide line we passed the higgly-piggly beach landscape of hummocks and pits on our way to the Ranger's station. We found only three labourers on site.

There wasn't much to see by daylight and one of the men suggested we return after dark. Near ten p.m., we donned headlamps to climb into the dinghy. As we got organized in the tender, we saw them everywhere – tiny baby hatchlings skittering around in the water beside the boat. Smaller than the palm of our hands they flailed in the current, so incredibly vulnerable, so apparently witless, acting on impulse to swim for the light. We quickly switched off our headlamps and waited for the hatchlings to move on before starting the engine to go ashore.

At the beach, they were everywhere in the shallows and on the sand, crawling over our bare feet. We marvelled at the sight of four females, all digging their nests above the high-water line. It was amazing to witness, but it was a sight we probably shouldn't have been seeing. Later on in our travels in Borneo, we learned that other cruisers who had visited the island had been told by the conservation officer not to come ashore. It seems the officer had been away on the day of our visit and the labourer we'd spoken to had little interest in enforcing the rules. I was horrified to think we'd done the wrong thing.

⚓

The picturesque anchorage of Santubong delighted us. Surrounded by verdant hills and rocky outcrops, it was an exotic setting in the quiet calm of a river mouth. With its handy dinghy dock, friendly people, a resident crocodile, and its proximity to the city of Kuching, it was a great spot to settle in for ten days. We wasted no time in sampling Borneo's delights, making day trips to Fairy Cave, Semenggoh Wildlife Centre for orangutan rehabilitation, and Santubong Cultural Village. We hiked locally, seeking out rock carvings, and farther afield in nearby national parks where we delighted in the pitcher plants the area is known for. The city of Kuching was also a fun distraction and provided wonderful provisioning at a shop called "Cold Storage," a place that sold all the Western goodies we loved so much.

Just as we'd been wowed by Kalimantan (Indonesian Borneo) months earlier, we were thrilling to the adventures Malaysian Borneo had to offer. In July, we were just beginning to sink our teeth into it and we resented having to break our stride.

On our schedule for 2012 was a mid-year trip back to Canada. Our last trip back had been a rushed affair upon the death of Nik's father in September 2011. At the time, we'd made some vague comments about returning for a Canadian Christmas, but once we were back in Asia, we knew our hearts weren't in it. Too soon, too expensive, too detrimental to our own schedule, too not where we wanted to be in December. And so, we put it off and settled on a July trip instead. It was still expensive and still took a month of time from Borneo, but a July trip to Canada was more palatable.

Saying we were going was one thing, but making it happen was another. As always, it came down to where we could leave the boat, how we could get there, and where the nearest airport was. Miri, Sarawak, Borneo, over 300 NM along the coast, was our answer. The only trouble was the marina there refused to take reservations and operated on a first come, first served basis. Knowing that a fleet of boats would soon arrive for the Rainforest World Music Festival, we chose to forfeit a trip up the Rajang River to make a dash for Miri to secure one of the three remaining berths in the marina for ourselves. We had a plane to catch.

We returned from sunny Canada to the oppressive heat of Borneo with our fourteen-year-old niece. As always, we made a special effort to play tourist and have fun – flying from Miri to Gunung Mulu National Park for a two-day visit to the famous limestone caves before sailing northeast through Brunei to Labuan and on to Tiga Island, where the very first season of the TV show *Survivor* was filmed. We "bathed" in a cold mud volcano, swam and snorkelled, paddled around on our stand-up paddleboards, and sailed on to Kota Kinabalu ("KK"), where we enjoyed a dockside stay at the luxurious Sutera Harbour Resort. In KK, we jumped on another small plane, this time to Sandakan, in order for our niece to visit the Sepilok Orangutan Rehabilitation Centre. It was an action-packed, fun-filled three-week vacation that ended in, you guessed it, PGD.

But when our niece left to fly home solo, there was no time for long faces. We still had a long bucket list for Borneo and we were geared up to check it off. Over ten days we harbour-hopped our way across the north coast before turning the northeast corner to sail down the east coast to Sandakan. After hastily reprovisioning in town we headed for the Kinabatangan, the second-longest river in Malaysia, our ultimate destination for the season.

Heading upriver on our second day, we crossed paths with our friends, Ken and Wendy on *Cop Out*. We were travelling in opposite directions but, wanting to catch up on one another's news, we decided to stop and anchor together for some social-izing and fun. The following day the four of us piled into their large dinghy to speed along the muddy river, stopping to drift and watch when one of us saw something of interest. While proboscis monkeys scrambled through the trees and impressive hornbills glided through the air, we chatted – the usual topics of where you've been, where you're going, and what's broken on your boat.

"What are your favourite places so far?" Ken asked.

"That's a tough one," Nik replied. "There's been so much. The Pacific was fantastic, that's for sure. We loved French Poly-nesia. We loved Vanuatu too."

"Vanuatu was wonderful," Ken agreed. "The people were fantastic. There was this one guy I remember, he gave us a huge pile of fruit and vegetables."

"Ezekiel!" I shouted.

"Yes!" Ken and Wendy replied.

"My name is Bible name!" Nik chimed in.

"Always nice to say hello!" I added, smiling at the memory.

Although we'd passed through Vanuatu years apart, we'd both pulled into the same anchorage in Port Sandwich and we'd both had the very good fortune of meeting Ezekiel and receiving his generous gifts.

I loved the braided social structure of the cruising life, the way our path crisscrossed with other cruisers, the way we had experiences – unique, but shared. We headed upriver the following day, still hoping to catch a glimpse of the elephants, while *Cop Out* carried on downstream, heading back to Phuket where they would sell their boat, to begin a new phase of their lives.

The many boats we'd met in the Sail Indonesia Rally had by now fanned out across Asia, each one with a different plan. Fellow sailors came and went, sometimes crossing our bow, sometimes disappearing in our wake. Although we came from diverse backgrounds, we had much in common. We didn't just love sailing – we loved adventure. We weren't dreamers, we were doers – always finding new ways to sample more from the smorgasbord of life, forever in pursuit of change.

In September 2012, Nik and I could feel a new phase coming too. As much as we loved Asia, we were on the other side of the world. Trips back to Canada were expensive. The falling markets had us thinking of going back to work. Concerns for our ageing moms tipped the balance and we decided on our next plan.

At Sukau, where overhead wires prevented us from exploring farther upstream, we turned *Green Ghost* around. We never did see the elephants of the Kinabatangan, but that was okay. We knew elephants were in our future. We were Africa bound.

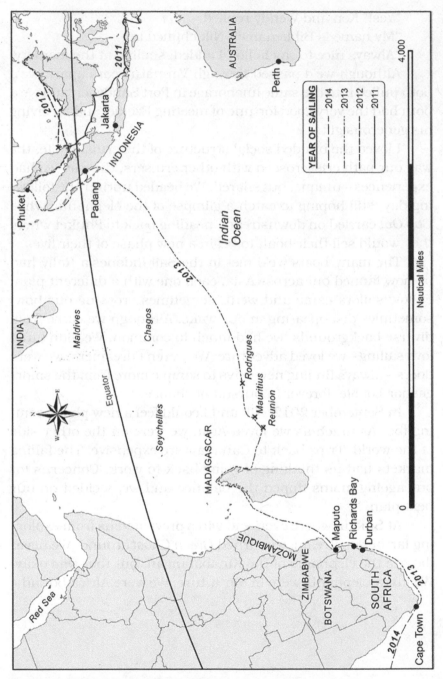

Figure 3. Indian Ocean Route Map

CHAPTER 22

Crossing the Indian

(October 2012 – May 2013)

We checked off all our remaining bucket list items in Asia, climbing Mount Kinabalu, the highest peak in Asia for my fiftieth birthday; visiting Brunei; and enjoying a month of land travel backpacking around Vietnam, Laos, Cambodia, and Myanmar before the end of 2012. We packed it all in.

Then, in order to get ourselves into position for our crossing to Africa, we retraced our steps, sailing *Green Ghost* back across the top of Borneo, past Singapore, up Malacca Straits through Christmas and the New Year, and back to Phuket, Thailand, our stepping-off point.

We had to psych ourselves up for this one. The Indian Ocean was a big step out, the kind of big step we hadn't taken in over a decade. We were younger when we set out to cross the Pacific. *Green Ghost* was younger then too. Upon our departure from Vancouver, between the boat and the crew, the *Ghost* was better prepared than we were. On the edge of the Indian, the opposite was true. It would be foolish to deny that you become a little complacent after so many years and so many miles. The boat was not as precisely tuned as it had been for the Pacific. Our gear was no longer new – it was well worn in but then, so were we. We were far more seasoned and that had to count for something.

❋

A couple on *Sea Bunny* kept a spreadsheet of all the boats that planned to cross the Indian Ocean to South Africa in the next year. If you wrote to them and asked to be on the list, you'd receive a monthly e-mail to keep up to date with the changing fleet.

In the Pacific, almost every boat had been headed to the Marquesas. From there, all the boats cruised together throughout the relatively narrow corridor of French Polynesia. The Indian Ocean was different – cruisers had a choice of routes. From the west coast of Thailand or Malaysia some chose a northern route, heading for the Andaman Islands, then Sri Lanka, the Maldives, and the Seychelles. Some chose the middle route over the top of Sumatra, striking out from the Sumatran west coast directly for the islands of Rodrigues, Mauritius, and Reunion. Still others sailed south from Singapore, down the eastern side of Sumatra, then west through Sunda Strait and southwest for Australia's Cocos (Keeling) Islands. Some sailed directly from Australia, possibly visiting Christmas Island before heading to Cocos (Keeling).

While most vessels eventually turned up in Mauritius or Reunion, there were about 3,000 NM to cross before all westbound vessels converged upon those distant locations. From Mauritius or Reunion there were further routing decisions to be made. Madagascar was in the way. Vessels had to choose whether to go up and over Madagascar or under it before reaching the ultimate destination of Richards Bay, South Africa, the usual end point for a southern Indian Ocean crossing. We'd chosen the middle route because the west coast of Sumatra is a surfer's paradise and Nik was hankering to get his boards wet again. We scanned the field of forty-two boats on the *Sea Bunny* spreadsheet to find there were only four other boats going our way.

⚓

Through March and April, we enjoyed a fantastic seven weeks, sailing from Phuket, Thailand, up and over the top of Sumatra, and then lazily cruising the east coast and the outer islands of Simeleu, Nias, Sipika, and Tanahbala in the company of *Moonfleet* and *Larissa*.

We checked out of Indonesia at Padang, a chaotic grimy city of over 800,000 on Sumatra's west coast.

Over our few days in Padang, our boat boy, Rio, helped us. We purchased diesel which, for some reason, had to be delivered under cover of darkness in beat-up jerry cans paddled out to us in a leaky dugout canoe. He set up a taxi to take us into town where we filled our propane tanks, bought groceries at the shop and veggies at the market. He explained that on our final day we would check out with the immigration officer, the customs officer, and the port captain. While the offices were clustered together south of town, Rio explained that we would have to make a trip north, across the city.

"The immigration officer is out of the office," Rio said. "But it is no problem, he has given the stamps to his son. You will go to his house for checkout. My driver knows the way."

Not your average set-up, but hey, this was Indo, so we went with it, knowing that all the driving would make for a full day of checkout procedures.

On our last day in Padang, Rio organized a taxi for us first thing in the morning. As we dinghied by the Canadian-flagged catamaran, *Tara*, Captain Jimi waved to us from his cockpit.

"Where are you off to so early? he asked.

"We're heading in to check out," we called back. "Departing tomorrow."

"I checked out yesterday," he called back. "I'm leaving to-morrow too."

We waved and carried on to shore where we jumped in the waiting taxi and eased into the busy Padang traffic. Our driver found the immigration officer's house without trouble.

We arrived at the front door and knocked. A heavyset young man greeted us as we entered the scantily furnished room. He was fat, no surprise. After many months in Indonesia we'd noticed the trend. While most Indonesians were slight of build, government officials and their families were universally fat. More money, I suppose. More disposable income.

"*Selamat pagi.* Good morning!" I said as I reached out my hand to shake his. I looked up to meet his eyes then looked away quickly when I realized there was only one – eye, that is.

"*Pagi,*" he responded, but I barely heard him. I was ashamed at how quickly I'd looked away from his face. What had happened to him, I wondered. His left eye was white – no iris, no pupil. I didn't dare steal another look for fear of staring.

Thank goodness, Nik's reaction was more direct and more caring. He shook the young man's hand and said, "My goodness, that's quite an infection you have there. Have you seen a doctor?"

Where I'd shown my horror, Nik showed concern. Why was that so hard to remember? When lost for words, think of a kind one. Yay, Nik, I thought to myself. Well done.

The home office was no different from Indonesian government offices. A big screen TV was blaring a daytime soap opera from its prominent position on the wall. We were introduced to a cousin who was hanging around. The cousin answered Nik's question.

"Yes, he has seen the doctor. He has some medicine now."

When I regained my composure and looked again, I realized that Nik had nailed it – the trouble was an eye infection. The young man's entire eyeball was covered in a yellow oozy pus. When he blinked, the pus squeezed out a little, but it didn't run down his cheek – it was too thick to flow.

"Well, that's good to hear," Nik responded.

We made small talk while the young man seated himself and opened our passports to cancel our Indonesian visas. Despite being unwell, he applied his stamps to both the ink pad and the passports with vigour. *Bam! Bam!* There were numerous papers to be filled out, signed, and stamped as well. *Bam! Bam! Bam! Bam!*

Now and then the young man would stop what he was doing, grab his T-shirt below the neckline and pull it up over his face, wiping a great smear of pus out of his eye. I watched from across the table and tried not to grimace. All I could think of was that glob of pus on the inside of his shirt sticking to his skin.

"Okay, sign here, here, and here," he said to us, pushing the papers across the table.

I cringed when Nik asked, "Can I borrow your pen?"

I signed too. Quickly.

We sat in the southbound taxi wishing we could be more than an arm's length away from our own hands. We still had the customs office and the port captain to go.

Hours later, our checkout paperwork complete, we dinghied back to our boat, through the harbour, passing Jimi on *Tara* again.

"How'd it go?" he yelled over to us.

"All good!" we said, giving the thumbs-up.

"You saw the immigration guy?" Jimi asked.

"Yep!" we called back over the noise of the outboard.

"How was ol' pus-eye anyway?" Jimi barked back. "Come over for a drink later! But wash your hands first!"

We were all thinking the same thing: with a 2,600 NM journey ahead, none of us wanted any part of ol' pus-eye along for the ride.

⚓

Ready for departure on the day we checked out with officialdom, we had a frustrating ten-day wait before the weather cleared for a go decision. We couldn't complain too much. We were anchored about 20 NM south of the city, off the lovely Cubadak Island Resort with *Moonfleet* and *Tara*. We ran out of time on our cell phone, we ran out of local currency, and we ran out of fresh fruit and vegetables too. Fortunately, WiFi at the resort kept us connected to online weather forecasts and strong radio signals allowed us to use our Sailmail on board without difficulty. In the evenings, we idled away our time in a most incongruous way – watching season three of *Downton Abbey* on DVD.

The Passage Weather website indicated a suspicious pattern developing that could become a tropical revolving storm (TRS). In the Bay of Bengal, north of the equator, the TRS formed slowly over the next several days, tracking towards Sri Lanka. A second low formed south of the equator and tracked south. We were right not to trust the two bull's-eye shapes. The depression evolved into a named storm, *Jamala*, with winds over forty-five knots. So we waited.

Tara departed on May 14 and a day later at 10:45 a.m., in the company of our friends aboard *Moonfleet*, we set out to cross the Indian Ocean.

We had a lovely sail through the afternoon, as a gorgeous moderate wind on our stern whisked us south and west away from the coast of Sumatra. After sundown, the wind died and we began motoring. Squid boats with their lights glowing over the horizon were a reminder that we were not yet far from land.

As ex-*Jamala* moved westward, a huge vacuum was left in her wake. We motored through the windless first night and through to the next morning, through the whole next day and the following windless, starry night. At low rpms, we made only three and a half knots per hour, heading more south than west as we sought out the trade-wind breezes that would fill in south of the equator.

After three days of mostly motoring, Nik emptied the sixty litres of diesel we'd stored on deck into the tanks. We were in good shape to continue motoring for another fifty or sixty hours, but after that we'd be getting antsy for some wind. In the meantime, we marvelled at the liquid surface before us – not even a ripple. We watched transfixed when six beautiful dolphins came to swim at the bow, perfectly visible through the glassy sapphire surface.

The longer, faster *Moonfleet* had pulled ahead, reporting back to us that they had light trades in their area of the not-so-high seas. Our hearts lifted when, after eighty-three hours of motoring southwest off the Sumatran coast, we too found wind.

☸

Nearly a week out I began to think some part of ol' pus-eye had found its way on board after all. I'd scratched an itchy area on my right forearm and it became infected. My skin became red and inflamed and soon developed patches of white pus. Antibiotic ointment didn't help. A fluid-filled pouch formed around the infected part of my forearm. When the infection began to spread and two more areas of inflammation cropped up on my hand and my bicep I started to worry about sepsis. Hundreds of miles from medical help, I didn't want to take any chances, and I began a five-day course of the roxithromycin we carried in our medicine kit. Fortunately, it did the trick, killing off the bacteria that had been flourishing on my arm.

☸

Our weather became squally and grey and the sea became lumpy and unpleasant. On the upside, we were doing over six knots in the direction we wanted to go, but the nasty weather began to take a toll on Nik. From his Pacific sailing days, he'd finally learned – without hesitation he applied a scopolamine patch and hung on for the ride.

In the more boisterous conditions, we thought we'd hit the luxury of the trade winds, but the bigger winds didn't last. As the system moved over us, we were again left in a windless vacuum, bouncing around on confused seas, having to start the engine again to make miles.

Our friends aboard *Moonfleet* were ahead and farther south. They reported forty-knot winds from their position.

No thanks. We preferred too little over too much, but we made slow progress and the Captain grew impatient.

"We should have paid the forty grand," he complained. "We'd be in Turkey by now." He was referring to the number of people we knew who had paid the big money to have their boats loaded on a freighter in Thailand and shipped to the Mediterranean.

"More than half a year's budget? For shipping? I never could have lived with that," I reminded him.

Still, it was frustrating. We were having trouble getting it right. At the edge of the trades we were experiencing drizzling rain and listless winds. At six to ten knots there was no real heart in them. They were directionless – now abeam, now on our quarter, now off our stern. With the lack of consistent pressure on our sails, *Green Ghost* was rockin' and rollin' in the equally confused seas. We did all we could to catch the zephyrs that came our way, but the lame wind was dumped from the sails every few seconds. The canvas slapped on the collapse and snapped back harshly on the fill. It was horrible to listen to and unnerving to contemplate the relentless shock loading on both the sails and the rigging. It was tough on Nik too. He always did more of the deck work than I did, which was not easy in his mildly seasick state.

Little did we know things were about to get worse. On our eighth day at sea, and just under 2,000 NM from Rodrigues, our planned destination, Nik woke me up in the late afternoon, jarring me out of my off-watch slumber.

"Jenn," he said, "we've got a big problem."

"What?" I mumbled, swimming up through the fog of sleep to the surface of consciousness.

"Our transmission," he said. "It's flooded with salt water."

CHAPTER 23

Wait and Hope

(May – June 2013)

"What?" I said again.

"I was checking all the fluid levels on the engine like I always do. There's no oil in the transmission. It's full of salt water."

I sat up. Nik's tense expression frightened me.

"So there's salt water where it isn't supposed to be?" I said, trying to understand.

"Yes," he said.

"Can more get in?" I said, with a rising wave of panic.

"What?"

"The salt water, can it just keep coming?" I asked, still trying to understand what was happening.

"No."

"So we're not sinking then?"

"No, we're not sinking."

"Not sinking. That's good."

"Yeah, but without oil in the transmission, we can't run the engine."

"Right. That's not good. But as long as we're not sinking we have lots of time to think about it."

"True."

On a sailboat, one might think, who needs an engine when you've got the wind? But the engine does matter. It matters because it charges your batteries and your batteries run your systems and your systems keep you safe and well. On most modern cruising boats, sailors rely heavily on their power supply. We had a major problem on our hands.

I got out of my bunk, Nik got out the engine manual, and we started brainstorming together. Nik explained that he was pretty sure that the copper tubes inside the heat exchanger had failed. A pinhole leak must have developed, allowing the cooling salt water that surged through the heat exchanger to enter the transmission while allowing the oil in the transmission to flow out. He stared into the engine compartment in the bilge. An idea for a solution came to him quite quickly.

"Maybe I can rig a bypass," he suggested. "That would remove the transmission oil cooler from the raw-water cooling circuit. If I rig a bypass, I can isolate the transmission and then we could still run the engine, just not in gear. We'll have no propulsion, but if we can run the engine, we can charge our batteries, and if we can keep the batteries charged, we'll be okay. But before I isolate it, to save the transmission, I've got to get the saltwater out."

To rig a bypass, he needed a length of hose with the right inner diameter to join the engine output directly to the raw-water exhaust. I went on watch in the cockpit while Nik put on a blue spandex body suit, donned a red cape, and set to saving the day. He dug deep into lockers of spare parts. He had purchased some spare lengths of hose before we left Thailand. A section of hose he had intended to use as a chafe guard on the anchor bridle had been squirrelled away for that someday project. It was the right diameter and the right length. Thank goodness for the bits and pieces crammed into the lockers. That one piece of spare hose saved the day.

Inverted, lying on the sole of the cabin head down in the bilge, Nik was able to construct a bypass to the heat exchanger. He also created a closed system for the transmission by joining the output to the heat exchanger directly back to the input for the transmission. He removed the salt water from the system by blowing through the tubing. He rinsed the circuit with diesel first, then added transmission fluid. We engaged the transmission briefly and found that the closed system held, but on inspection we were disappointed to see that the transmission fluid was pink in colour – some salt water remained inside and we didn't have enough fluid left to flush it and fill it a second time.

Nik remained distraught over our predicament. In situations requiring mechanical/electrical know-how, beyond a calming influence and moral support, I didn't have much to offer. He felt the pressure squarely on his shoulders. While he was hand-wringing over unanswered questions, I reminded him that we were not alone. Just like that TV gameshow, we had a lifeline – we had Sailmail. I suggested we get outside advice.

I began to write e-mails to people we thought might be able to help. To fellow sailors who were more knowledgeable diesel mechanics, we asked if, in a pinch, 15W40 motor oil could be used in the transmission. We requested research from our brother-in-law, writing: *the transmission is a BorgWarner Velvet Drive, model number 10-17-012, gear box ratio of 2.57:1. Can you contact BorgWarner and find out how long we could get away with engaging the transmission without cooling?* To cruising friends Taffy and Shirley on the sailboat *The Road*, already at the island of Rodrigues, we asked: *Are there repair facilities on the island or should we head straight for Mauritius? Can you put us in touch with the Port Captain? We may need a tow on arrival.*

Our contacts were happy to assist. Our brother-in-law kept us entertained with his wit, writing back: *Apollo 13 ... this is Houston. I will call the manufacturer and report back.* We received plenty of information from our sources, including information direct from BorgWarner, news of a mechanic on Rodrigues, and a contact e-mail address for the Harbour Master at Port Mathurin who was standing by, nearly 2,000 NM away, ready to tow us through the reefs into port when our mast crested his horizon.

We learned that we could use motor oil to fill the transmission and we could engage the transmission for roughly four minutes without cooling before bad things would start to happen. Confident with our temporary fix, we were ready to sail on to Rodrigues as planned.

But sail on, we could not. Within a day of losing our transmission we found ourselves on a windless sea. We'd never seen the ocean so flat. It was so calm, I entertained myself by taking photos of my near perfect reflection in the deep blue water, of our speedometer reading 0.00 knots, and of our fishing line hanging limp and pathetic off the stern. A quiet anxiety set in.

We were going nowhere. Our sails slapped relentlessly. Frustration prevented us from sleep. We reminded ourselves that even if the engine was working we'd be concerned about fuel consumption, but that didn't mitigate our impatience. We were restless captives, unnerved by the irrational thought: what if the wind *never* came back?

To distract ourselves we jumped overboard. With masks and snorkels we hung weightless in the sapphire crystal blue, staring down into shafts of sunlight probing 16,000 feet of water. Small fish sparkled like jewels many feet below. It was another world, both beautiful and forbidding.

I made a pizza and we sat in the cockpit to watch a movie on the laptop. But these diversions were nothing but a brave front. We were disquieted. We despaired. At day's end our GPS position indicated we'd moved 30 NM in the previous twenty-four hours. While a one-knot current had been pushing us, thankfully in the right direction, we made only 6 NM by sail. Much like our spirits, our mileage was at a record-breaking low.

That night I finished reading my book, *The Count of Monte Cristo*. The last line could not have been better suited to our situation. "All human wisdom is contained in these words: Wait and hope!"

⚓

When the wind returned in gentle seven- and eight-knot puffs we were delighted. Such light air gave us a good boost on the still-flat seas. A magnificent full moon kept us company through the quiet night and we thrilled to see the speedometer flash numbers at us once again. When you've been going no-where, it's amazing how fast two to three knots can feel.

We'd chosen to sail a more northerly route after leaving Padang, hoping to find ten to fifteen knots of wind. We stayed at nine degrees south while we made more westing, wanting to avoid the blustery twenty-five-knot trades farther south. Mean-while our heartier friends on *Moonfleet* had gone south more quickly, down to eleven degrees before heading west, putting them in robust trade winds earlier in their trip. On our nightly radio schedule, they were reporting winds in the twenty-five gusting to forty range and speed records to boot. In hindsight, we realized that hanging around farther north had put us at a greater risk of being becalmed, a risk we regretted taking now that we were engineless. Perhaps we should have been more ag-gressive on our southerly mileage. On the other hand, we were glad to be in gentle conditions when the oil cooler failed. Effect-ing that repair in twenty-five to forty knots of wind would've been terrible. In sailing, and in life, every choice you make has consequences.

On our twelfth day at sea we finally found the trades. Twen-ty- to twenty-five-knot southeasterlies were upon us together with an endless parade of dark grey squalls bringing rain, rain, and more rain. The seas built to three metres. In the heavier weather, we reefed down and changed the watch every three hours instead of our usual four. We were finally making tracks, chewing up the miles to Rodrigues.

"Should have bought a catamaran," the captain grumbled when we learned over the HF radio that our friend, Jimi, had already arrived in Mauritius.

Nik was happier a few days later when conditions eased for his fifty-first birthday. We were treated to a beautiful sailing day with sunny skies and continued progress on a favourable course, albeit at decreased speeds. I made a chocolate birthday cake, lopsided despite the gimballed oven. The best gift was the sound of the fishing line singing at sunset. Nik reeled in small yellowfin tuna in the fading light.

On our twentieth day at sea we encountered our first freighter, the first of several we would see over the next few days. The alarm rang out on our AIS, letting us know that a ship, projecting its own AIS signal, was within a ten-mile range. Fantastic technology – you hear it even before you see it. *Solar Orion* was eastbound on the Durban-Singapore shipping route and would pass with a closest point of approach of 2 NM on our port side. Close enough for photos, not close enough to smell the exhaust – just the way I like it.

Our spirits lifted with the sign of life and the pleasant sailing conditions had us smiling. As always, in good conditions, it never occurs to me that it won't last. But dawn came grey, rainy, and miserable and we found ourselves back in unpleasant conditions for two days. We were becalmed again. Three-knot zephyrs zipped every which way, causing a rolling motion and slapping sails. Our wind indicator spun in circles.

"Maybe we should burn out the transmission just to get there," Nik muttered, frustrated by our lack of progress.

"Go to bed. When you wake up maybe there'll be wind," I offered.

But there wasn't any, not on his shift and not on my next shift either.

Finally, fifteen-knot winds filled in from the south, the sky cleared, and we were sailing in a consistent breeze on a beam reach straight down the line to our destination. Happiness restored.

We arrived in Mathurin Harbour, Rodrigues, at eight a.m. on a Sunday morning after a twenty-five-day passage. Nearly as long as our crossing from Mexico to the Marquesas back in 2001. Arriving on a Sunday meant we incurred overtime charges at the customs office, but at only US$66 we didn't care. It was a small price to pay.

Because of our Sailmail correspondence with Port Captain Gilbert Mallet, Port Mathurin was expecting us. As instructed we called in on VHF Channel 16 upon our arrival outside the reefs. Despite our inconvenient timing, the little tugboat *Albion* came out to meet us with its crew of three volunteer Coast Guard members and Captain Mallet himself. My eyes welled with tears as they waved us good morning and threw us a towline to attach to the bridle we'd already made up. What good people, I thought. What fine people you meet on the sea.

CHAPTER 24

Madagascar

(June – September 2013)

After spoiling ourselves with a month in each of the two islands of the Republic of Mauritius (Rodrigues and Mauritius) and ten days of magnificent volcanic hiking on the visually stunning (but very expensive) island of Reunion, our thoughts turned to completing the final stretch on the Indian Ocean. Our ultimate destination, Richard's Bay, South Africa, became our focus.

In the Mascarene Islands, a new part for our oil cooler had been ordered from the U.S. and after Nik's expert installation we were good to go. There was only one problem – Madagascar was in the way. Over a thousand miles long and 350 miles wide (1,580 kilometres long, 579 kilometres wide), it was a significant obstacle. We either had to duck under that large island landmass or go over the top. Sailors who choose the southern route are unlikely to stop, mainly because of a dearth of attractive anchorages and an excess of questionable officials at the southern end of the island. A route over the top of the country, on the other hand, provided good opportunities for coastal cruising.

Madagascar was a destination completely foreign to us. Ranking among the ten poorest countries in the world, known for its corrupt officials and petty crime, it was not a place we'd ever planned to go. If it hadn't been for a chance meeting in a taxi, we never would have.

Back in Sumatra, in the small town of Lahewa on Nias

Island, we ran out of cash. We rented a taxi with three other cruising couples to make the hour-long drive to the nearest ATM in Gunungsitoli. In the back of the van, introductions were made between sailors and the usual facts were established: which boat were you on, where had you come from, and where were you going. A French-speaking couple said they were headed for Nosy Be.

"Madagascar? Why there?" Nik asked.

"We live there," they answered.

It was no wonder I hadn't recognized the flag flying off the back of their yacht.

"You *live* in Madagascar?" I asked, surprised. Madagascar? Wow. When you say it out loud, exotica oozes from every syllable.

"Yeah," they answered, blasé about their home address.

No doubt they rued the moment they let on to their Malagasy roots because for the rest of the taxi ride we hammered them with questions. We kept up our enquiries over a shared lunch and continued our interrogation on the return journey. By the time we were back on *Green Ghost* we had our minds made up.

A mixture of coast-hopping and idling in anchorages was far preferable to the non-stop mad dash across difficult seas that the southerly route promised. Armed with some local advice and a few anchorage notes from other cruising sailboats, we set out to discover the wonders of Madagascar – a biodiversity hot spot where over 90 percent of the wildlife is found nowhere else on Earth.

⚓

Whales. They were everywhere. And these whales were way too close. It was late August, right in the middle of the humpback whale breeding and calving season. Thousands of them migrate from Antarctica to Madagascar each year, and our destination, Ambodifototra on Île Ste. Marie (now called

Nosy Baraha), was one of the best whale-watching ports on the east coast. We'd spotted a few of the majestic cetaceans from a distance. Longer than and twice the tonnage of our boat, from a distance was just fine with us. But it wasn't the humpbacks that gave me the greatest scare. On our final miles into Île Ste. Marie, an unusual sound made me look up from the book I was reading in the cockpit.

"*Phhssst!*" It was the unmistakable sound of a marine mammal exhaling.

I jumped up and looked aft off the port quarter to see dark shapes disappear under our hull. I kneeled on the cockpit seat, gripped the stern rail, and looked straight down at our rudder. On either side of it was the great bulbous head of a pilot whale. At only half the length of our boat and a tonne or more in weight, they weren't nearly as large as the humpbacks, but the fact that two of them had decided to take up positions on either side of our rudder was mighty disconcerting.

"Ho-leeeee shit! You're beautiful but get away from there!" I said aloud. They did as I requested and moved off without incident.

⎈

"*Green Ghost, Tegan,*" came over our VHF radio.

"*Tegan, Green Ghost,* go ahead."

"Welcome to Madagascar! How was your trip?"

"Thanks, Janet. It was pretty boisterous on the last day, but fine overall. We're glad to be here."

"Good to hear. We just wanted to give you a heads-up regarding check in. The customs official here is demanding US$40 in local currency from every boat. We're pretty sure it's graft. He won't say what the charge is for and he doesn't give a receipt."

"Did you pay it?"

"We didn't pay it on the spot because we didn't have any local currency. He was insistent, so we told him we would have to go to the bank and bring the money to him later. We've been to the bank now, and we're planning to go ashore to make our payment in a few minutes."

"I hate this kind of thing," I said.

"Yeah, me too. We probably wouldn't pay it if we were leaving soon, but we're going to be here for a couple of days, and knowing they have a boat and can come out and harass us, well, we just don't want to put ourselves in that position."

"Yeah, I hear you," I said.

"When we're in the office, do you want us to let them know you've arrived?"

"Sure. Tell them we'll come to their offices tomorrow morning, if that works for them," I said, hoping to head off an on-board visit by the officials.

"Will do. Talk to you later. *Tegan* out."

The news of a corrupt official made our first taste of Madagascar a sour one.

The following day we checked in with *Haven*. Over the years, we'd learned that corrupt officials were less likely to make illegal demands when faced with a small crowd. But not this guy – he had balls. Balls and chins – obviously he'd been collecting graft money for years. In a country of underfed people, this customs officer looked like Jabba the Hutt. Money was demanded of us and we too used the excuse that we couldn't pay a fee until we'd visited an ATM.

Through the next day we canvassed other sailors in the anchorage. Had they paid the charge? One boat had flatly refused and departed the anchorage the next day. Every other boat had caved.

The following day we were in town, picking up some vegetables and having a cold beer on the porch of a hotel when Jabba himself roared up on a motorbike that looked like a kid's toy under his enormous frame. He was unimpressed to see us spending our local currency on cold beer when we still hadn't thrown cash in his direction.

"You have been to the bank. You have money. You will pay me," he demanded.

His appearance on the scene unsettled us and we caved too. We were disappointed with ourselves for giving in, feeling we'd only reinforced his sense of entitlement, making things worse for boats arriving after us. For what it was worth, in an e-mail to the Canadian Consulate in Antananarivo, Nik reported the officer, but we doubted it would have much effect.

A spate of thefts in the anchorage at Île Ste. Marie further unsettled us. Our friends on a large catamaran were boarded in the night. While they slept, several items were stolen from their cockpit, including their chartplotter, their VHF radio, and the captain's shoes.

A day trip to the tiny Île aux Nattes to see black-and-white ruffed lemurs soured our experience further. Our outing required hiring a manned lakana, a traditional wooden outrigger canoe, to be ferried across a narrow channel that separated the islet from Île Ste. Marie. Settling on a price with our canoe-man and ensuring we were talking about a return fare, we were adeptly delivered to the sandy beach on the far side. When our captain refused payment, insisting we pay upon our return, I became suspicious. Sure enough, back on the big island at day's end our canoe-man insisted on double the amount we'd agreed upon. Our paddler made a great show of his dissatisfaction, tucking his hands in his armpits, refusing to take our money while insisting we owed him twice the amount. Voices were raised, locals gathered round.

I began to get the feeling this was daily entertainment. No doubt his antics often worked, and tourists often paid, either shamed into remuneration in front of the poor locals or frightened into paying by the ever-growing mob of young men. It was an amount no more than C$5, but it was the principle of the thing. Already tired of being viewed as a walking ATM and still harbouring resentment towards the crooked customs agent, we refused to pay. In the end, we gave him the agreed upon amount, leaving our money at his feet, before speeding away on our rented motorbikes. It was an unpleasant ending to a day of sightseeing. Being a tourist in Madagascar was challenging at every turn.

Not only was the social environment confronting, the physical environment was challenging as well. The east coast is the rainy part of the country and after experiencing several days of showery conditions we were keen to move on, up, and over the northern cape to the west coast, known for its sunny weather and warmer, more tranquil waters.

It was more than 300 NM to Cape Amber and the straight-line nature of the northeast coast did not offer many places to stop. The entire coastline is a lee shore exposed to the strong southeast trade winds and of course to the swells generated by them. From May until October winds at Cape Amber are high. Our strategy was to sail to Antsiranana (formerly Diego Suarez), 30 NM short of the northern cape, where we would wait for fair weather before rounding it.

We travelled northbound up the east coast in building conditions with winds reaching thirty to thirty-five knots through the afternoon. There were gusts close to forty and massive following seas. *Green Ghost* surfed down the face of the waves with our speedometer showing twelve knots at times – something we'd never seen before. The conditions were the most challenging we'd faced on the whole of the Indian Ocean. On one occasion, we were thrown over on our port side so heavily that our life ring was dunked in the sea and ripped off the rail. It seemed we were destined to lose a life ring in every ocean that we crossed.

We arrived in Diego Suarez with three reefs in our mainsail and both of us exhausted from hanging on tightly for the three days and two nights it took to get there. Navigating into the harbour was made challenging by the fact that our charts were off by more than half a mile – the worst error we'd ever encountered on electronic charts.

We had only a short rest in the well-protected harbour because the opportunity to round the cape presented itself more quickly than we expected. The guide books tell you to round the point of land "with one foot on the shoreline" – in other words, stick close to shore. It was an exhilarating ride up and over the top and fantastic sailing down the northwest coast, where the winds remained very strong but the seas were magnificently flat, giving us great speed and big distance, and allowing us to make the anchorage at Nosy Hara by nightfall. We were the only boat in the anchorage and we planned to spend a day there, doing nothing, resting up, reading books, and relaxing.

In the morning, we were approached by a small boat carrying five young men. One spoke French very well. He told us that the island was a park and we would have to pay a 15,000 ariary entrance fee per person. He had a cash box and a receipt book that he waved around, but he wore no uniform. We explained that we were not planning to go ashore and therefore we would not be entering the park and we would not pay the fee. He argued hard, arm-waving that the whole area was a park, a marine park, and that the charge applied even for anchoring. Suspicious, we disagreed with him and insisted that we would not pay. When his friends started asking us for whiskey and cigarettes, the legitimacy of the cash box and the receipt book evaporated. We held our ground and they eventually let it go and went away.

Once again, we were left in a quandary. Had we been right to stand our ground? In a country where the average annual income was around US$400, asking for a little money from someone who likely had an income one hundred times greater probably seemed like a pretty reasonable thing to do. The amount they'd wanted was only about C$5, but, again, it was the principle of the thing. We couldn't go through Madagascar handing out C$5 to every person we met – could we?

Later we learned from an Internet search that a marine park had been created in the bay at Nosy Hana. It was a project between WWF and the local communities. We felt terrible. We eventually learned that three other boats that stopped in the same bay later in the season were not asked for payment. Perhaps we'd put the young park officer completely off his job.

⚓

We moved on to another difficult-to-pronounce location, Andranoaombi. We chose to anchor well away from the village, hoping to give them some privacy and have some of our own.

Chief Mohmeen and his son came out in their dugout canoe. Mohmeen's French was good enough for us to converse at a basic level. He wondered why we'd anchored so far from his village. Our choice of location was less respectful than we'd hoped. Never mind privacy, we'd forced the chief to paddle a long distance to perform his duties.

Realizing we were receiving a formal welcome from the chief, we offered him a small gift and handed him a T-shirt. He thanked us and took a papaya out from under his seat, handing it to us in return. He asked us if we had any school supplies that the children of the village might use. We'd prepared for this before departing the Mascarene Islands and we were pleased to hand over a stack of notebooks and a box of pencils. Chief Mohmeen thanked us profusely.

We looked for something for his son and found a smaller T-shirt. Tomatoes appeared and were handed to us. While Nik asked the chief about his family, I went below to rummage through some second-hand clothing we had on board specifically for this purpose. I managed to find something for each of his other children as well as a dress of mine for his wife. He smiled broadly and suddenly bananas and mangos appeared from the dugout. It was a beautiful interaction, so gently conducted, the most amiable trading I've ever done. We were not at all offended when Chief Mohmeen asked shyly if by chance we might have some sugar on board.

"Oui!" I said and went below again. It was easy for me to get more sugar – we'd be in town within the week. It was not so easy for him. I poured most of the sugar I had into a Ziploc bag for transport.

"C'est parfaitement blanc!" he said, eyes wide as I handed

it to him. He'd never seen sugar so highly refined, so perfectly white.

His final request was for power. He hadn't thought to bring it with him, but back in the village he had a cell phone with a drained battery. The village had no electricity, so he asked us, if he brought the phone to us, would we be able to charge it.

"Certainement," Nik answered. It seemed such a small request.

Mohmeen and his son paddled off. He never did return with his cell phone. I guess we'd anchored just too far away.

There was plenty of trading to be done in Madagascar. At Nosy Mitsio many local canoes came out to us at anchor. All wanted to trade lobster, not for cash, for goods. It made sense. There was only one shop on Mitsio, so trade goods were more useful than cash. T-shirts, shorts, fishing line, swim fins, masks and snorkels, hooks, school books – all were valued items. We had lobster for dinner four nights in a row.

Our interactions with locals were becoming more pleasant. As we travelled south down the northwest coast we were approaching the island of Nosy Be, the largest and busiest tourist resort in Madagascar, a hot spot for South African vacationers. Perhaps our interactions were improving because we were dealing with locals who had more experience with foreigners and were better skilled at bridging the culture gap.

An exotic sounding place, the words Nosy Be mean only "big island" in the Malagasy language, but the main town bears the more evocative name of Hell-Ville. The place was named for Admiral de Hell when the French colonized Madagascar in 1840, not for any more apt reason. Indeed, we found there was nothing hellish about it. In the anchorage off town, we were immediately adopted by boat boys Jimmy and Rasta John, who charged a couple of dollars a day to procure just about anything for us. They arranged laundry, propane, and diesel and they kept an eye on our dinghy and on our boat when we went ashore.

✸

After a pleasant time in Hell-Ville, we continued south, making stops in every location that was noted for interactions with lemurs. We couldn't get enough of the gentle primates. Whether engaging with a semi-tame animal taken in as a pet in a local village, or watching wild sifakas, a lemur with black hairless faces framed by silky white fur, we thrilled at every moment with this most remarkable species.

Farther south, we stopped at the Alcatraz of Madagascar, Nosy Lava, a former island prison. We took a walk through the prison ruins and were soon joined by two teenagers, a young boy and an older girl carrying a baby on her hip. With a few words of French and a good deal of arm-waving they showed us around the place, taking us to see the stone-walled damp prison offices where we were fascinated to find the prison records, dumped from the rusty filing cabinets and strewn about on the floor.

An older man appeared out of nowhere, telling us he was a prison guard (unlikely) and that we had to pay him (also unlikely). He disappeared when we gave him a pack of the Malaysian cigarettes we still had in our trading stores.

After a tour around the prison and much picture taking, we went back to the beach and our dinghy, thinking about heading home to rest from the heat of the day. The teenagers remained with us. The young man was quite interested in our inflatable and our outboard.

We didn't make a habit of inviting local people on board. The reasons were manifold; we liked our privacy and we didn't want to create temptation or stir up envy by flaunting our comparative wealth. But these teenagers were charming, their enthusiasm affected us, and we did something we'd rarely done before – we invited them out to the boat.

They enjoyed the speed of the dinghy ride and the cool shade of the cockpit. We showed them around inside, indicating where we slept, pointing out the small toilet and shower.

We showed them our instant flame on our propane stove, how water poured freely from our taps, then we pulled cold drinks from our tiny refrigerator. I imagine it was a lot to take in. I had one last piece of baby clothing on board, a tiny T-shirt that read, "I'm the little brother." Although the wee baby was a girl, I gave it to the eighteen-year-old mom, who was thrilled to have something new for her daughter. I gave the fifteen-year-old boy a spare pair of sunglasses.

With the visit over, we offered to take them back to shore. They didn't want to go back to the prison. They wanted to be taken to the far northern end of the beach where a couple of dugouts were pulled up on the sand. En route, Nik allowed the young man to drive the dinghy, which pleased him so much. With his new sunglasses on, he stood up and struck a pose of great confidence, roaring up to the beach with his hand on the throttle, showing off his piloting skills to the local fishermen on shore. We landed and they disembarked, heading up the path and over the hill with the fishermen who were carrying buckets of sea urchins back to their fish camp.

So often we heard stories from other cruisers who boasted of their interactions with local people. So often we asked ourselves why we didn't try harder to be more open, more welcoming, and more relaxed with the people we met on our voyage. Pleased with ourselves over the enjoyable contact we zotted back to *Green Ghost* to idle away the afternoon reading and drinking cool drinks in the shade.

An hour later we heard a noise against the hull. Our young friend was back. Alone, he'd paddled out to us in one of the dugout canoes. He no longer had the sunglasses I'd given him. With an earnest look on his face, he wasted no time tying up to our boat. Then he hopped up on deck without need of invitation.

I stepped out of the cockpit to sit on the coach house roof. Nik stepped out as well. We didn't know why he was back, but we thought it best to have our discussion out on the side deck, not in the cockpit.

"Je couche ici," he told us.

"I think he wants to sleep here," I said to Nik.

"Je couche la-bas," he said, pointing below decks.

"Non, pas possible," Nik responded. "Parce-que, demain, nous allons," Nik used short bursts of carefully enunciated French.

"J'irai avec vous," he came back.

"Is he saying he wants to go with us?" I asked Nik.

"I think so," Nik responded to me. Then to the boy, "Non, non, pas possible, pas possible. We go very far. Um, nous allons tres, um, tres … what's the word for far? Beaucoup de miles. Nous allons beaucoup de miles, demain."

"Je viens avec vous," he insisted.

"Oh, my goodness," I said to Nik. "Now what do we do?"

The young man went on to speak at length in Malagasy. A French word popped up here and there. It was something about his mother, and something about Mahajanga, a settlement farther down the coast. We tried to explain that we were not going there, that we would be travelling far away, to South Africa and then, all the way to Canada. He was persistent, but of course he could not win the argument. Thwarted, he eventually climbed down off our deck into his dugout, utterly dejected. We waved him goodbye, trying to sound cheery and encouraging, but we were both feeling much the way the boy looked.

Madagascar. It was like no other place we'd ever been. Our very existence there unleashed a series of butterfly effects. Our impact, however small, threatened unforeseen consequences at every turn.

I went to bed thinking of our adoption file, closed so many years ago. Nobody had chosen us. And here was this young man, desperate to paddle out of his own life, ready to jump on board, grab a berth, and go to sea. "Beaucoup de miles" was no problem for him – he relished the thought. I wondered what would become of him, what prospects he had. I wondered what would've happened if we'd simply said, "Okay."

⚓

By late September we'd made our way south to Moramba
Bay, the jumping-off point for many cruisers planning to cross
the Mozambique Channel. It was a lovely protected spot to sit
and wait for weather. The shore was lined with baobab trees
and inhabited by shy sifakas. We delighted watching them in
the trees, where they leaped athletically, always maintaining
an upright position. On the ground they moved more comical-
ly, hopping sideways in an upright galloping motion, bouncing
along on their hind legs with their arms held up for balance.

A walk on a nearby island led us to a massive baobab tree
that was reported to be fifteen hundred years old. Nature was
a balm for us in Moramba, just what we needed to combat the
rising tension in the growing fleet.

On a world map, Madagascar looks like it is tucked in beside Africa, but the channel is wider than it looks. It is a 1,200
NM journey to Richards Bay, South Africa. Like any offshore
passage, choosing the right weather window was imperative.

Several other boats already in the bay had sailed south
from Nosy Be earlier, hoping to get a jump on the crossing.
While we'd idled our way down the coast, they'd been waiting,
kicking at the stall for departure. But no weather window had
materialized. As a result, when we arrived in Moramba Bay,
there was an air of impatience in the fleet.

Fortunately, the small group of boats was well provided for
by young men from the nearby village who came out in canoes
offering items for trade: mangos, bananas, papayas, tomatoes,
eggs, fish, and lobster. We were surprised at the prices being
paid. It was the last stop in Madagascar for every boat in the
anchorage and it was well known that Malagasy currency was
worthless outside the country. Cruisers tossed their big bills
at the locals without much thought and in some cases, sailors
handed over the last of their Malagasy currency outright. By
the time we turned up in the bay the economy was well out of
whack. The local salesmen were so enamoured with their big-

spending customers that not a single canoe approached us, the unknown newcomers.

When the weather cleared for a go, our fellow sailors departed. Electing to let the seas in the channel calm down before we set out, we chose to depart a day later. After the mass exodus, micro-economics took over. The market demand dropped instantly. The vendors rushed in, oversupplied. We were canoed six times that day – and prices for everything had plummeted.

It was a delicate economic system and it made me reflect on the country itself. In Madagascar, I felt that every action I took or didn't take set off a ripple of consequences both in the place I was standing and in myself. Corrupt officials had caused my mistrust of all Malagasy and it followed that I treated honourable people with suspicion, preventing them from doing their job. A gracious village chief restored my faith in humanity, but petty thieves stole it back again. We were satisfied and generous in one moment and displeased and guarded the next. We couldn't settle on a way of being in Madagascar. It was a precarious existence, swinging on the end of a pendulum between trust and treachery. I sensed that in Madagascar, no one is ever just passing through. Every person tips the balance and leaves the place changed. Maybe the same can be said of everywhere you go. In many places we'd visited I felt like a drop in a bucket, but here, I felt like a drop in a teaspoon.

In the end, we left the anchorage with Ar25,000 in our coffers, equivalent to about C$12. Those three folded bills still rustle around in my travel kit. They do me no good at all. Perhaps it was stupid of us not to toss our last currency into a passing dugout as we departed. Perhaps it was a missed opportunity: the very best kind of ripple effect that we failed to initiate.

CHAPTER 25

Africa

(October 2013 – February 2014)

We departed Moramba Bay with strong easterly winds that made for beautiful sailing on our first day out. The wind was aft of the beam and the seas were flat as we charged southwest, hugging the northwest coast of Madagascar and heading toward Cap Saint-André. From the cape, our destination was Richards Bay, South Africa, about a thousand miles on a diagonal path across the Mozambique Channel at a bearing of 218 degrees.

The channel was notorious for the fronts that marched across it and for its strong and unpredictable currents. After departing the Madagascar coast, the goal was to get to Richards Bay before the next front came in. If you didn't make it, there were few places to hide. To cross it, you needed a strategy. First and foremost, you had to avoid getting caught in a big south-westerly blow, particularly once you were on the west side of the channel in the fast south-flowing Agulhas current. Our charts indicated twenty-metre seas could form in such conditions. These were dangerous waters.

As the wind became southerly, we found ourselves beating into a brisk fifteen to eighteen knots, spray a-flying as we punched into two-metre seas on a westerly course. When conditions eased and backed to the east, the sailing was easier and we enjoyed a more comfortable ride. But the currents confounded us.

"That's strange," I said to Nik. "The compass on the binnacle shows us on a perfect southwest heading of 225 degrees, but the autopilot says our course over ground is 168 degrees."

"That doesn't make sense," Nik answered.

"I know," I said as I looked around for metal objects hanging off the binnacle, thinking something magnetic was interfering with the compass.

Although our bow was pointed in a southwesterly direction, because of a strong current, we were actually moving in a direction that was east of south – we were sailing sideways.

At another point on the journey, we noticed that our speed over ground read 0.0 on the knot metre, while the boat knots read 3.0. In other words, we were sailing forward at three knots into three knots of unfavourable current and although our heading was perfect for a Richards Bay landfall, we were standing still. In both cases, in order to get through the strong eddies, the foresail was furled and the engine went on.

On day eight we entered the fast-flowing Agulhas current on the western side of the channel. It gave us a two-knot boost, but it wasn't enough. On the morning of our tenth day, with about sixty hours of sailing to make Richards Bay, the weather forecast predicted that the next front was expected in approximately sixty-four hours. We were so close, but we weren't willing to risk it. If we were a few hours late, or if the front was a few hours early, we would find ourselves in the Agulhas current as the front arrived – the most dangerous place to be in a big southwesterly blow. We made the choice to play it safe and detour to Inhaca Island off Maputo, Mozambique, 30 NM off our course.

"Dammit!" I heard Nik say in the cockpit.

"What's happened?" I called up from my bunk.

"The genoa halyard's let go and the sail is sliding down the forestay! Can you come up here and give me a hand?"

We hastily rolled the slumping genoa up on the foil and unfurled the smaller staysail, which slowed our speed toward shelter. Although it had been a difficult decision not to carry on to Richards Bay, we now knew we'd made the right choice. If we'd pushed our luck and made a run for it, the genoa failure would've ensured that we lost the race with the approaching weather. We would've found ourselves on a section of coastline where there was nowhere to hide. Instead, we were safely at anchor when the bad weather arrived on time and in force.

The anchorage at Inhaca wasn't much to see, but as the saying goes, any port in a storm. While we waited, we socialized. Roger and Sue of *Wapiti*, the only other boat in the anchorage, had ducked out of the weather just as we had. Although we'd been chatting on the radio net together as we crossed the channel, we'd never met, but that didn't stop them from planning a party. Learning it was my fifty-first birthday, they invited us over for a delicious curry lunch. They even had a gift-wrapped birthday present for me and a card to go with it. Their generosity epitomized the cruising world, and made a birthday holed up off the coast of Mozambique an even more memorable affair.

While we waited for the weather, we pulled the genoa down and found that the webbing loop that was stitched into the head of the sail had worn through. I sewed some new webbing on, we rehoisted the sail, and we were shipshape once again.

After three nights and two days, we were able to resume our journey. From Inhaca south to Richards Bay was a mad dash. By now we understood that although the weather forecasting could be inaccurate for the Mozambique Channel, the South African meteorologists had it dialled in when it came to predicting coastal weather. We had only 200 NM to go, but it was a narrow window of opportunity in mixed conditions and we had to make use of every hour. Nik was in a state of high anxiety. I admit that I was too. It was the first time I'd felt nervous about a departure.

Everything went according to plan. After several hours of tacking into south-southeasterlies, the winds backed to the northeast on time and exactly at the strength predicted by the forecast, allowing us a due south run. For the final sixteen hours to Richards Bay, with three reefs in the mainsail and a tablecloth of genoa unfurled, we made our final fast dash to South Africa.

Moonlight lit our way until one a.m. when the moon set,

leaving me on watch in the ink-black night. Nik had gone to bed an hour earlier, instructing me to wake him for the final approach. Friends, already in Richards Bay, had reported to us that the harbour entry was well-marked and that the electronic charts for the area were spot on. This was a good thing as the timing was such that we couldn't avoid arriving in the dark.

The twinkling lights of Richards Bay were a welcome sight. We'd left Madagascar over two weeks earlier and, as always, we were both looking forward to someone else's cooking and a long walk on shore. As I approached the harbour entry I was feeling confident with my position, using the C-map charts on the chart-plotter on the binnacle and the Navionics charts on the iPad as confirmation of our position, but as we neared the harbour entrance something didn't look right. There was something between us and Richards Bay. As we bounced along, the lights in town appeared and disappeared, now blocked out by a black silhouette, now peeking out from behind it. I couldn't see what the object was, but something as black as the night itself stood between us and the channel and obscured the lights of town.

"I need some help up here," I called down to Nik.

"What's up?" Nik asked as he came into the cockpit, still groggy. He hadn't had much rest.

"There's something big and black between us and the channel but I can't figure out what it is."

Nik grabbed the binoculars and went out on deck. Bracing himself against the mast he took a good look forward. "It looks like a black hill," he called back.

"That's what I thought. But how can it be? There's no island on the charts."

We rolled up the genoa to slow down and to improve our visibility. I steered to skirt the object, keeping the black mass to our port side. Closer, we could see that a single tiny white light marked the apex of the monolith. Closer still, we could differentiate some colour – rust red near the waterline, black on top. Nearer still we could make out some white markings, and two huge anchors against the black hull. The mystery object was the bow section of a modern ocean-going bulk carrier sticking up above the water's surface. But where was the rest of her? Was the stern section still attached, resting on the sea floor? We couldn't believe no one had mentioned this monstrous hazard to navigation on the way into Richards Bay, but then for anyone entering the port by day, it was so obviously a shipwreck, it needed no explanation. It was only by night that the wreck posed a threat.

We learned that the 273-metre MV *Smart* had run aground two months earlier as she exited the harbour in ten-metre seas. It surprised me that no one had boarded her bow section to spray paint the words Not So in front of the ship's name.

Free and clear of further obstacles, we rocketed into a slip at Tuzi Gazi Marina, tying up at three a.m. and beating the forecasted thirty-knot southwesterly front by eight hours. Despite the late hour, once *Green Ghost* was tied up, we quietly walked up the docks together to perform a ritual we hadn't done in twelve years. We held hands and jumped onto African soil, then we turned around and walked back to the boat to go to bed. We'd made it.

We soon moved over to Zululand Yacht Club where most of our friends were tied up. We immediately plunged into the social scene at the laid-back community-oriented ZYC. On Braai nights, steak dinners could be purchased for about C$12 per couple and at happy hour on pub nights, rounds of half a dozen drinks were only C$7. But it was the camaraderie that was intoxicating. We felt part of something, part of a sailing community, one of a small number of people who had sailed a boat from Australia to Africa. We settled in and paid for a month at the dock.

At one of the social nights Nik was asked about our trip by a local sailor. The man listened intently while Nik enthusiastically told our story. When Nik was finished, the man looked at me.

"Do you have kids?" he asked.

"No," I replied.

"Yeah, well, I didn't *think* so. You can't do *that* with kids."

It was a line we heard often and it always put me on the

back foot. My sense of cozy inclusiveness vanished. Although the comment was probably nothing more than a practical observation – that sailing with two adults is logistically easier than sailing with a family – it always struck a wounded part of me. The comment pointedly excluded us from the drudgery of parenting and suggested that being childless was nothing but a lucky perk that made all we'd accomplished so much easier. I wondered if I'd ever stop flinching. Probably not. I suppose it will always define me, that broken part of my heart. In response, I was speechless.

"But you *can!*" Nik chimed in, always good at saving the moment with his cheerful disposition. "You *can* do this with kids. The Copelands, the Martins, the Wilcox family ... they all did it decades ago. And these days there are many more. We've met so many wonderful cruising families. You *can* do it with kids. It would be an amazing enriching family experience!"

"Yeah, well, not with my kids." He stopped us.

There was no changing his mind.

⚓

We were determined to make the most of our time in Africa. Hiring a car with our friends Bruce and Kerry from *Haven* we took off on a road trip in pursuit of the big five: one car, two couples, three weeks, four countries, and over five thousand kilometres of fun. Africa surprised us at every turn from the nearby white rhinos of Hluhluwe Game Reserve to the semi-tame cheetahs of Emdoneni Game Farm to the adventures farther afield.

We drove 1,700 kilometres to Kasane, Botswana, for a couple of days in Chobe National Park before a day trip across the border into Zimbabwe to see Victoria Falls. From there we headed south and west to Maun, into Okavango River country.

We'd read that the Old Bridge Backpackers was a good place to arrange a boat trip up the Okavango Delta, a UNESCO World Heritage site and one of the Seven Natural Wonders of

Africa. Kerry and I, forever the planners, approached the administration desk in the open lobby.

"We'd like to speak to you about a river trip," Kerry said.

"Yes, what kind of trip are you looking at?" the manager replied.

"Well, there are four of us, and we're thinking we'd like to do a four-day, three-night trip up the river and then upon our return, we're thinking we'd like to do two days and one night in Moremi Game Reserve."

"And when would you like to do this?"

"Tomorrow."

The manager smiled widely. "You're optimistic, aren't you?" he said with a note of sarcasm.

"Yes, we are!" Kerry and I said in unison, laughing out loud.

"Let me make some calls. Help yourself to a coffee, have a seat by the bar, and I'll get back to you shortly."

"Well, he didn't say 'no'," I said brightly to Kerry as we stirred whitener into our strong coffee.

In under an hour the manager came to us and told us he had it all arranged – a guide, a cook, a crew, two boats, and reservations upriver. We were in. It was only later that we realized that our last-minute booking probably meant we got a less experienced team.

The following morning, we handed our gear to the camp assistants, keeping only our daypacks with us as we climbed into the shallow draft river boat with our soft-spoken guide, Alec. It was a treat for all of us. We didn't have to operate the vessel, we didn't have to navigate; all we had to do was sit back and enjoy the scenery.

The Okavango Delta was fantastic. Wildlife was everywhere: elephants at the water's edge, fish eagles perched in the trees, crocodiles slithering in from the banks, and hippos idling in pools. Amazed at Alec's eyesight and delighted by his commentary, we found he was a fantastic guide and we were awestruck every mile of the journey.

It was the beginning of the rainy season and the water

level was low. Navigating the braided river system was not easy, something we appreciated after bottoming out a few times. Now and then Alec would stop the boat and lift the outboard to carefully pilot through extremely shallow patches; other times he'd perform a similar routine to clear weeds caught in the propeller.

At one bend in the river, Alec stopped the boat to check the propeller. With the prop clear, he scanned the water surface then gunned the boat, passing through an area of tall reeds at top speed. As we rounded the next corner, a hippo on shore charged the water, covering the short distance to the water's edge with remarkable speed. We flew past, heading upstream to a great lunch spot.

We set up our folding chairs in the shade of a large tree and pulled out our picnic lunch. On the quiet savannah, we had a chance to ask Alec questions.

"That hippo back there, the one that ran into the water when we went by, I guess the noise of our engine frightened him. Is that what they do? Do they run for the water when they're frightened?" I asked.

"No. Not frightened," Alec explained in cropped sentences.

"Oh?" I said.

"Hippo was charging us."

"Oh," I said again, embarrassed at my naiveté.

"That is why I make sure, no weeds."

"So how did you know to do that? Is that hippo always in that spot?" Nik chimed in.

"Yes, always there," Alec answered.

"Does he always charge the boats?" Bruce got in on the questioning.

"Yes. Bad hippo," Alec answered, straight-faced.

"Does the hippo ever *get* the boat?" I asked, horrified.

"Sometimes." Alec replied. "Sometimes they bite it."

"If they bite it, then what happens?" I needed to understand this. We hadn't been given the lowdown on the emergency exits.

"If the boat has hole, I drive it up on the bank," Alec answered.

"Then what?"

"Then you run."

I doubted very much anyone would have much of a chance outrunning a hippo, so this last part struck me as futile. I knew that hippos caused more deaths than the other wild animals in Africa, but for some reason I'd imagined them being dangerous to folks on foot near the water's edge. It hadn't occurred to me that they would attack a twenty-foot tinny roaring through their territory at top speed. This business of being in the African bush was not to be taken lightly.

After lunch, we carried on upriver, seeing beautiful wildlife at every turn. In one area where the stream was very broad, Alec slowed our boat and began arm-waving and shouting. There was another boat much like ours on the far side of the river.

"That is Captain," Alec explained to us afterward.

"Is that our gear?" Nik asked.

Back at the backpacker's dock, there had been two boats: ours, which carried us, our daypacks, our picnic lunch, and some chairs, and a second boat that carried all the camping gear – the tents and sleeping bags, our larger packs, the food, and the rest of the team.

"Yes. Captain doesn't know the river. He is on the wrong side," Alec said evenly. I wasn't sure if it was a problem. Deeply concerned or utterly delighted, Alec's face always looked the same. His tone of voice never seemed to change.

On we went, taking in all the Delta had to offer, never tiring of another elephant sighting, the flight of a crested crane, or the dash of impala from the water's edge.

It was late in the afternoon when Alec stopped the boat midstream and turned off the engine to give us complete quiet. He'd done this a few times since lunch. It was a moment to take in the sounds of the Delta, to appreciate the natural beauty in peace. But Alec wasn't delighting in bird calls, he was listening for the sound of an outboard motor.

"Alec, why are we sitting in this spot?" Bruce asked after ten minutes or more.

The sun was sliding down the afternoon sky. In the distance, we could see towering anvil-shaped clouds and rain on the horizon.

"I am listening for Captain," Alec explained. "He is behind us."

Caught up in viewing wildlife, we hadn't paid much attention to the fate of Captain and the gear, but Alec had. He'd been fretting all afternoon.

"How far is it to the campsite?" Nik asked.

"Not far," Alec answered.

"Why don't we just go to the campsite and wait for Captain there?" Bruce asked.

"No, Captain must arrive first," Alec answered.

We waited another ten minutes. No sound was heard. The sun sank lower.

"Alec, shouldn't we go to the campsite? We don't want to be out on the water in the dark, do we?" Kerry chimed in.

"We don't want to be on shore in the dark," Alec replied. "No fire."

"I have a lighter," Nik announced. He dug in his daypack and held it up like a prize.

Alec's eyes lit up. "Good," he said and he started the motor.

Finally, on shore, Alec instructed us to collect firewood, but not to go out of his sight. It was against park rules to gather wood on the Delta, unless it was an emergency. Our camp wood was in the supply boat – it was an emergency. As the rain moved toward us, we collected wood with greater urgency, amassing a large pile, enough, we hoped, to last the night.

We unloaded the boat. It didn't take long. We had only five chairs and our daypacks. Between us we had one litre of water, one slice of bread, and some dried plums.

Soon we had a roaring blaze and we gathered around it, straining to listen for the sound of an outboard above the noise of the crackling fire. Alec explained that a fire was considered a matter of safety in the bush at night – a fire kept most animals away. Good to know, I thought. Most, I noted. As darkness

descended upon us a few drops of rain began to fall. Fortunately, we were on the fringe of the storm cell. The clouds passed at
a distance, grey curtains of rain streaming out of the night sky,
intermittently illuminated by forked lightning.

"You can sleep. I will keep watch," Alec told us.

"We'll take turns," Kerry offered.

"If there's one thing we're used to, it's keeping watch,"
Bruce added.

Alec agreed, but insisted upon taking the first shift. Bruce
and Kerry stretched out on the ground to try to get some sleep.
Nik and I elected to doze off in our chairs. Before sleep settled
upon us, we heard it – the distant sound of an outboard engine.
Captain and his crew arrived to save the day, or, in this case,
save the night.

"Oh, what a trip!" Captain said as he came ashore. "My
heart was very hectic for you!"

I smiled at his expression. He was clearly rattled. There was
much discussion between the guides and many apologies to us,
the customers. We brushed it off – no harm done. Besides, the
prospect of the five of us alone, unsheltered and unarmed for
a night in the African bush, made for a terrific story. Not quite
Naked and Afraid, but *Unprotected and Somewhat Concerned*
might've been an accurate title.

We pitched in to unloading the cargo and setting up the
tents while the safari staff set up the camp kitchen to start dinner. We learned that Captain had twice gotten stuck. On one
occasion, in order to refloat the boat, the crew had unloaded all
the cargo onto the riverbank and walked it piece by piece upstream to deeper water, where they were able to reload without
bottoming out. They may have been less familiar with the river
than the other guides, but they got the job done.

In the morning, we set out from camp for a walking safari,
which was a lovely hike across golden bushland, except for the
moment when we were charged by a bull elephant. It was the
one time a sudden urgency possessed Alec, although he still
addressed us in his usual short sentence structure.

"Elephant! Run!" was his only command.

We did run and the elephant stopped short, happy to have us off his section of the savannah.

Bad hippos and territorial elephants aside, our road trip through southern Africa was a terrific experience. But after three weeks of land travel, it was time to get back to our element. The sea was calling.

⚓

Although we'd made it safely to Africa, the Indian Ocean was not yet behind us. We wouldn't leave it in our wake until we rounded the Cape of Good Hope. And the journey around the cape, with its notoriously windy conditions, was no small undertaking.

We were up against the same weather challenges. In southern African waters, the biggest weather concerns for sailors are the low-pressure cells that move from west to east across the southern Atlantic and affect the southwestern area of the cape, causing strong winds and heavy seas. The depressions march through at a rate that makes rounding the cape in one long passage virtually impossible. To add to the challenge, there are relatively few, relatively widely spaced ports of call.

We took the first step and made the 90 NM trip from Richards Bay to Durban without trouble, but there was still nearly 900 NM to Cape Town. We waited in Durban for eight days, sitting out a forty-knot blow, before venturing out on the next round of good weather.

To aid our weather information, and as an added safety measure, we'd joined the Peri Peri Maritime HAM radio network, masterfully controlled by Roy, a resident of Durban. Radio check-ins with Roy became a highlight of our dash around the Cape. I called in twice daily to give Roy our position and get an update on when the next cold front was due to arrive. After I introduced myself as Jennifer, Roy, like many South Africans (and Brits and Aussies), immediately began calling me Jenny, a nickname that has always made me cringe. There are only two people who have ever gotten away with repeatedly calling me Jenny, my father-in-law and Roy.

Departing Durban with a solid northeast wind filling in behind us and the strong southwesterly-flowing Agulhas current beneath us, *Green Ghost* flew south for the cape. We recorded our fastest time ever, sailing 224 NM in a twenty-four-hour period, nearly double the mileage of a typical day. At that speed, we made East London Harbour in good time and Roy waved us on.

"You'll make Port Elizabeth at this rate," he advised on the afternoon schedule.

Another 135 NM to the safety of Port Elizabeth, and the weather held. Another 200 NM to Mossel Bay, and still the weather held.

We'd been at sea for a couple of days. The sailing was good but demanding in the cold. We wore pants and socks and fleece jackets to keep us warm on the night shifts and slept poorly, chilly in our bunks. We were reminded of our sailing roots back in Vancouver – seals in the tea-green water, mountains on the shore, and cold feet. As we passed each port in favourable conditions, Nik began to lament.

"We're missing opportunities for a good rest at anchor."

"Are you kidding me?" I said. "We're so lucky to be making it this far. They say if you can make Mossel Bay, you're in a good position to wait for weather to round Cape Point. We might do this thing in two hops."

"But have you seen this?" Nik held out a picture of Knysna, an idyllic brochure photo of a serene blue-green harbour on South Africa's southern coast. "It looks so beautiful. We're going to miss all these places," he grumbled.

Later, I checked in with Roy.

"Peri Peri Net, this is the sailing vessel *Green Ghost*."

"Good morning, Jenny, good morning, Jenny. Jenny on *Green Ghost*, go ahead with your position, go ahead with your position." Roy had a habit of saying everything twice.

I gave him our position and asked, "We've got to make a decision here, Roy. We're just off Mossel Bay, 220 NM to go to Simon's Town. How does the weather look? Have we got another forty-eight hours before the front?"

"Keep going, Jenny, keep going, Jenny, keep going, keep going!" he yelled into his mic. "You've got the weather window of the decade, the weather's going to hold for you, it's going to hold for you, you'll go all the way to Cape Town on this, you'll go all the way to Cape Town!"

I hung up the mic, looked at Nik, and made my announcement.

"If you want to see Knysna, we can rent a car. This boat's going to Cape Town."

"Hard-ass," he said, but he couldn't argue with me – we were going to make it from Durban to Cape Town in a fast five and a half days. Like Roy said, it was the weather window of the decade.

Rounding the most southerly point of Africa, Cape Agulhas, and the sight of the more famous Cape of Good Hope, was a thrill for me. I recalled the stories of Bartolomeu Dias and his search for a trade route to India. When I sat in my grade school social studies classes, I never imagined that one day I'd be here at the cape on my own boat. It was the only one of the five great capes we'd round on our trip. It wasn't just a point of land, it was a magnificent rite of passage, a seafarer's coming of age. For us, it was the end of the long haul across the Indian Ocean and the threshold of the Atlantic, our home stretch.

"You've got to come up here and look at this!" I yelled down to Nik.

"I'm sleeping," he replied.

"But we're passing the cape. It's amazing!"

"I'm sure it's very nice," he said, turning over in his bunk.

I was in awe of the place. Nik, not so much. He napped on his off shift as we passed the famous landmark. Me? I clipped on, stepped out on deck, and, with the cape as my backdrop, took selfies like mad.

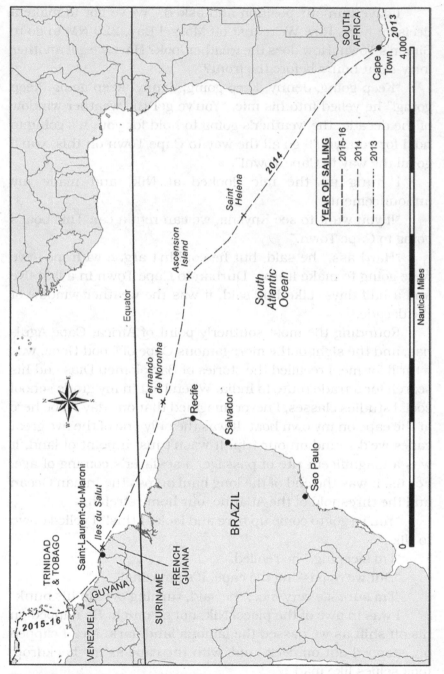

Figure 4. Atlantic Ocean Route Map

CHAPTER 26

St. Helena

(February – March 2014)

It was hard to imagine that we'd never wanted to sail to Africa. The pirate activity in the Gulf of Aden had prevented us from sailing from Asia to the Med and forced our cruising route south. Africa, as it turned out, was nothing short of magic.

Africa had gravity. A coastline both dangerous and thrilling, a countryside exhilarating and enchanting, wildlife like nothing we'd ever seen before, and peoples with an origin so ancient, I felt a profound sense that I'd stood at creation's ground zero. In Africa, I had warmed my soul at the hearth of humanity.

We set out to cross the Atlantic with our senses filled by Africa. Since arriving in Richards Bay four months earlier, we'd sailed for only one week. We were rusty, but our confidence upon departure was high. With no hurricane season in the South Atlantic (only one has ever been recorded in history), there was no angst over leaving too late or too early. Besides, we finally had seasickness licked, so the Atlantic didn't threaten Nik the way previous oceans had. The Atlantic was a kinder ocean. With its consistent trade winds and fewer squalls, we were certain it would be a shorter, more enjoyable passage.

We were excited at the prospect of heading home. Being in the northern hemisphere would mean that our cruising season would be in Canada's winter months and our off-season would be in Canada's summer. We imagined all kinds of possibilities for home-based off-season fun.

So we allowed ourselves to believe that the Atlantic was

the small one, the easy one. We didn't consider the fact that it was also likely to be the most tiring. There were so few places to stop. Unlike the Pacific with its many island groups, or the Indian where we rested for a nearly a month in each of the well-populated islands we visited, our route across the Atlantic offered only three remote stops: St. Helena, Ascension Island, and Fernando de Noronha. We planned a five-day rest at each one.

On an excellent weather forecast that promised southeasterly winds for a straight week, we sailed out of Cape Town on a Wednesday morning in late February 2014. Dolphins saw us off and seals and penguins waved goodbyes as the beautiful backdrop of Table Mountain disappeared in our wake. With 1,750 NM to go to St. Helena, we settled in to enjoy the ride, expecting a two-week trip.

One day into the passage we downloaded weather files and saw that the weather forecast had changed dramatically. Rather than the promised southeasterly winds, we were to expect a bout of northwesterlies, the very direction we were trying to go.

Sunny skies became overcast and by late afternoon on day three we were motoring into light adverse winds. By nightfall, we were beating into it, heeled over, galloping over the oncoming waves. In the increasingly uncomfortable conditions, we got down to basics: sleeping (not well), eating (not much), and trying not to get flung off the toilet seat at the wrong moment (not easy).

Our four-hour watches had become habitual. I always took the midnight to four a.m. shift which probably sounds like the short straw, but it had its upside. By doing the graveyard shift, the other two of my three watches were in full daylight. This made sense because I did most of the food preparation at sea. On the eight a.m. to noon watch I would ready food for Nik when he came on at lunch. On the four to eight p.m. watch I would prepare dinner for both of us. I got the sunsets, Nik got the sunrises. We were used to it, but it was still tiring. Day by day, watch after watch, the bags under my eyes grew into a complete set of luggage.

The first half of the trip had been dominated by the weather patterns that affect the Cape area, which meant either too much wind or none at all. The adverse conditions abated by day five when we lost the wind altogether and then at the start of the second week, we found it again. Finally, back in the trade winds – consistent, moderate breezes from the south-southeast – we could sail directly downwind, with the sails set wing-on-wing, straight down the course line to St. Helena.

⚙

We'd seen few other vessels on the journey, so when a twenty-eight-metre fishing vessel crossed our bow, we were keen for a chat. Nik picked up the radio mic.

"Fishing vessel, fishing vessel, this is the sailing vessel *Green Ghost, Green Ghost.* Can you tell me if you are towing nets? Over."

"No Eeenglish, Español, Español," came the reply.

"Yo hablo Español," Nik replied boldly.

I looked at him in surprise. He didn't speak Spanish.

A torrent of Spanish came back at us and went on for a couple of minutes.

"That'll teach you, Mr. Yo Hablo Español," I said, laughing.

"Which one of my many expressions do you think would be an appropriate response?" Nik said.

"Hmm. 'Dos cervezas, por favor' ought to do it," I said, teasing him about his proficiency at ordering "Two beers, please."

When the Spanish-speaking captain finally finished, Nik fessed up.

"Um, sorry, no comprendo." Then he asked simply, "We go okay?"

"Okay. Si. Go okay," came the reply. We could hear a chuckle in the responding voice and we carried on to St. Helena.

⚙

We'd been sailing under a dull grey canopy for more than a week. The overcast skies frequently showered us with smatterings of rain. The disappearance of both the sun and the moon was depressing and disorienting. With no golden orb arcing through the sky and no moon through the night, we had no astronomical touchstones to remind us that we were still on planet Earth.

On our eleventh day at sea, I caught a glimpse of the setting sun in a gap of clear sky at the horizon. It was a relief to know that the fiery yellow ball was still up there, that we hadn't made a wrong turn and ended up on planet Water, where one might sail forever without ever finding a shore.

☸

We sailed swiftly in superb conditions for the last stretch. Under sunny skies, in pleasant trade winds, we sighted sea birds and scattered flights of flying fish as we made the final miles north and west.

St. Helena was a fourteen-million-year-old lump of eroded volcanic rock in a remote part of the Atlantic. I imagine it looked godforsaken to Napoleon, when he was exiled here in 1815, but to us, after two weeks at sea, it was a beautiful sight.

The island slopes off steeply in all directions, providing no natural harbours. There was only one reasonable anchorage off the capital, Jamestown, on the leeward side of the island. Deep and plagued by strong gusts that came barrelling down the northwestern slope across the anchorage, it wasn't ideal. Fortunately, the St. Helena government had installed sturdy moorings for visiting yachts which could be used at a charge of one GBP (British pound sterling) per day – a great bargain for the security they provided. We took one and settled in among the half-dozen other cruising boats already in the harbour.

There was a bit of a knack to getting safely on land. Despite being on the leeward side of the island, there was a notable swell at the dinghy dock. To assist those disembarking at the cement wharf, a crosspiece had been erected between two vertical pilings. From the crosspiece hung a rope three inches in diameter. The idea was to stand up in your bobbing landing-craft, grab onto the moveable rope, and swing yourself to the safety of the wharf. It involved a bit of coordination and there were some wet feet for those who missed.

When we finally did get ashore I had the worst case of sea legs. It was the opposite of seasickness. I was so used to everything moving that for the first day, I felt nauseated to be on solid ground where nothing moved at all.

"I could live here," Nik announced (not surprisingly) as we strolled into town.

"I could too," I agreed. "I'd rent a Georgian stone house, hide away in it, and write a book."

"It looks like the perfect place for that," Nik agreed.

We fell in love with Jamestown, where one-sixth of the island's four thousand people lived. The Georgian buildings were so well preserved that a walk up Main Street was like walking through a living museum. Discovered by the Portuguese in 1502, the island had been Dutch (1633) and eventually became British (1658). The closely packed shops and buildings built alongside the island's only continuously flowing freshwater stream formed a narrow linear settlement at the bottom of the steep-sided valley. With the stone walls, the fort Castle of St. John, St. James' church, and the gun batteries on the cliffs, we felt as though we'd stepped back in time more than three hundred years.

We paid a local Saint (as the islanders referred to themselves) for a tour. Robert spoke English as both a first and a second language. When he spoke to us he was perfectly understandable, but when he spoke to other islanders in the local dialect, we didn't have a clue what he was saying. He greeted his neighbours with an expression that sounded something like, "Yorride orwah?" which I later learned translated into "Are you all right, or what?" It was the Saints' way of saying, "Hi, how are you?"

Robert had driven the local school bus for twenty-odd years and gave a great island tour, taking us to all the hot spots, including the place Napoleon spent his first night in exile, the cottage where he spent his next seven weeks, and the house where he lived in exile for several years before his death in 1821. Mr. Bonaparte got a lot of press on St. Helena. At times, it was a bit over the top. After seeing all the places he'd ever laid his head, we were also taken to see what was no longer his grave. The French wanted him back, so his body was exhumed and returned to France in 1840. Being dutiful tourists, we took the ten-minute walk down a grassy path through the woods and snapped a couple of photos of the place where Napoleon isn't buried.

After a few days of fun stretching our legs ashore, we turned our attention to our onboard jobs. Nik always felt a rig inspection was important after an offshore passage, and ever since finding a broken clevis pin and the so-close-to-letting-go forestay when we arrived in Rodrigues on the Indian Ocean, he was hyper-vigilant about inspecting the rig after every offshore passage.

Nik got in the bosun's chair and tied it to the main halyard. Using a winch, I cranked him up to the first set of mast steps, then kept the halyard taut as he climbed from there. He paused to inspect each of the attachment points where the standing rigging was secured to the mast. Now and then he called out to me to lock him off at a certain position so that he could dangle in the bosun's chair, hands free, to take a good look at the rig.

The forestay is a wire rope that goes up the front of the boat from the bow to the top of the mast and keeps the mast from falling backward. The backstay runs from the stern to the top of the mast and keeps the mast from falling forward. The shrouds are wire rigging on either side of the mast that keep the mast in column by restricting movement from side to side. All the stays are important of course, but at least with the shrouds there are two sets: one set that reaches to close to the top of the mast (uppers) and another set that reaches about halfway up the mast (lowers). It was at the upper shrouds where Nik paused for a long while.

"We've got a problem up here!" he called down.

"What's wrong?" I yelled back.

"The tang on the port side is broken! Three mil stainless snapped like a potato chip!"

A tang is simply a piece of sheet metal that is used to attach the shrouds to the mast. *Green Ghost* has double tangs, so although one tang had broken, the assembly continued to keep the shroud attached to the mast. Still, we thought we ought to fix it. The shrouds were attached to the tangs and the tangs were attached to the mast with a large bolt. We had a small sheet of three-millimetre-thick stainless steel on board in our spares locker. All we had to do was unbolt the broken tang, take it ashore, and ask a local tradesman to fabricate a new one from our spare sheet metal. There was just one problem. We could not unbolt the tang. Over three days Nik tried everything. He tried anti-seize, he tried his propane torch, he tried some whack-it-with-a-mallet persuasion. Nothing worked. The bolt would not budge.

In the end, we jury-rigged it. I went up and tied a spare line around the mast above the upper spreader. We led the line to the deck, through a block and back to a winch. If the tang broke completely, the installed line would take over and support the mast. We put two reefs in the mainsail to reduce the stress on the mast above the upper spreaders. We did all we could, but the breakage was a nuisance and a worry. Not only had we been delayed by our repair work, but with less sail area, we'd be sailing with reduced speed for the remainder of our crossing.

We were in our usual mindsets. I was optimistic that we'd supported the mast well and that the rig would be okay. Nik fretted. With so many Atlantic miles ahead of us, he wanted the confidence of sailing with a perfectly robust rig. I believed that we'd manage whatever came our way, but Nik felt the weight of the world on his shoulders. If the rig failed in some way, he knew it would be his greater strength and mechanical know-how that I relied upon to fix it.

Despite my outward optimism, inwardly I admitted that the breakages were getting me down. The challenges of cruising were beginning to overshadow the joy. We were both looking forward to getting to Trinidad, docking the boat, and walking away for a while. We were beginning to feel we needed some downtime from cruising.

But getting to the Caribbean required several more passages. So, after ten days at St. Helena, we set out on the 700 NM journey to Ascension Island.

As it turned out, the rig was the least of our worries.

CHAPTER 27

Ascension

(March – April 2014)

The ocean was a vast expanse of whitecaps in the relentless trade winds. Sitting in the cockpit, looking astern, all we could see was the next wave coming. Standing at the wheel, looking forward, all we could see was the backside of the wave that just went past. We called them HOS's – horizon obliterating swells. They crowded in on the *Ghost*, their crests peaking in a translucent glacier blue, collapsing into a frothing white whoosh behind us.

Despite the big motion, we got into our offshore routine quite quickly, settling into life with attachments. At sea, it seemed, I always had something on my head. On the morning shift, it was sunglasses. Off watch for the afternoon, I'd have ear plugs jammed in and an eye patch keeping daylight out while I napped. Back on watch at four p.m. the sunglasses were switched out for a headlamp at sunset, then at eight p.m. it was back to ear plugs, but no eye patch was required to sleep in the dark. At midnight, the ear plugs were out and the headlamp was back on. Back to bed at four a.m. and the headlamp came off, the ear plugs went in, and the eye patch was back in position in preparation for sunrise. It was an endless change of headgear.

The water temperature was 20°C, fifteen degrees higher than it had been in Cape Town. We were back in the tropics. We were noticing the warmth and humidity in the air too. The fridge iced up, the fans were on, and scantily clad sailing was back. Life was hot and uncomfortable, but we were chugging along making good mileage toward Ascension.

Then, our trusty third helmsman, "Otto," gave up the *Ghost*, literally and figuratively. Three hundred nautical miles from our destination our electronic autopilot stopped working and we didn't have a backup. Our mechanical autopilot, Digger, had not been working properly for a long time and we'd been lazy about repairing it, relying on Otto instead. With no backup system, there was only one solution – hand-steering.

It is physically demanding and mentally tiring to have to hand-steer at any time, but worst of all to have to do it *all* the time, particularly with a short-handed crew. We shortened shifts to three hours. At first, I was optimistic – *we can do this!* But two hours into my first shift and thoroughly exhausted, I started counting. Over 300 NM, with two reefs in the mainsail, about seventy hours, divide by two, thirty-five hours ... a dozen shifts each – it seemed an impossible task. *Keep going, Jenny!* I heard radio Roy's voice in my head. One more hour. I told myself, *This won't last.* Contemplating manageable time frames and concentrating on encouraging mantras was the only way I was going to get through it.

Conditions required two hands on the wheel. Arm, shoulder, and back muscles were constantly engaged. There was no reading, no curling up behind the dodger out of the wind, no grabbing a snack or making a warm beverage. On shift, you couldn't leave the wheel for a moment, not even for a bathroom break. Off shift, rest took precedence over everything else. Meals were simplified – grilled cheese sandwiches, scrambled eggs, and canned beef curry were our saviours.

We'd heard horror stories from other sailors about "that time the autopilot failed," but we'd never experienced the situation ourselves. It was a marathon of physical effort resulting in a fatigue so complete, I felt exhaustion at a level I'd never experienced before. After hand-steering for three nights and two days I had new respect for anyone who has hand-steered for longer. We were spent, but we knew we were lucky. It was only 300 NM – it could have been worse.

While St. Helena felt remote, Jamestown had been a civilized village and a quaint mid-ocean settlement. By comparison, Ascension was a wild windswept place, the rugged back of beyond. The unearthly landscape of barren lava flows and volcanic cinder cones looked like a scene from a sci-fi movie. Even so, we were happy to see it. Like Rodrigues was in the Indian Ocean, Ascension was our little slice of oh-thank-goodness in the Atlantic.

As at St. Helena, there was no natural harbour at Ascension. The broad swell of the South Atlantic bent around the island, creating notable motion even on the lee shore. The swell in the anchorage, the waves surging upon the beach, and the strong winds that wrapped around the island added to the uncivilized setting. We arrived mid-morning on a Friday and set our anchor on the second try.

"Hey, check these fish out," Nik said to me as he returned from lowering the anchor at the bow.

"I know, they're everywhere!" I said.

The small black fish were about eight to twelve inches long and they stood out starkly in the aqua-green water. There were hundreds of them swimming about. Like seagulls at a seaside picnic, it seemed they'd come to see if anything good was on offer. I tossed a crust of bread in and we watched in astonishment at the instantaneous mob feeding. The surface became a thrashing swirl of black bodies as dozens of the fish hungrily swarmed the tiny crust. In seconds, there was nothing left but a frenzied school of bread-predators searching for a second morsel of food.

"God help you if you fell in," Nik said.

"No kidding," I answered. "Death by piranha. I wonder what they are."

We wasted no time launching the dinghy and going to shore, to check in with the officials and get Internet access.

In the port captain's office on the long cement pier I made small talk while we got the paperwork done.

"We noticed many small black fish in the harbour as we came in," I said. "There must be hundreds of them."

"Thousands," Kitty George, the port captain, replied.

"Yes, I suppose you're right, thousands," I agreed. "What are they?"

"We call them blackfish," she said with a completely straight face.

"Of course," I said, trying to remain serious, but wanting to giggle. "That makes sense."

We purchased WiFi access from a humourless woman at The Obsidian, the island's only hotel. We wrote an e-mail to a marine electronics dealer in the U.K. and ordered a brand-new autopilot, hoping we might be able to get it on the next flight.

Pleased with our efficiency, we went looking for something to eat. The hotel wouldn't feed us because they needed several hours' notice to prepare a meal. The saturnine proprietress sent us to a snack bar called The Saints.

"Do you have a lunch menu?" Nik asked over the counter.

"Today is chicken nuggets and french fries but we're out of chicken nuggets," came the reply.

"Okay, thanks. Maybe we'll come back tomorrow," Nik said.

"Tomorrow is tuna sandwiches and french fries," the cook announced.

"Okay, thanks," Nik said, holding back the temptation to add "for the warning."

We learned that the next nearest place to get a meal was either the British RAF base, an eight-kilometre uphill walk, or the U.S. Air Force base, also a long walk from the wharf. Ascension wasn't much of a tourist destination. It reminded us of a remote mining camp – not so much a place to live as a place to work. The population of eight hundred worked for the British government or the U.S. military. As a result, for people passing through, there was limited entertainment.

Sick of our own cooking and desperate for a meal, we bought two frozen pizzas at a little grocery shop, went back to the boat, ate pizza, drank beer, then slept for eleven hours straight.

☸

We'd allotted five days for a stop at Ascension. We were keen to get our repairs done. The new autopilot would be shipped to the military airport in Bristol, England, spend two days clearing security, and then it would arrive on the semi-weekly flight. We anticipated a week-long wait – not bad, not too far off schedule.

But everything took longer than planned. It took five days just to finalize the order and another five days for the parcel to arrive in Bristol. There, it was placed on the manifest for a flight departing in six days' time.

We made daily trips to shore, walking up the long cement wharf to the small cluster of buildings that were Georgetown, spending a small fortune (5 GBP per hour) at The Oblivion, to use their weak and intermittent WiFi to check progress.

The delay caused a series of inconveniences. We'd had to apply for permission to visit Ascension before we left St. Helena, and we'd already overstayed our permit. Two extensions to our Permit to Stay were required while we waited. We worried about our propane. We were more than halfway through our forty-pound supply and there was no LPG (liquid petroleum gas) for a thousand miles in any direction. Our credit card expired at the end of May. We'd expected to be in Trinidad by then to receive it, but the way things were looking, that wouldn't be the case. We could feel our plans for an Ontario summer slipping away.

Worst of all, our delay wreaked havoc with our social life. *Moonfleet* had stayed on at Ascension hoping we could sail on together to Brazil. But when our delay became ever longer, we encouraged them to leave without us.

"We'll see you in South America!" I shouted to Diane as we passed *Moonfleet* in our dinghy.

Diane and Alan were preparing to weigh anchor for departure.

"But we've been together for nearly two years!" she shouted

back. "I hate to go without you!" She looked truly upset at our parting.

"Don't worry, Diane!" Nik called back. "We'll be right behind you. We'll catch up to you somewhere, I know we will!"

Alan, the consummate captain, swung *Moonfleet* out of the anchorage as we went ashore to check e-mail.

Our optimism vanished at The Oblivion when we received the news that our shipment would be delayed another full week.

☸

As we had on the Indian Ocean, we'd continued to operate a radio net on the Atlantic. It started with just the two of us, *Moonfleet* and *Green Ghost,* but by the time we reached Ascension we had a dozen boats on the roll call.

"Good morning, everyone. This is *Green Ghost, Green Ghost,* Charlie-Foxtrot-Golf Seven-Two-Three-Seven with the Atlantic Crossers' Net. Is there any emergency traffic? Any emergency traffic come back now." Pause. "Nothing heard. Let's start the roll call. *Eliana, Eliana,* this is *Green Ghost, Green Ghost,* how copy?"

The comeback was barely discernible. We could tell it was Dave on *Eliana* responding to our call, but attempting conversation was fruitless – his voice was too faint to decipher. With our stationary existence, we were getting farther and farther away from our comrades travelling west.

Being left behind was hard on our hearts. Upon our arrival at Ascension almost every boat on the roster was behind us on passage. Over the course of our stay, every boat passed Ascension, some even arriving in Brazil while we sat stationary. By our last few days on the island, the fleet was so far west of us that we were having tremendous difficulty transmitting and receiving. It only made sense to transfer net control to the boats in the middle of the pack.

It was depressing that we had to give up the very net we'd started. It wasn't a control thing. It was, after all, much easier to be the guy who called in than to be the guy who ran it. It was about the people. Time and time again on our journey we'd found that it wasn't just about where you were. It was about the people you were with – and we were no longer with our people.

But we were slowly becoming Ascension Islanders.

When a poster at The Saints snack bar touted free dance lessons, we dinghied ashore in the dark. An Ascension Airline hostess had a thirty-six-hour turnaround and while she was there she gave salsa lessons. There were three of us in the class – us and a German guy on his way home from a conservation contract in the Falklands.

We squeezed the salsa lesson into our busy schedule of checking out the museum (open on Monday evenings and Saturday mornings only), seeing the fort, lunching at the Saints Club (too many french fries, too many times) and going to the beach with a conservation officer after dark to watch green turtles lay their eggs at the second largest nesting site in the world (the largest being in Costa Rica).

Each night in the anchorage, under starry skies we would hear the sharp exhalations of female turtles making the last few hundred metres of their long journey. They swam all the way from Brazil just to lay their eggs on the beach at Ascension.

Twice we shared a rental car with other cruisers and tried to make a day of it. Even though we drove every paved road on the island at the posted speed limit of thirty kilometres per hour and stopped once for coffee and another time for snacks, we'd done it all by two p.m. At about ten kilometres by thirteen kilometres, Ascension isn't that big.

We watched the people, the vessels, and the turtles come and go. And we waited.

⚓

We'd been fortunate to have relatively good conditions, making our trips into the wharf reasonably easy for most of our stay, but the good conditions didn't last. At times, a dangerous swell was present in the bay. The locals called them "rollers" and the port captain had warned us that when the rollers came in, the wharf was untenable, and we should not attempt to go ashore.

The difficulty in landing was one of the reasons many cruising yachts didn't bother to stop at Ascension. Even on a gentle day, the broad Atlantic swell kept the water level in constant motion at the wharf's side. You had to have your wits about you when you approached the cement structure in a small boat. Picking that sweet spot, that safe moment to step out of the dinghy between crest and trough, was not for the faint of heart.

While on Ascension we'd had the experience of coming into a dry wharf, the lower landing baking-hot in the sun, only to step out of the dinghy and get soaked to the knees without warning. Bare feet and shorts were a must.

We learned not to put items down on the landing. The safe thing to do was to unload one person (me) and then have the dinghy operator (Nik) hand over one item at a time. I would take each one, and scramble up five or six cement stairs before setting the item down safely high and dry on the wharf. It was a tricky process, transferring our backpacks, our computers, our cameras and shoes.

Even the emptied dinghy was in peril. We couldn't leave it tied up adjacent to the wharf. It would've been damaged by abrasion from the up and down of the swell. A stern anchor had to be used to hold the dingy off the rough cement.

One day we were on shore for some mid-morning distractions when we saw a catamaran arrive in the anchorage. Later, we met the crew in the grocery store. The four sailors were from Brazil. They had stopped only to get water, refuel, resupply, and send e-mail. They carefully spent every last coin of their British currency at the shop, while their captain went off in search of Internet access.

A little later, when Nik and I wandered back down the wharf to head home we saw the Brazilians already there. From a distance, we could see them walking down the cement staircase, all four of them, carrying all their goods to the dinghy landing.

"Uh-oh," Nik said, and we quickened our pace.

As we reached the end of the pier we saw the four sailors crowded onto the small landing with their jerry cans of fresh water and fuel, and their bags of groceries as well. The captain was struggling to pull their dinghy alongside. The wharf was wet, which should have been a clue, but they were distracted with the task at hand and they were not paying attention to the sea.

"Um, you might want to …," Nik began to warn them.

At that moment, a rogue swell rolled in, noiselessly rising up, engulfing the small wharf, and soaking the Brazilians thigh high. Then, the water receded, floating all their jerry cans and gathering up all their groceries in one wet sweep. Every single item was sucked into the sea.

There was chaos on the landing. Two Brazilians managed to jump in their dinghy. They struggled to get their outboard started. The jerry cans floated, partially submerged in the ocean. The grocery items spilled from their bags, canned items sinking, buoyant items bobbing in the swell. A pale head of cabbage bounced on the surface just briefly then disappeared in a dark swarm, a mob feeding frenzy of blackfish.

"I'm going in!" Nik shouted.

Not having access to our own dinghy with the Brazilians blocking the landing, Nik set down the bags he was carrying, threw down his backpack, tore off his T-shirt, kicked off his shoes, and dived in. He swam straight for the cabbage now twenty metres away. If there was one thing we knew, salad mattered. In a few powerful strokes Nik pounced on the produce. He grabbed the cabbage with one hand, tearing it away from the scavengers, triumphantly holding it high in the air. But he was too late. In those few seconds, the cabbage had been reduced to the size of a golf ball.

Nik looked at it, shook his head in disbelief, tossed what was left of it back to the blackfish, and swam for our dinghy. The would-be coleslaw was history – it was time to save the other items. In our own dinghy, Nik assisted the Brazilians in recovering their grocery bags and their jerry cans from the water.

✺

While we waited for the new autopilot to arrive, we went up the mast again to take a look at our reinforcements and make sure everything else was okay. Our jury rig looked fine but, I was alarmed to find a one-legged cotter pin where the forestay attached to the top of the mast. We'd had this problem on the Indian Ocean, having found that same cotter pin sheared right off upon our arrival at Rodrigues. We replaced it again, but it worried us because we didn't know the cause.

I'd relaxed a little and enjoyed our Ascension distractions on shore, but Nik remained feisty and hyper through much of our stay. He was seeing the bigger picture. It wasn't just a matter of waiting for the new equipment; once it arrived, he was the guy who had to install it, and he fretted about the responsibility. What if, after all this time, he couldn't make the new autopilot work?

When our long-awaited parcel finally arrived late in the afternoon of our twenty-fifth day on the island, we excitedly unpacked the boxes, read the directions (me) and looked at the parts (Nik). We hoped to have the unit installed and tested by the end of the following day.

But the next morning Nik got up and put his clean laundry away, a task that had been left undone for a week. Then he made the bed. He never makes the bed. I knew what was happening – these were avoidance tactics. I understood. As long as the new equipment remained in the box, it represented our escape. Once we got started on the installation, if anything went wrong, if there was some extra part that we'd need that would take another three weeks to arrive, well, neither one of us could face that outcome. We wanted to wallow in the positive possibility just a little while. So we both had a second cup of coffee and tidied up the boat, enjoying the feeling that an exit was possible, before we set to the task of proving it.

It took all day for Nik to complete the installation. I helped out as assistant, doing some of the satellite jobs, and locating tools that had been in hand one moment and were lost the next. The following day we picked up the anchor and moved in circles around the harbour testing the new equipment on all points of sail. All good.

We reanchored and went into town to complete our check-out procedures. Immigration stamped our passports OUT, the port captain handed us our clearance papers, garbage was dropped off, groceries were picked up, and we made one last visit to The Oblivion to send e-mail.

"I can't believe it, but tomorrow's Friday," I said as I looked at the calendar back on the boat.

"Don't even start," Nik said.

"Well, you know what they say, 'Never leave port on a Friday.' The last thing we need is more bad luck."

"I'm not listening to that superstitious hocus-pocus," Nik said. "It's probably some bullshit British Navy saying. I prefer the Serbian expression."

"What's that one?" I asked.

"Fuck Friday – we're outta here."

After twenty-eight days, we pulled out of the harbour at Georgetown, leaving the tiny island of Ascension in our wake.

CHAPTER 28

Fernando de Noronha

(April – May 2014)

The trade winds blasted us off Ascension's leeward shore and rocketed us out onto the big blue. As the island disappeared in our wake, I contemplated the folks we'd met who lived on that tiny island, only ten by thirteen kilometres in size, for more than twenty years. This wandering soul couldn't understand how they did it. And yet my feelings were mixed. After so much angst over our month-long stay, it felt strange to be leaving. I knew I'd never see Ascension again. I wondered, Had I lapped it up? Had I made the most of my time there? The island had been good to us, a safe haven, a unique experience. But as always, we were pushing on, seeking more of the same, but different.

You'd think we would've been bright-eyed and well-rested, but oddly we were both dejected and tired. In its own way, the delay had been exhausting. Gear failure was a given in offshore sailing. You'd think we'd learn how to take it in stride. But we could never completely relax when *Green Ghost* wasn't fully operational. Gear failures always took a toll, rattling our nerves and eroding our resolve. The long wait had crushed our momentum. Having lost so much time on Ascension, we'd given up on the idea of cruising continental Brazil. We decided to sail to Fernando de Noronha, then on to French Guiana, and then straight to Trinidad.

☸

"Did you hear that?" Nik asked me in the afternoon our first day out.

"What?"

"I thought I heard something like a thunk, thunk, thunk."

I listened carefully for a moment. "I'm not hearing it."

Out of practice with the sounds of being at sea and too used to things going wrong, Nik looked around, scanning the deck and the rig, then looking over the stern at our rudder.

He was hearing things. There'd been no *thunk, thunk, thunk* in the afternoon, but later that evening a loud bang followed by a *slam, slam* and a *flap, flap, flap* had both of us wide-eyed and scrambling.

"Turn on the spreader lights," Nik called from the cockpit.

I leapt from my bunk and flipped the switch.

"The lines for the downwind pole have gone slack," Nik said. "The pole has collapsed. I think it's broken."

"Oh, geez. Give me a sec and I'll come up," I said, dressing to assist him in the cockpit.

The foresail, no longer supported by the pole, was flapping around. Nik quickly furled it, then put on a harness to go forward to take the pole down and secure it on the mast.

Another gear failure on our first night at sea was distressing. We were sailing with reduced mainsail due to the broken tang discovered in St. Helena. The thought of having to sail the remainder of the Atlantic without a downwind pole to improve the efficiency of our foresail was terribly discouraging.

"What's the diagnosis?" I asked when I got up for my morning watch.

"Haven't got my feet dirty," he replied.

He meant feet wet or hands dirty, but for once, I left it alone.

"I'm going to sleep for a couple of hours, then I'll get up and get at it."

We juggled the watch schedule through the afternoon so that Nik could examine the pole. He found that the line that secures the pole in its telescoped-out position had chafed through at its attachment point inside the pole. An afternoon of dismantling began. Out came the liquid wrench, the impact screwdriver, the hacksaw, and the torch to deal with seized bolts. There was some violent persuasion with the rubber mallet accompanied by a great variety of swear words. There were stripped threads, sheared heads, and rivets that had to be drilled out. Replacement bolts and rivets of just the right size were located from the bowels of the tool chest. With no manual to assist him and the motion of the ocean complicating every move, Nik worked through the afternoon. By sundown, we had an operable pole. Once again, yay, Nik.

We relaxed into the pleasant conditions of the voyage. Sunny skies and a fifteen-knot southeast breeze gently guided us toward Fernando. Portuguese man o' war jellyfish drifted by. The moonless nights were star-filled. Each night, on my graveyard shift, I watched Mars slowly setting to the west. Saturn sat a little higher in the sky. Later I watched the lovely Venus rising in the east, so bright she cast a beam across the water from the horizon to our home.

⚓

"That sounds like Dave," Nik announced.

Morning and night, we faithfully tuned in to the prescribed channels for the Atlantic Crossers' Net.

"I think that's Mike now," I chimed in.

Reception was so poor we made a guessing game of it.

"That's Diane!" we said jointly, thrilling in the familiarity of her voice.

But transmission and reception remained poor, and most often everyone sounded like Charlie Brown's teacher: "Wah-wah-wah."

When we were unable to talk to anyone on the net, I wrote e-mails to friends and family instead. I described the sea state, the wind strength and direction, and the forecast of what was to come. I spoke of the moon, knowing that my family and friends, wherever they were, would be seeing the same: the waxing and waning, the rise and the set. Each note gave a latitude and longitude and a miles-to-go countdown. We were disconnected from people but hyper-connected to our physical world. When I read back over my e-mails from that time, I feel the intense kinship we had with the sea and the sky, our acute awareness of our own well-being. What I wrote – the small details of building winds, the number of apples left in the fruit bowl, the thumbnail of the crescent moon, the damp sweaty smell of our laundry – the minutiae, all of it was important to us. I realize now that none of these details mattered much to our followers back home. They put up with my fine-point fixations for the four words at the end of each transmission – *All well on board*.

"Are we there yet?" Nik asked on the ninth day out.

"Not yet," I replied.

We'd met other sailors who told us they loved the offshore legs so much that they felt depressed as they neared their destination, knowing their passage would soon be over. We didn't feel that way. For us the getting there was taxing, the being there was grand. At times, at sea, we became quite grouchy.

That night, the wind died with the sunset and with insufficient sail, we were moving oh-so-slowly and rolling around a great deal. *Kalunk, kalunk.* A repetitive noise began. The straps holding the propane tanks snug in the locker had loosened, allowing the tanks to slide around. *Kalunk, kalunk.* Frustrated by this disturbance to his night watch, Nik decided to put a stop to it.

He lifted the hinged cockpit seat and leaned it back to rest against the coaming. He should have kept one hand on it because of course, on the next big swell, the boat rolled to port and the hinged lid closed heavily, right on his head.

He reacted quite violently. There was the shock of being attacked by a locker lid, there was the immediate testosterone-fuelled inanimate object rage, and, of course, there was the excruciating pain. Then there was the bleeding. Next came the cursing, the heavy-heeled stumble down the companionway, the noisy flailing in the head as the door was slammed shut and cupboard doors were flung open. There was an encore of swearing with bitter curses along the lines of, "We never have any first aid equipment on this boat!" and something more about the whereabouts of the Band-Aids.

"What's happened?" I asked, sitting up in my bunk.

I got no reply.

I got out of bed and stood outside the closed door. "Are you okay?" I said, trying to open the door.

"Don't open it! The drawers are open!" he shouted from inside. If the vanity drawers were pulled out in the head, you couldn't swing the door open without damaging the woodwork.

"Tell me what's happened!" I demanded.

There was more cursing and many contemptuous remarks about our first aid supply.

"Get a grip on yourself, for heaven's sakes!" I yelled through the door. "Tell me what's happened! Have you hurt yourself?"

"This is bullshit!" came the reply. "We never have any bandages on this boat!"

"Just because you don't know where they are, doesn't mean we don't have any!" I shouted back.

"If I can't find them, what good are they?"

I had only one response.

"Why you not marry Thai girl? Thai girl very niice!"

It was a ridiculous scene. While the two of us engaged in a full-on domestic row through a slammed bathroom door, *Green Ghost* carried on, oblivious, under a starry sky, lurching and rolling across the dark Atlantic.

I sat on my bunk with a "Hmph!" and waited for Nik to calm down.

When I was finally let into the head, I found Nik with a blood-soaked wad of toilet paper up against the back of his skull. He had an inch-long gouge in his scalp. It bled, as only head wounds can, but it was a clean cut and, with pressure, the bleeding soon stopped. I flushed it with saline solution, applied alcohol and an antibiotic cream. I was sure it would heal up just fine left on its own and, eventually, it did.

⚓

After a slow and gentle eleven-day ride, the islands of Fernando de Noronha appeared. The skyline was stunning, dominated by the phallic Morro do Pico and pierced by dramatically eroded volcanic rock silhouettes in every direction. The shoreline was sand-fringed with beautiful beaches of golden muscovado sands tucked between the headlands.

We arrived in the anchorage with perfect timing – 8:30 p.m. ship's time, just late enough that the officials had gone home for the day, not too late for cocktail hour, and still early enough for a proper night's sleep. We anchored off the steep rocky headland beneath an old fort, Forte de Nossa Senhora dos Remédios.

"Did you hear that?" Nik asked once the engine was off.

The Atlantic swell slapped the near-vertical cliffs at the shoreline, forcing air through fissures and crevasses, producing a sound like a fire-breathing dragon.

"Ah! The Dragon of Fernando!" I said, a little overly dramatic. (What can I say? I was reading *Game of Thrones* at the time.)

"I've never heard a blowhole so loud."

We went below, poured ourselves generous G&Ts, and later fell asleep to the hissing respirations of a sea dragon.

Despite the thrill of making landfall, on our first day in the anchorage we dug deep into our locker of self-control and remained on board to complete our job list rather than making a beeline for the famed beaches of Fernando.

We didn't normally get cheeky with officials, but anchoring fees at Fernando were expensive. So we decided that a little cheekiness was worth the risk. In the customs office, when asked what day we'd arrived on the island, we answered coyly.

"Arrive here?" gesturing to our feet. "Today," we said, suggesting the truth – that we'd only just come ashore that day.

There was a flurry of Portuguese among the men in the office, but our claim went unchallenged, even though *Green Ghost* had been anchored in full view of the port captain's office for the previous two nights. We were given a table of costs that escalated for a three-, four-, or five-day stay. We pointed to the four-day option and were given a bill for R$1,060 (about C$500) to sleep at anchor in our own bed, at hotel *Green Ghost*.

Knowing that Fernando was expensive, I'd anticipated an island of high-end development and a clientele to match, but I was wrong. The sparsely populated island is rugged and natural. The tourists were mostly vacationing Brazilian nationals dressed down in comfortable go-to-the beach clothing. On the beaches themselves, much less was worn – much, much less. My cheek-encasing bikini seemed downright frumpy next to the fashion sported on Fernando. No one does butt cheeks like the Brazilians. Even the men were in tiny togs.

The local Baía do Sancho had recently turned up on a list of the Top Ten Beaches in the World. Naturally, we had to see it. To get there we took a bus to a national park, passed through the park gateway, then proceeded along a raised walkway through lush green forest to a vertiginous platform perched on a cliff. We descended through a hole in the platform, climbing down two long vertical stainless-steel ladders, squeezing through the narrow crevice in the basaltic rock. Once on the sand at the bottom, we were surrounded by a crescent of high cliffs on one side and the sapphire sea on the other. We swam and snorkelled, enjoying the company of turtles and rays and the ever-present eye-popping sight of the few other tourists in their oh-so-tiny Brazilian swimwear. There was no doubt this beach had earned its place on the list of the best.

Perhaps in reflection of our long-faced stay on Ascension we were determined to have as much fun as possible in our ninety-six hours on Fernando. We were all-in, ignoring our budget, splashing out on an expensive meal at a fancy restaurant overlooking the port, trying out premium versions of the national drink, caipirinha, the taste of Brazil.

We rented a dune-buggy – a green machine on a Volkswagen chassis with fat tires and low gearing – and felt particularly authentic when Nik brought his surfboard ashore. We ripped around on the rough dirt tracks hunting for the best surf spots. A surfboard in a dune buggy – it felt so very Barbie and Ken.

Four days of fun on Fernando had been a welcome respite and had energized our flagging spirits. On deck on our final evening, we readied the boat for offshore. We knew what had to be done: lifting and securing the outboard and the dinghy, checking the rigging, stowing any items left lying around, plotting our course for the morning. The tasks were so familiar now, we barely had to converse. As we quietly worked together we marvelled again at the loud exhalations, the ever-present bellowing that pulsated with the roll of the sea. Soon, *Green Ghost* was ready. Change, it seemed, was as inevitable as the next breath of a dragon.

CHAPTER 29

One Hundred and
One Atlantic Nights

(May – June 2014)

I got a Brazilian. Cold, that is. I suppose my immune system wasn't up to interacting with the South American population on Fernando. Retribution crossed my mind – shades of historic voyages and transmission of disease – only this time it was the English (descendant) going down.

We were en route to French Guiana. At 1,300 NM, it was another long passage and it wasn't much fun being at sea with puffy eyelids, packed sinuses, and a dripping nose. Had I been at work, I would've stayed home, but you can't take a day off when you're offshore sailing. So I took my watches with a box of tissues. Fortunately, conditions were gentle and, because of our watch schedules, I got to go back to bed every four hours.

The wind was only four to six knots, much too light for a seventeen-ton boat with a double-reefed mainsail. We were in the doldrums again, sailing only eight of the first thirty-seven hours of the voyage. After three days, northeast winds filled in, putting us on a beam reach and we began to make good mileage toward French Guiana. This was a big change from months of southeasterly wind patterns and, although we were still two degrees south of the equator, the conditions suggested that we had crossed into the weather patterns of the North Atlantic. Our speed was improved by the north equatorial current that moves up the South American coast. With a full moon lighting our nights, no squall activity and the gentle wind, we settled in to enjoy the last leg in the open Atlantic.

But the northeasterly didn't last. Within a day we were back in light air. The Intertropical Convergence Zone (ITCZ), that writhing movable band of calm, toyed with us. Our daily mileage dropped off and I began fretting over our schedule.

I used small Post-it Notes for planning. Knowing we aimed to be in Trinidad by mid-June, I worked back from there, calculating mileages and counting days based on average speeds. I worked out what time was left over and allocated time in each port. I was always moving my sticky notes around. An extra day in Fernando moved everything back a bit, a few days of fast sailing bought back some time. Nik, on the other hand, rarely looked at my scheduling. He didn't like the constraints of a calendar. He believed we could swing by the coast of Brazil, we could spend a week at Dégrad des Cannes near Cayenne, we could visit the European Space Centre at Kourou and still see Devil's Island and Saint-Laurent-du-Maroni. He was the idea-man. He lived in a world of endless potential, where time was ever-expanding and all things were possible. But I was the girl with the calendar and I drove the itinerary in real time. Or so I liked to think.

In reality, I wasn't driving anything. The weather was driving the itinerary and the windless conditions were driving us both nuts. At times, we had a boat speed of less than one knot. Thankfully, the three-knot current allowed us to eke out hundred-mile days, but the slow pace played on our minds. When our patience waxed we would sit back and enjoy the calm conditions, peacefully reading books and celebrating the free ride in the current. When our patience waned, we would curse our predicament, throw down our books, flip on the engine, and burn more diesel.

Despite our frustrations, we both realized that transiting the global weather-defining zones gave us a connection to something bigger than ourselves. Crossing the doldrums was something every sailor on a transequatorial passage had to do. It didn't matter what century you were in. It didn't matter what fancy technological advances you had on board. Getting through the doldrums on a sailboat was an exercise in patience and belief. I fell back on my usual mantra: *This won't last, this won't last, this won't last. We will emerge.* And we did.

⚓

"What's the drill this time?" Nik asked me.

"What drill?"

"We're about to cross the equator. I bet you've got something up your sleeve."

I didn't. Was I becoming indifferent? We were already shell-backs after all. Did we really need a big celebration?

"Remember our first crossing in the Pacific? I died my hair blonde," he recalled. "Then, when we crossed back, there was the little beach party on that muddy mangrove shoreline in Indonesia. You dressed as a mermaid and I dressed as a pirate."

"Yeah, I remember," I said, smiling. "We were the only two people in costume!"

"What did we do when we crossed south again, off Sumatra, wasn't it?"

"You slowed the boat down for me and I swam across," I said.

"Oh, yeah," he smiled. "So what is it this time then?"

I looked at Nik. He was wearing next to nothing in the heat. I looked down at myself and suggested, "I suppose we could just run around naked."

Nik smiled, the way he always did when he heard the word naked. Dropping his Fijian sarong, he took off for the bow.

"Counter-clockwise!" I shouted. "For the storms of the north!" I dropped my own sarong and took off after him.

A pod of pilot whales passed at a distance as we crossed the equator into the northern hemisphere. It felt good to be home.

As we neared the coast of South America we sailed into Sargasso Sea. The greenish-brown seaweed formed large rafts, some of them much larger than the boat. There was a thickness to the masses, a little bit of elevation, and from a distance, you could fool yourself into thinking they were sandbanks glistening in the sun. The seaweed made a swishing sound as it brushed by our hull and wreaked havoc with our fishing line, which had to be reeled in.

Finally, the ITCZ passed. Goodbye, gentlest passage ever. Hello, shrieking winds, creaking floorboards, and the dull thud of waves walloping our starboard bow. Salt spray everywhere, dead flying fish stinking up the deck, horizon-obliterating swells – it never ceased to amaze me how strong winds transformed a calm body of water.

In the lumpy conditions, I chose basmati rice and prefab chicken tikka in a foil pouch for dinner, thinking it would be simple to make: boil one, heat the other. But it wasn't an easy meal. It was meticulous work picking bugs from the rice with a teaspoon. We hadn't been in a large grocery store since leaving South Africa nearly three months earlier. As always, toward the end of an ocean crossing, our supplies were getting low.

We crossed onto the continental shelf in the night and our depth sounder found bottom. After eleven days at sea, we arrived at Devil's Island and anchored off the old French penal colony, a place made famous by author Henri Charrière. Although happy for a rest from the boisterous conditions, it was slightly unsatisfying stepping ashore. Devil's Island was just off Kourou, French Guiana. We could see the mainland of the South American continent only 7 NM away. It wouldn't feel like we'd crossed the Atlantic until we set foot on that shore.

After two nights of rest, we departed mid-day on an overnight to the mouth of the Maroni River, the boundary between French Guiana and Suriname. In the morning, on the flood tide,

we carefully picked our way 20 NM up the broad shallow basin
to the town of Saint-Laurent-du-Maroni. In on-again/off-again
rain showers, we anchored in behind the wreck of an old ship,
the *Edith Cavell*, with one other cruising sailboat.

Distracted by the tasks at hand – launching the dinghy,
lowering the outboard, loading up the garbage, and finding the
check-in paperwork – we dashed ashore between rain squalls
all business as usual. In our hurry, we forgot our usual ritual.
It wasn't until later, over baguette sandwiches in a local café,
that we realized we'd forgotten to celebrate with our usual
jump to shore. We'd officially crossed the Atlantic Ocean from
Africa to South America. The Caribbean was only a short hop
away.

Saint-Laurent-du-Maroni was the centre of the French
penal colony system and the landing point for convicts from
France. For nearly one hundred years (1852 to 1946), crimi-
nals sentenced to prison and hard labour were off-loaded at
The Transportation Camp and later distributed to various
other prison locations in the country, Devil's Island being one
of them. We toured the quartier disciplinaire and peered into
the cell marked #47, with its miserable moldy plaster walls, its
plank bed and rusted leg shackles. It was the cell everyone came
to see, to lay eyes upon the famous name scratched into the
cement floor: *Papillon.*

⚓

I'd hoped for toucan and scarlet ibis sightings as we flew upstream in a twelve-metre dugout canoe. A huge outboard roared
on the transom. The river tour guide explained to me that it was
not the right season for the former and not the right location
for the latter. Instead our tour group stopped on the Suriname
side of the river and toured Maroon villages and Amerindian
settlements where big black ladies in wide skirts and undersized
bras cooked large rounds of manioc flour atop circular iron
grills over a fire. Young men constructed dugout longboats from

impossibly big logs, and little children ran around in their undies or in nothing at all.

On the water, kingfishers poised on branches, hunting at the river's edge, and birds of prey soared overhead. The green jungle was dotted with bright flowers, some like giant calla lilies, while others looked like fireworks bursting in flight. Up one narrow tributary we saw butterflies so magnificently blue they made peacocks look underdressed.

Above the small town of Apatou, our tour ended with a drive through the rapids, something that can only be done when the river is bloated by the wet season rains. It was frightening flying at high speed through such turbulent waters in a boat that hardly seemed made for the task. In the moment we shot the rapids, we had the most violent torrential downpour we'd had all day – under ball caps and huge blue ponchos topped with bright orange life jackets we stayed remarkably dry as the water flew over, under, and all around us.

At the fixed-menu lunch stop, we tried some stewed meat in a tomato-based sauce.

"What do you think this is?" Nik said as we tucked into the hot lunch.

"Looks like chicken," I said.

"It's not chicken," he said. "See?" He separated a tiny bone from his meal and pushed it to the side of his plate. "That's no chicken bone."

"Well, it tastes like chicken," I insisted, having taken a bite.

"I heard the guide use the word 'Pak.' I think it's one of those guinea pig-like critters that we've seen running around on the grass."

"Tastes like chicken to me," I insisted again, as I removed a short hair from my helping.

After a week of rest, we picked up our anchor as the tide turned to ebb. We made good time with the currents, both fluvial and tidal, and we were quickly whisked out to sea. We were soon back to being uncomfortable, scooting along on a beam reach in more than twenty knots of wind. We didn't hesitate to take seasickness medication. Our sea legs were long gone after resting up in the oh-so-still Maroni River. Soon, the salt spray was flying and we were hanging on for the ride. *Green Ghost* sped along, racing for Trinidad.

⚓

I got up for my morning watch to find a small puddle of long-life milk pooled up against the fishing tackle locker. Flakes of once-moist cereal had dried hard on the counter, the floor, and the companionway stairs.

"Cereal killer," I playfully accused Nik in the cockpit.

"Yeah, and we're short one bowl," he replied in a monotone. He was not in the mood for my humour.

In the boisterous conditions, he'd lost control of his breakfast as he turned from the galley to climb the companionway stairs. He'd made it to the cockpit, where he was flung against a winch, chipping the bowl in the fall. In utter frustration, he'd flung the lot into the sea.

I understood his short temper. A beam reach in twenty-plus knots was a ridiculous way to live. Big waves soaked our starboard deck, swooshing up against the galley porthole and rushing astern, soaking the cockpit cushions before sliding back into the sea. I'd been reciting my mantra again. It seemed I'd been reciting it an awful lot lately.

Days before, in the doldrums, when we'd been idling away our time, Nik had been scheming and dreaming all kinds of future long-distance voyages. He was full of thoughts beyond Trinidad, making plans for Newfoundland, Labrador, Greenland, Iceland, maybe Europe, and the Med. His musings got me thinking, Was I really up for more sailing?

Physically I'd begun to find it more difficult. I used to be stronger. My grip strength had deteriorated. Any kind of intense manual work left my hands aching for days. My stomach wasn't up to it either. With our four-hour schedule, I ate when on watch, and slept when I was off. There'd been too much lying down after eating and I'd developed uncomfortable acid reflux symptoms. Popping Nexium, Zantax, or any other antacid remedy had become part of my routine anytime we were at sea. Menopause had a negative impact too. My body thermostat was wildly out of whack and my episodes of total nuclear meltdown that some called hot flashes were terribly uncomfortable in the tropical heat.

I was feeling tired. I was looking forward to a change. But I wondered – was the fatigue I felt real? Were we looking for a finish line because we were truly tired? Or was it the finish line itself that was causing my tolerance to dissolve?

☸

Between the coastal current and the strong trades, we flew at eight and nine knots, knocking off the 605 NM journey to Trinidad in just over four days, and setting a new record for our second fastest day ever – 193 NM on our last full day at sea.

In the late afternoon of June 7, 2014, after 5,600 NM, and 101 Atlantic nights, we sighted the northeast tip of Trinidad, a shadowy silhouette of land barely discernible through the humid haze. As I stared ahead at our final destination, I reflected on our crossing. There'd been a lot of keeping the chin up on the Atlantic. With that in mind, I went below.

"What are you doing?" Nik said, seeing me bum-up and head-down in the bilge.

I triumphantly held up my find.

"Looks like cheap bubbly," he said.

I put the green bottle in the fridge and smiled.

"Tastes like champagne to me."

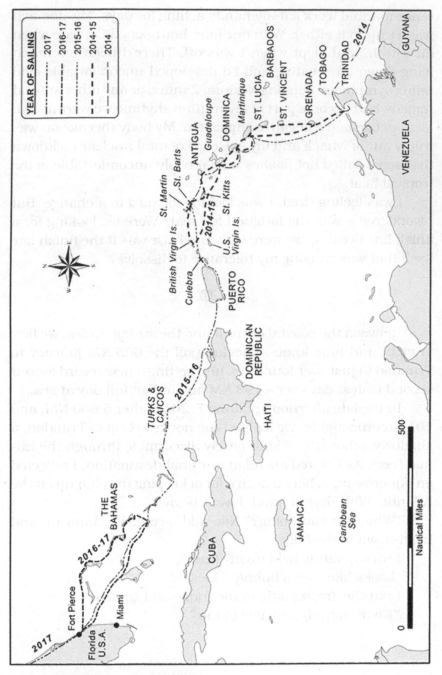

Figure 5. Caribbean Route Map

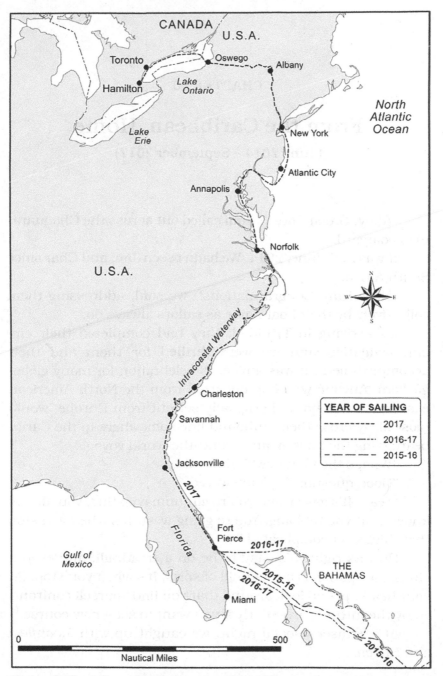

Figure 6. East Coast North America Route Map

CHAPTER 30

From the Caribbean, Home

(June 2014 – September 2017)

"Ahoy, *Green Ghost*!" Jimi called out across the Chaguaramas boatyard.

It was mid-June, 2014. We hadn't seen Jimi and Char since South Africa.

"Hey! *Tara*! Congratulations!" we said, addressing them collectively by their boat name as sailors always do.

By arriving in Trinidad, they had completed their circumnavigation and we were thrilled for them and their accomplishment. It was a place of celebration for many globe-girdlers. Anyone who had departed from the North American east coast, or who had originally set out from Europe, would most likely cross their outbound line somewhere in the Caribbean, tying the knot on an around-the-world voyage.

"What's the plan now?" Jimi said.

"Good question," Nik answered.

"Yeah. It's easy when you're circumnavigating, you always know what you're doing. You're going west. It's when you stop that things get complicated."

He was right. It's easy to be on a treadmill, and even a circumnavigation is a treadmill of sorts. It's when you stop, lift your head up, and look around that you find yourself confronted by the future, particularly if you want to set a new course.

At a cruiser's social night, we caught up with *Moonfleet* and *Haven*.

"Are you going through?" Bruce asked, referring to the Panama Canal.

"No," I said, "it doesn't make sense for us."

"Captain Hard-ass has relented," Nik chimed in.

In Asia, I'd harboured the dream to complete a circumnavigation – it was that goal-oriented nature of mine, that determination to do things thoroughly, to bring things to a perfect close. At that time, the Indian Ocean lay ahead of us, and having convinced Nik to sail across it rather than ship the boat to the Med, I believed a full circle was a possibility. After all, after Africa, there was only the Atlantic left.

"I'd still *love* to be able to say we did it – a circumnavigation is such a remarkable achievement. It's just that it doesn't make sense for us now. If we go through, we'd need to get up to Zihuatanejo, Mexico, to cross our outbound line. Either that, or we'd have to sail to the Marquesas again, then maybe up through Hawaii, north then east back to Vancouver. Either way, *Green Ghost* would end up on the west coast, a long distance from where we want to be.

"Nik's thinking he'd like to go back to work," I went on with my monologue, "and we want to be around for our moms a bit more, so it makes sense for us to be closer to Ontario. We don't want to leave *Green Ghost* the way we did in Australia, it's too hard on the boat. Either we live near the boat and we use it, or we sell *Green Ghost*."

I flinched a little when I said it. Aside from those few hours on the hellish trip across the Gulf of Carpentaria, selling *Green Ghost* had never seriously crossed my mind. But things were changing now, I could feel it. We were entering a different phase of life.

☸

Although still a long way from Canada, arriving in the Caribbean felt pretty close to home. A direct flight from Trinidad to Toronto took less than six hours. Hurricane-free from

December 1 until May 30, the Caribbean offered the perfect winter destination for frozen North Americans seeking a tropical thaw. Better still, Trinidad sat just below the hurricane zone, providing year-round safe storage for vessels.

Arriving in Trinidad was an end-point for us. We'd been living and travelling full-time on *Green Ghost* since we'd moved back on board in Queensland, Australia, four years earlier. For us, it was about as long as we enjoyed living at no fixed address. We wanted a break from the adventure, some time off the roller coaster and a place to call home.

Five weeks after arriving in Trini, *Green Ghost* was high and dry on the hardstand, the mast was pulled, the rig work done, the boat was covered with a shrink-wrap canopy, and we were on a flight to Toronto. In three more weeks' time, we'd emptied our storage locker and we were unpacking boxes in our one-bedroom apartment in Burlington where both our mothers lived. We were cashing in our full-time world cruising life to become part-time sailors.

⚓

We relished the ease of the Burlington life – having a car to swing by one of six fully stocked grocery stores within ten minutes of our front door, a mailbox, a couch, a TV, the Internet. We thrilled at the simple things: water from the tap, an endless supply, so refreshing and cold or so soothing and hot, whatever we wanted. Electricity was included in our rent, as were laundry facilities, a weight room, and a pool. Recycling made us feel good and garbage runs were easy – when the bin was full we put a bag down the chute in the hall. Life's basics were effortless in land life, but the split life made boating more complex.

⚓

After a lengthy repatriation in Canada, we returned to Trinidad to complete maintenance work before setting out to explore the busy Caribbean as seasonal cruisers. We expected some pretty plain sailing. After all, the next country was a day sail, at most a single overnighter away.

We weren't too surprised at the number of sailors – we'd expected the Caribbean to be crowded – but we were surprised by the sailing. We found it was quite difficult to sail north from Trinidad at Christmastime. Though we were often within eyesight of our next destination, it was never a cakewalk to get there. The intensity of the trade-wind conditions between the islands was challenging. Finding ourselves beating into the weather all too often, we came to understand that The Windward Islands are so-named for a reason.

Despite the brisk conditions, an international fleet of vessels was always on the move. There were many North American sailors who had coast-hopped their way south from homes on the eastern seaboard. There were European would-be world voyagers, revelling in the accomplishment of their first ocean crossing. There were the folks who'd crossed the southern Atlantic – South Africans or perhaps Europeans who were completing their circumnavigation. There were Aussies and Kiwis with two oceans in their wake, and west coast North Americans with three oceans down and only Panama standing in the way of closing their loop. The Caribbean was a crossroads like no other.

As we made our way north from Trinidad to Grenada, and on to Saint Vincent and the Grenadines, St. Lucia, and Martinique, we found that the fleet was not only multi-national, it was multi-directional too. Just when we'd met some terrific folks on the beach, we'd learn they were leaving the next day, heading south. The chance of seeing each other again was slim. Our globe-trotting buddies had struck out in their own directions. *Moonfleet* and *Haven* had gone west through Panama, others were headed northeast back to Europe, and some had left their boats in Trinidad and flown home for a rest. In the Caribbean, there was no defined fleet. We felt a bit lost, not because we were alone, but because we were alone in the crowd.

❂

"Oh my God," I said as I surreptitiously peeked out one of our portholes, spying on a sailboat anchored next to us off Dominica. "The woman on that charter boat is rinsing her bedsheets in the sea!"

"Oh boy. They'll be stinky and itchy tonight," Nik said.

"And all that fine salt working its way into the mattress – forever damp ... Ugh! How is it that people don't know?"

"Well, we didn't know," Nik reminded me. "You've got to remember, we've been at this a long time. Cut them some slack. Some charter boaters are pretty green behind the ears."

"Wet," I answered.

"Well, I'm sure she'll hang them to dry."

"No, you mean wet," I said. "As in wet behind the ears, as in just born."

He looked at me blankly. I was doing it again.

"A newbie is either wet behind the ears, or they're green, but they're not green behind the ears. That sounds like they're going moldy."

"Whatever," he said. "You know what I mean."

Nik was right, we'd been at this a long time and we'd learned a lot over the years. We weren't finished with learning either. We still made mistakes. We still accidentally dropped things off our boat, or inadvertently conversed on Channel 16, we still, on occasion, docked the boat imperfectly, or landed the dinghy poorly on a beach ... Sure, we still resorted to yelling at one another now and again – we just did it a lot less often.

❂

Though the boisterous and demanding weather patterns surprised us, we could handle the Caribbean sailing. It was the neighbourhood that took time to get used to. We'd crossed oceans in such great company and we missed the folks who put in the hard miles, our intrepid blue water friends. For that first season in the Caribbean, I couldn't shake the feeling that I wasn't with my people.

I was used to boats that were full-time live aboard, not part-time holiday properties. I was used to voyaging sailors, not vacationing ones. Offshore sailors were all-in. Caribbean sailors had houses and cars and whole lives they lived back home. Their time on board was short term – a few months' winter break. They weren't on a 'round-the-world mission, they were mostly just hanging out. And so the vibe was quite different – the anchorages felt less like Everest base camp and more like Ever Rest trailer park. I felt like I didn't fit in.

I couldn't get used to the dogs. Few long-distance cruisers travel with pets. There was the issue of quarantine in new countries, and of course the problem of bodily functions, walks, and exercise. Dogs were nearly impossible offshore, but in the Caribbean, dogs were a sailing accessory. They were everywhere.

Dogs stood at the prow of fast dinghies, nose to the wind. Dogs barked their displeasure at passing boats, defending their spot in an anchorage. They slept on decks, they were walked on the beach, they ran for Frisbees in the surf. Doggie play-dates were arranged on the radio, sometimes in mock doggie voices. I found the new neighbourhood confounding. It was all a bit too suburban for me – the very thing we'd strived to leave behind.

⚓

In time, I came to appreciate that Caribbean sailors had defined their own dream, their own way to enjoy life on the water. Toward the end of our first season, after exploring the Lesser Antilles from Trinidad to the British Virgin Islands and back, I settled into it. I had to, because after all, we'd become part-time vacationing sailors ourselves.

In our second season, we cruised through the northern islands and ended in Fort Pierce, Florida, where we stored *Green Ghost* for the summer. On our third winter getaway, we spent the entire season in the Bahamas. Our proximity to Canadian friends and family meant multiple rendezvous each winter. We enjoyed an unprecedented amount of entertaining and a slower pace, just hanging out.

As part-time cruisers, *Green Ghost* endured cyclical periods of desertion, intense maintenance, and heavy use. We left her alone in a boatyard for more than half of every year. Like closing a seasonal cottage, but much more involved, we spent days in April doing maintenance projects before storing the boat on the hardstand for the summer. Seven months later, we'd undo all the mothballing and re-establish the systems for the sailing season ahead.

We soon noticed that our fun-to-work time ratio was way out of whack. In our part-time sailing calendar, we spent four or five weeks doing maintenance on the hardstand for every four or five months of good times on the water. It was a very different schedule to our ocean voyaging days when we hauled the boat every eighteen months for bottom painting, but otherwise kept it livable while we kept it going. It seemed to us that seasonal sailing involved more work.

It wasn't just the part-time schedule that was to blame. There was a backlog to address on our must-do list. This was in part because of the age of the boat and also because we'd not had access to as many goods and services in the far-flung places we'd been. Some of the work was self-inflicted, because once we were up on the hardstand, we fell victim to the while-we're-at-it disease and took extra time to address the nice-to-do list as well. The seasonal to-dos, the must-dos, and the nice-to-dos made for some very long lists. I could sense another change coming as the maintenance fatigue wore us down.

☸

Nik pined to work again. He liked the idea of one more kick at the can. It was in part a longing for the relief of a paycheque and the things one could buy. But he also missed the camaraderie of work, the professional setting, and the accolades for a job well done. He figured, if he wanted another shot at it, he ought to return to the workforce before he got too old.

Me? Although I'd often thought that having a positive closing chapter to my career would be a feel-good happy ending, I was less driven to corporate work. I didn't long for it the way Nik did.

To suit our changing interests, together we hashed out a plan.

Closing the loop on a circumnavigation wasn't in the cards for us, but we both liked the idea of closure, of some kind of suitable ending to our tale. Our solution was to bring *Green Ghost* home. Back in Canadian waters, we could plant the flag for completing the journey: Vancouver to Toronto – the long way around.

⚓

"Vancouver, Canada? You're a long way from home!" A couple approaching in their dinghy had read our port of registration on the transom.

"We sure are!" Nik replied. We were anchored near Fernandina Beach, Florida, having started our northbound journey up the Intra-Coastal Waterway (ICW).

"What was it like going through The Ditch?" the man asked us, referring to Panama as he stopped his dinghy to chat.

"Oh, we didn't come that way," Nik answered. "We came the long way around."

"Around Cape Horn! That's brave!" the woman said, impressed.

"No, not that way," Nik explained. "We came the long, long way."

A look of confusion flashed on their faces, as if for a moment they'd forgotten that the earth was round.

"You mean ..."

"Yeah, the really long way – from Vancouver across the Pacific to New Zealand then Australia, then up through

Asia, from Sumatra across the Indian to Madagascar and South Africa, around the Cape, and then finally across the Atlantic to French Guiana, up to Trinidad, then up through the Caribbean to here ...," Nik said, opening his arms in a wide gesture.

"Wow! What a journey!" they said together.

"Yes, it was!" I chimed in.

"You must have a few stories," the man said.

"Oh yes," we said collectively. "Yes, we do!"

We had many similar interactions as we brought *Green Ghost* north, up the ICW to New York City, then on up the Hudson River, to the Mohawk River and the Erie Canal. We emerged onto Lake Ontario at Oswego, New York. From there, we sailed for Canada.

☸

"Will you be needing any fuel?" the young man at the fuel dock asked as he helped us with our dock lines.

"No, thanks, I've just pulled in to phone Canada Customs. They told me I couldn't declare our arrival until I was actually standing on the ground in Kingston," Nik said.

"Oh, okay," the young man replied.

Nik stepped ashore to assist with securing the boat. When he finished I could see that he was smiling broadly. He approached the young man. "It's been seventeen years since I've stepped off this boat onto Canadian soil. Looks like you're the welcoming committee!"

The young man was speechless with surprise and he stiffened a little as Nik engulfed him in a great bear hug.

"We're home!"

We hung a banner from our lifelines and flew the flags of all the countries we'd visited from our flag halyards as we made our journey west along the lake. Family members and friends celebrated our homecoming with parties in Kingston, Oshawa, and Etobicoke.

So many years ago, we'd chosen our path. We'd chosen to live our lives in a specific way. We'd set out with a dream to sail to Australia and a belief that we would figure the rest out from there. One day at a time, we'd done it. We'd sailed the long way home.

As we continued westbound toward Burlington I looked up at the courtesy flags fluttering in the breeze. So many memories were wrapped up in each one. I thought of all the good people: the laughing hardware shop attendant in Zihuatanejo who knew exactly what electrico ppfssst ppfssst meant, the generous Ezekiel, our fellow sailors who saved *Green Ghost* from drifting away in Maumere, and Port Captain Mallet and his team of volunteers who skillfully towed us in through the reefs at Rodrigues. I thought of the artistry of Polynesian tattooists and of Tongan voices raised in song. I recalled delighted greetings of "Hello, mister!" and smiling children asking, "Bonbon?" Sure, now and then, we met a bad hippo, but there were so few. As one wise Fijian marina manager had said, "People everywhere are the same, mostly good."

As we bounced over the wake of a passing motorboat, I thought of the difficult conditions we'd endured. So many times, I'd used my mantra, *This won't last, this won't last, this won't last.* And it never did. We sailed through the rough moments, at times hanging on white-knuckled, but in time we always found sunshine and fair winds.

I turned to look at Nik at the helm and I saw my familiar reflection in his sunglasses. Windblown as usual, I was still me. My core sense of self felt unaltered. All the miles hadn't changed who I was. But I knew that in its own way the voyage had defined me. I'd become an offshore sailor, an adventurer in a steamer trunk with a mast. How acutely I felt my good fortune. I sensed that I'd set myself free. How constraining it is to be defined by others. How liberating to decide who you'll be.

284

Glossary

Glossary definition sources are as follows:

[1] https://www.merriam-webster.com
[2] https://www.nauticed.org/sailingterms
[3] Personal knowledge

Other online sources where individually noted.

AIS – Automatic identification system. An automated, autonomous tracking system used on ships and by vessel traffic services on shore for the exchange of navigational information. AIS-equipped terminals electronically exchange vessel information by VHF radio signal. Static information such as the vessel's name, type, and length, as well as dynamic information such as the vessel's position, course, and speed, can be communicated. The information can be received by other vessels or base stations within range and can be displayed on a chartplotter or computer monitor.
Source: www.marinetraffic.com/hc/en-us/articles/204581828-What-is-the-Automatic-Identification-System-AIS-
Accessed March 12, 2020

amidships – In or toward the part of the ship that is halfway between the bow and the stern. [1]

anchor bridle – A loop or length of line attached to the anchor chain by a chain hook or other method that takes the strain of the ground tackle off the windlass and redistributes it to two points, usually to deck cleats on either side of the bow (or stern cleats if the bridle is being used on a stern anchor). See also bridle. [1, 3]

antipodean – Relating to a place diametrically opposite on the globe. [1]

astern – Behind or toward the stern of a ship. [1]

atoll – A ring-shaped coral reef or string of closely spaced small coral islands, enclosing or nearly enclosing a lagoon. [1, 3]

Autohelm – The brand name of an electric autopilot marine device. [3]

autopilot – A device for automatically steering ships. [1]

Awlgrip – A brand name for marine paint products designed to both beautify and protect the hull of a boat above the waterline. [3]

bare poles/running under bare poles – Travelling with the wind astern and no sails deployed. In strong wind conditions, the pressure of the wind on the hull and the mast(s) alone will generate a forward velocity. [3]

batten – A thin narrow strip of wood or fibreglass or other rigid but flexible material which, when inserted into a fitted pocket in a sail, helps to support the sail's shape. [1, 3]

beam – The width of a ship at her widest part. [1]

beam ends – Literally the ends of the beams in the deck framing, used to refer to the sides of a ship. The term is used to describe a vessel that is inclined so much on one side that the beams approach a vertical position. It may describe an extreme situation in which a vessel is about to capsize, but more often it means the vessel is heeled over forty-five degrees or more, as in the expression, *"It was so rough, she was standing on her beam ends."* [1, 2, 3]

beam reach/beam reaching – Reaching is the tack sailed by a ship with the wind coming just forward of the beam, on the beam, or aft of the beam. When reaching, the wind is striking the side of a vessel at any angle from 60 to 160 degrees. When the wind is at about 90 degrees to the vessel, the wind is striking the vessel on the beam. Therefore, a beam reach, or beam reaching, is sailing with the wind on the beam. [1, 2, 3]

beam seas – Swells or waves that approach the vessel on the beam, a potentially dangerous situation in heavy weather. [3]

beating – Sailing a course as close to the direction of the true wind as possible, also referred to as close-hauled. The sails are trimmed close to the centreline of the vessel. This point of sail allows the vessel to travel upwind, diagonally to the wind direction. [3]

Beaufort scale – The Beaufort wind force scale is a scale in which the force of the wind is indicated by numbers from Force 0 to Force 12. Each number relates not only to a specific wind speed but also to observed conditions on land or at sea. [1]

berth – (noun) Sufficient distance for maneuvering a ship, or an amount of distance needed to maintain safety; a place where a ship lies at anchor or at a wharf or dock; a bunk where a seaman sleeps. [1]

berth – (verb) To bring a vessel into a berth. [1]

bilge – The part of the underwater body of a ship between the flat of the bottom and the vertical topsides, the lowest part of a ship's inner hull where any leakage collects. [1, 3]

binnacle – A stand or housing for the ship's compass, usually placed where it is easily seen from the helm. [1, 3]

block – A wooden or metal case with one or more sheaves or pulleys and having a hook, eye, or strap by which it may be attached. Used to gain mechanical advantage or as a fairlead. [1, 3]

bommie – An Australian expression for coral reef, typically columnar in shape and rising higher from the bottom than the surrounding reef. These may be a hazard to navigation particularly at low tide. [3]

boom – A horizontal spar that supports the bottom edge (the foot) of a sail. [1]

bottom side – Refers to the wetted surface of a boat, the part of the hull in constant contact with water that is typically painted with anti-fouling paint to prevent marine growth. [3]

bow – The forward part of the hull of a ship, sometimes used in plural, bows. [1]

bridle – Any loop or length of line attached to two points to spread the force of a pull. On a sailboat, typically spreading a load of lifting or towing forces. See anchor bridle. [1, 3]

brightwork – Varnished woodwork on a boat; may also refer to polished metalwork. [1]

breadcrumb trail – As in a GPS breadcrumb trail, is a series of successive locations usually depicted as a dotted line on the visual display (chartplotter). The line graphically represents the course that has been taken. This allows users to keep track of their successive locations and to backtrack inbound exactly along the outbound path taken. [3]

broach – To veer or yaw dangerously so as to lie broadside to the waves. [1]

Cape Horn – A geographical location, but also a brand name of mechanical self-steering equipment for sailboats. [3]

catenary – The curve assumed approximately by a heavy uniform cord or chain that is perfectly flexible but not capable of stretching and that hangs freely from two fixed points. [1]

chain hook – A hook that securely attaches to a link on a chain. [3]

chain plate – A metal plate which is bolted to the side of a ship and to which the shrouds are fastened. [3]

chartplotter – An electronic device used in marine navigation that integrates Global Positioning System (GPS) data from a GPS receiver with an electronic navigational chart (ENC) and displays both the ENC and the position, heading and speed of the ship on a screen typically located at the helm station or the navigation station of a vessel. The chartplotter may also display other data from radar, automatic information systems (AIS), or other sensors.
Source: www.web.archive.org/web/20110204212414/http://www.marinegpschartplotter.co.nz/what-is-a-chartplotter.html Accessed March 12, 2020

circumnavigate/circumnavigation – To go completely around especially by water. Among offshore sailors the term usually implies a sailing trip that involves transiting every longitude of the globe. A circumnavigation is completed when you cross your outbound track. [1, 3]

clew – The lower aft corner of a sail, or a metal loop attached to the lower corner of a sail. [1]

clevis pin – Part of a strong u-shaped metal fastener used in sailboat rigging. Holes at the ends of the prongs on the u-shaped clevis accept a bolt-like pin, the clevis pin. The combination of a clevis and a clevis pin is commonly called a shackle.

close-hauled – See beating.

close reach/close reaching – A tack sailed by a ship with the wind well forward of the beam but not as close-hauled as possible. This sailing course lies between beam reaching (when the wind is perpendicular to the side of the vessel) and beating (when the vessel's course is as close to the direction of true wind as possible). This point of sail allows a vessel to travel upwind, diagonally to the wind direction. [1, 3]

cockpit – A space or compartment from which a boat is steered, piloted, or driven. On a sailboat, usually an open well located aft in which the helmsman sits to steer, and which offers some protection and safety for the crew. [1, 3]

cockpit coaming – A vertical surface or raised frame designed to prevent entry of water. It usually refers to a raised section of deck or a low rim around an opening in the deck of a ship such as around a hatchway, or, in this case, around the cockpit. [1, 3]

companionway – A ship's stairway from one deck to another. [1]

compression post – A vertical stainless steel post that stands between the base of the mast and the keel. The post, which supports deck-stepped masts, transfers the weight of the mast to the keel and prevents deck damage (compression) from the weight of the mast and from the pumping forces of the mast. [3]

cutless bearing – Or shaft bearing, is a bearing on the driveshaft of a marine vessel, usually made of brass with an inner fluted or grooved rubber lining. The bearing is lubricated by the surrounding water that enters the grooves when the shaft is rotating. Source: www.cruisingworld.com/how/check-shaft-bearing-hard/ Accessed March 12, 2020

Dall's porpoise – A black-and-white porpoise of temperate and arctic waters of the rim of the North Pacific Ocean. [1]

davits – A small crane that projects over the side of a ship, for lifting and lowering, lifeboats, anchors, or cargo. In the case of a recreational sailboat, usually in pairs, used for lifting, lowering, and stowing the dinghy. [1, 3]

depth sounder – An instrument for measuring the depth of the water beneath a ship, may be mechanical or electrical. [1, 3]

dodger – A hood or windscreen forward of the cockpit that protects the crew and the companionway from wind and spray. Can be soft and removable; made with a metal frame and canvas material, or hard and permanent; constructed from wood, metal or fibreglass. [3]

doldrums – A part of the ocean near the equator abounding in calms. Also called the Intertropical Convergence Zone (ITCZ). [1]

dorade – A horn- or scoop-shaped opening in the deck of a ship which allows fresh air to flow below deck while preventing water from entering. [3]

downwind – In the direction the wind is blowing. [1]

downwind pole – A spar used on sailboats to support and control a headsail (a spinnaker, genoa, or jib) when sailing downwind. This pole may be a fixed length or telescoping. One end of the pole is attached to a track on the front of the mast, the other end is attached to the clew (aft corner) of the foresail. If the pole is telescoping, it can be adjusted for the amount of sail unfurled. When sailing downwind, it is advantageous to "pole out" the foresail because the roll of the vessel in following seas will cause the foresail to repeatedly fill and collapse. This causes stress on the sail, the rig, and the mental well-being of the crew. When deployed, the pole supports the sail, gives it some shape, and prevents it from collapsing. A downwind pole isn't a mandatory piece of gear, but it is desirable on a cruising sailboat. On *Green Ghost* our downwind pole is about 3 metres long when not extended, and weighs about 60 pounds. [3]

drogue – Also called a storm drogue; a cone-shaped device made of flexible material that is dragged from the stern of a boat on a long line. Its purpose is to provide resistance to stabilize and decelerate the vessel, particularly in heavy weather. A drogue prevents broaching by keeping the hull perpendicular to the waves and prevents pitchpoling by preventing the vessel from speeding down the slope of a large wave and burying its bow into the back of the next one. [1, 3]

drop the hook – An expression that means to lower the anchor. [3]

ease – To lessen the pressure or tension especially by slackening (as in "ease the sheets"), lifting, or shifting, to maneuver gently or carefully, to moderate or reduce especially in amount or intensity; or to allow the helm to turn back a little after being put hard over (as in "ease the helm"). [1]

ebb tide – The state of the tide when it is falling; the period of time during which the tide is falling. [1]

EPIRB – An acronym for an emergency position-indicating radio beacon. [3]

evaporation plates – Part of a compression refrigeration system; specifically, the plates that are installed inside the area to be cooled, that is, inside the insulated refrigerator or freezer space. The evaporation plates draw heat from the area to be cooled. [3]

eye of the wind – The direction from which the wind is blowing. [3]

foil – Part of a roller furling system. The stiff length of extruded plastic or metal that is attached to the entire leading edge of the sail to be furled. [3]

foredeck – The part of a ship's main deck that is near the bow. [1, 3]

foresail – The sole or principal headsail on a sloop, cutter, or schooner. [1]

forestay – The cable, line, or stay that runs from the head of the foremast to the foredeck or bow of a ship, used to support the mast. [1, 2, 3]

foretriangle – The triangular space formed by the foredeck, the foremast, and the forestay of a sailing vessel. [3]

forward – At, toward, or near the bow of a vessel. [1, 3]

furl (verb) – To wrap or roll a sail close to or around a spar or a foil. [1, 2, 3]

furled (adjective) – Wrapped or rolled closely around a spar or a foil. [1, 3]

furling line guard – A part of a rolling furling system. A guard that prevents the furling line from coming off the furling drum. [3]

furling system – A system that allows the furling or reefing of a sail by rolling it around a rotating spar or foil. Roller furling is often used on foresails, but may also be used for mainsails. [3]

G&T – A gin and tonic. [3]

galley – A kitchen or cooking apparatus in a ship or plane. [1]

gallows/boom gallows – A U-shaped structure that supports the boom when the mainsail isn't in use. [3]

genoa – A large foresail, or jib, that substantially overlaps the mainsail. [1, 3]

Gouda – A mild cheese of Dutch origin that is similar to Edam but contains more fat; or the smell of our boat after fourteen days at sea in the tropics. [1, 3]

GPS – An acronym for Global Positioning System. A navigational system using satellite signals to fix the location of a radio receiver on or above the earth's surface, also referring to the electronic instrument so used. Garmin is one name brand of GPS instruments. [1, 3]

green flash – A momentary green appearance of the uppermost part of the sun's disk at sunrise or sunset that results from atmospheric refraction. The green appearance lasts for no more than a fraction of a second. [1, 3]

ground tackle – All of the parts of the anchoring system: the anchor, chain, cable, or rope and other tackle used to secure a ship at anchor. [1, 3]

gybe/gibe – The act of changing a vessel's course when sailing downwind, steering the stern of a boat (and the leech of the sail) through the eye of the wind, causing the sail and boom to swing from one side of the vessel to the other. [1, 3]

halyard – Any line used to vertically hoist or lower gear (a spar, a sail, a flag, etc.). [1, 3]

HAM radio – Also known as amateur radio, is the use of a specific part of the radio frequency spectrum for the purposes of non-commercial exchange of messages. The amateur community is well recognized as providing valuable communications assistance during times of disaster and emergency.
Source: www.ic.gc.ca/eic/site/smt-gst.nsf/eng/sf10281.html
Accessed March 12, 2020

harness – A safety device worn by seamen which can be fastened to lifelines, shrouds, or jacklines to prevent the seaman from going overboard. [3]

harden – To take in, or to take up any slack in (as in "harden the sheets"), the opposite of ease. [3]

hardware – The item of equipment necessary for a particular purpose; metal ware such as tools, fittings, cutlery, or utensils. [1]

hatch – An opening in the deck of a ship, or the covering for such an opening. [1]

head – Specifically a ship's toilet, but often used in reference to the room in which the toilet is located. [1, 3]

head (of a sail) – The uppermost corner of a sail. [3]

headsail – A sail set forward of the forward-most mast. [1, 3]

heave to/hove to – To halt the headway of a ship by positioning the jib aback and the rudder turned sharply to windward. This action is generally used to take a break from weather or sea conditions, or to provide time to attend to matters other than sailing the boat. The action is performed by steering the bow through the eye of the wind without tacking the foresail. The foresail is instead allowed to back (the wind pressure is on the forward side of the sail). The helm is then turned hard over in the opposite direction (as if to tack back again) and fixed in this position. It may be necessary to ease the mainsail slightly to further prevent forward motion [1, 3]

heel – (noun) A tilt (as of a sailing vessel) to one side; the extent of such a tilt. [1]

heel/heeled over – (verb) To lean or tip temporarily as from the action of wind or waves. [1]

helm – A lever or wheel controlling the rudder of a ship for steering; the position on the vessel where the steering device is located. [1, 3]

HF radio – High Frequency radio is the International Telecommunication Union (ITU) designation for the band of radio frequency electromagnetic waves between 3 and 30 MHz. Used aboard boats, HF radios allow for long-distance radio communications.
Source: www.web.archive.org/web/20131031020427/http://www.itu.int/dms_pubrec/itu-r/rec/v/R-REC-V.431-7-200005-I%21%21PDF-E.pdf Accessed March 12, 2020

hot bunking – A term to describe using the same bunk for two people working shift work on opposite shifts. While one person sleeps, the other is on watch. When the watch changes, the sleeper vacates the bed to go on watch and the worker going off shift lies down in a bunk still warm from the other person's body. [3]

hull speed – The maximum speed attainable by a displacement hull vessel. [3]

Intertropical Convergence Zone (ITCZ) – A belt of low pressure encircling the Earth near the equator where the northeast and southeast trade winds converge, also known as the doldrums.
Source: www.skybrary.aero/index.php/Inter_Tropical_Convergence_Zone_(ITCZ) Accessed March 12, 2020

iron genny – Also iron jenny. A tongue-in-cheek phrase used to describe a vessel's engine. [3]

jackline – A rope or line that leads from the cockpit of a vessel along the decks to the bow. The line is securely fastened at both ends. The line is used as a safety device. Using a carabiner attached to a safety tether that is attached to his/her safety harness, a seaman can clip onto the jackline and move freely fore and aft along the jackline, always being securely attached to the vessel. [3]

jib – A small triangular headsail set forward of the staysail and mounted to the forestay. [1, 3]

jury rig – (noun) A piece of equipment made in a makeshift fashion. [1]

jury rig – (verb) To erect, construct, or arrange in a makeshift fashion. [1]

kedge/kedging – To move a vessel by means of a line attached to a small anchor dropped at the distance and the direction desired, accomplished by taking an anchor and rode (still attached to the vessel) in a smaller vessel (dinghy) out to the desired location, and deploying it. The crew aboard hauls in the rode, usually with the aid of an anchor winch, drawing the vessel toward the anchor. [1, 3]

knot – A unit of speed equal to one nautical mile per hour, or 1.852 kilometres per hour (approximately 1.15078 mph). [1, 3]

lee/leeward – The side of a ship or area that is sheltered from the wind; the lee side, the side opposite the windward side. [1]

lee cloth – A piece of cloth held taut in a vertical position along the open side of a sleeping berth, used to secure a sailor at rest in his/her bunk. [3]

leech – The trailing edge of a fore-and-aft sail. [1]

lie ahull/lying ahull – The act of waiting out a storm by dousing all sails and simply letting the boat drift. [2]

lifeline – A line along the outer edge of the deck of a boat or ship, supported by stanchions to help prevent crew and passengers from falling overboard. [1, 3]

lines – Any rope used for a specific task on board a boat. [1, 3]

line brake / line clutch – A mechanical device that holds a line (rope) securely and does not allow it to move. [3]

luff – (noun) The forward (leading) edge of a fore-and-aft sail. [1]

luff – (verb) To turn the head of a ship toward the wind. When close to the eye of the wind, the sails will take air on the lee side and begin to ruffle in the wind. When luffing, a sailboat eases and slows. [1, 3]

MV – An abbreviation for Motor Vessel. [3]

Melmac – A brand name of durable plastic dinnerware known to be virtually unbreakable. [3]

main/mainsail – An abbreviation for mainsail/the principal and largest sail on the mainmast. [1]

mainsheet – The line by which the mainsail is trimmed and secured. [1]

motu – A Polynesian reef islet with vegetation. [1]

nautical mile – Abbreviated NM. The length of one minute of arc of a great circle on the surface of the earth. An international unit equal to 6076.12 feet or 1.15 statute miles, or 1.85 kilometres. [1, 3]

navigation lights – The lights required to be displayed from a boat or ship at night, including a port sidelight (red), a starboard sidelight (green), a steaming light (white facing forward, if underway using engines), and a stern light (white facing aft). [3]

navigation station/navigation table – An area with a seat and a large desk surface on which navigational charts can be unfolded and used, or more typically in modern-day sailing, where a navigational computer would be located, together with other instrument displays, where all systems of a vessel may be monitored. [3]

over-canvassed – An expression meaning that too much sail is up for the wind conditions, referring to a time when all sails were made of canvas. [3]

PACTOR modem – A special type of device that converts digital signals (such as those produced by a computer) to radio signals (such as those produced by an SSB radio). The modem is used to send and receive digital information, for example e-mails, by radio. [3]

Panga – A low-cost, modest-sized, lightweight, open fibreglass skiff used by fishermen in the developing world, designed specifically to use minimum outboard horsepower. Other key design features include a high bow, a narrow waterline beam, a flotation bulge (structural foam) along the gunwale, and a flat peak which makes the boat easy to pull up onto a beach and quick to plane at low hoursepower. [3] and Source: www.allmandboats.blogspot.com Accessed March 12, 2020

PGD – Post-guest depression, an acronym we used in jest for the feeling that descended upon us after guests left *Green Ghost*, a feeling of boredom, melancholy, and restlessness. [3]

pitch-pole – To capsize by being turned end over end. [1]

plane – (verb) To skim across the surface of the water. [1]

pole – See downwind pole.

port/port side – Refers to the left side of a vessel when looking forward. [1]

port tack – The tack on which the wind comes from the port side of a sailing vessel. [1]

porthole/sliding porthole – An opening such as a window in the side of a ship to admit light and air. Portholes are usually small with a sturdy weather-tight closure that may be a hinged glass cover or, in some cases, a sliding glass pane. [1, 3]

preventer – A control line rigged from the boom to a fixed point on the boat's deck to prevent or moderate the effects of an accidental gybe. [2]

Profurl – The brand name of French-made furling systems for yachts. [3]

pulpit – A railing around the bow of a vessel, useful as a secure hand-hold at the bows for a seaman on lookout or tending to the anchor or the sails. [3]

pushpit – See stern rail.

quarter – The stern area of a ship's side. [1]

radar – An acronym for radio detection and ranging. A system consisting of a synchronized radio transmitter and receiver that emits ultra-high frequency electromagnetic (radio) waves and processes their reflections for display. Used for detecting the presence, direction, distance, and speed of other vessels and for detecting and locating surface features. It is particularly useful for vessels operating in reduced visibility. [1, 3]

radio net/radio schedule – An agreed schedule for making contact with one or more other vessels at a certain time on a certain frequency, usually on long-distance (SSB or HAM) radio. [3]

reef – (noun) 1. A part of a sail taken in or let out in regulating size. 2. A chain of rocks or coral or a ridge of sand at or near the water's surface. [1]

reef – (verb) To reduce sail by taking in a reef. [1]

rigger – A person who fits out a sailboat with rigging. An expert in all aspects of the masts, spars, stays, lines, blocks, and other hardware installed above deck. [1, 3]

rivet/rivet gun – A rivet is a headed metal pin or bolt used for uniting two or more pieces by passing the shank through the hole in each piece and then beating or pressing down the plain end to make a second head. It is installed with a rivet gun (a pneumatic hammer) or with a smaller tool, called a pop-rivet gun. [1, 3]

roadstead – A place less enclosed than a harbour where ships may ride at anchor. [1]

rode – A length of rope or chain used to attach an anchor to a boat. [1]

roller furling – A sail management system that furls or reefs a sail by rolling it around a stay or a rotating foil. Roller furling is most often used on foresails but can be also used for mainsails. [3]

SSB radio – In radio communications, single-sideband modulation (SSB) is a technology that dramatically increases the efficiency of a radio's amplifier. SSB radios are able to harness the phenomenon of skip (where radio waves are reflected or refracted between Earth's ionosphere and the ground) to deliver significantly longer-range transmissions than line-of-sight VHF radios often found on sailboats. These radios provide a global communication network that allows simultaneous communications with multiple parties (radio nets). SSB radio also enables users to send and receive e-mail, call individual phone lines, issue two-way emergency broadcasts, and participate in radio nets. Operators can also receive AM, FM, and shortwave radio stations for news, sports, music, and other broadcast entertainment. Source: www.cruisingworld.com/single-sideband-radios-endure/ Accessed March 12, 2020

Sailmail – A radio based e-mail system designed for boat owners voyaging in remote areas. The system uses a PACTOR modem and an SSB radio to send and receive digital information by radio. [3]

sailplan – Formally, a set of drawings showing various sail combinations recommended for use in various situations. In practice, sailors may refer to their sailplan as the sails they have employed to produce the desired speed and comfort. [2, 3]

salon/main salon – The term means cabin, or the main area that serves as a dining room or a place to sit and socialize below deck. Also called a saloon. [3]

scope – The length of rode (line, chain, or a combination of both) deployed when at anchor. The length, or scope, is dependent on water depth and weather conditions. [3]

scopolamine – An organic complex found in the nightshade family of plants and used for preventing nausea in motion sickness. Transdermal scopolamine is administered through the skin via an adhesive patch, usually applied to the hairless area of skin behind the ear. To be effective, scopolamine must be administered at least four hours before exposure to an environment likely to cause seasickness. [1, 3]

sea berth – A bunk aboard a vessel that is comfortable to sleep in when at sea. A sea berth is typically handy to the navigation table and handy to the helm, often located amidships or in an aft cabin. [3]

self-steering gear – Either mechanical or electronic equipment that automatically steers a vessel while underway, maintaining a chosen course without human action. Also called autopilot and Autohelm. [3]

sheet – A line (rope or chain) used to regulate the angle at which a sail is set in relation to the wind. [1]

shrouds – Ropes or wires (usually in pairs) leading from a ship's masthead to the chain plates on the hull to give lateral support to the mast. [1, 3]

single hander – A person who customarily sails without the help of a crew. [3]

snuffer/snuffer line – A long tubular sleeve of fabric (much like a sock) that is pulled down over the spinnaker to douse the sail so that it can be lowered to the deck. The snuffer line raises and lowers the sock. Also called a spinnaker sock. [3]

sole – The deck or floor of a cabin or the cockpit. [3]

spinnaker - A large triangular headsail flown in front of the vessel and used when running before the wind. The spinnaker fills with wind and balloons out in front of the boat when deployed, referred to as "flying the spinnaker." Usually constructed of lightweight nylon, often in bright colours. [1, 2, 3]

spinnaker sock – See snuffer.

spreaders – In general, a device (such as a bar) holding two linear elements (such as lines, guys, rails) apart and usually taut. On a sailboat, spars (spreaders) are mounted on either side of the mast. The shrouds, attached at the masthead, pass over the spreaders to their attachment point at the chain plates on the ship's hull. The spreaders are used to widen the angle of the shrouds at the top of the mast, making them more effective. [1, 3]

spreader lights – Electric lights mounted on the spreaders, providing light for the deck below. [3]

stanchion – An upright bar, post, or support, typically mounted around the perimeter of a ship's deck, used to support the lifelines. [1, 3]

starboard/starboard side – Refers to the right side of a vessel when looking forward. [1]

starboard tack – The tack on which the wind comes from the starboard side of a sailing vessel. [1]

stays – A strong line or wire cable used to support a mast. [1]

staysail – A triangular fore-and-aft sail hoisted on the inner forestay. [1, 3]

stern – The rear end of a boat. [1]

stern rail – A secure railing extending around the stern of a vessel, used to keep crew secure in the cockpit. Sometimes referred to as the pushpit (as opposed to the pulpit on the bow). [3]

stop-knot – A knot used on the end of a rope so that the rope will not pass through a block, grommet, or fairlead. [3]

stream warps – A heavy weather tactic in which long heavy lines are streamed from the stern of the vessel in order to slow the vessel down and to keep the vessel aligned with the wind direction and perpendicular to wave direction. [3]

storm tactics – Any exceptional measures taken to safeguard a vessel in storm conditions. Typically, tactics beyond lying ahull or heaving to, and including more drastic measures such as streaming warps or the deployment of a sea anchor or drogue. Tactics that attempt to hold the bow into the sea and hold the vessel's position, or tactics that slow the boat down if running with the wind. [3]

tack – (noun) 1. A sailing direction to windward; 2. The lower forward corner of a fore-and-aft sail. [1, 3]

tack – (verb) To change the direction of a sailing ship when sailing close-hauled by turning the bow through the eye of the wind and shifting the sails to the opposite side. [1, 3]

tender – One that tends, such as a ship employed to attend other ships; a small boat for communication or transportation, to ferry passengers and cargo between ship and shore and to perform tasks alongside the hull; a dinghy. [1, 3]

tinny – A slang Australian and New Zealand term for a small open aluminum boat. [3]

topsides – The top portion of the outer surface of a ship on each side above the waterline. [1]

trade winds – A wind blowing almost continually toward the equator in the latitudes from near the equator to about 30 degrees north and south of the equator. In the northern hemisphere, these winds blow steadily from the northeast. In the southern hemisphere, these winds blow steadily from the southeast. [1]

transdermal anti-nauseant/antiemetic – A medicated adhesive patch that is placed on the skin to deliver medication through the skin into the bloodstream to suppress nausea and vomiting. [3]

transom – The planking (or other material) forming the stern of a square-ended boat. [1, 3]

Tropic of Capricorn – The parallel of latitude at 23 degrees 26 minutes south of the equator and that is the southernmost latitude reached by the overhead sun. [1]

TRS – Tropical revolving storm, referred to as hurricanes in the Atlantic Ocean and northeast Pacific, typhoons in the northwest Pacific, and cyclones in the southern hemisphere (south Pacific and southern Indian oceans). All three kinds of storms are the same – an organized system of clouds and thunderstorms with a low pressure centre around which winds of gale force or more blow spirally inwards, anticlockwise (anti-cyclonic) in the northern hemisphere and clockwise (cyclonic) in the southern hemisphere. These storms originate over tropical or subtropical waters.
Source: www.cultofsea.com/general/what-is-a-trs-or-a-tropical-revolving-storm/ Accessed March 12, 2020

V-berth – The berth located in the bow of a vessel, so called because of its V-shape. [3]

VHF radio – A Very High Frequency radio. A marine VHF radio refers to the radio frequency range between 156.0 and 162.025 MHz. Transmission power ranges between 1 and 25 watts. It is a relatively short-range radio, also referred to as a line of sight radio because transmitting and receiving antennas must be able to see each other to establish communications. Source: www.offshoreblue.com/communications/vhf-capabilities.php Accessed March 12, 2020

weather cloths – A piece of cloth tied vertically taut between the stanchions, the life lines, and the toe rail at the stern of a vessel to enclose the cockpit, providing protection from wind and spray as well as providing privacy for the cockpit. [3]

weatherfax – A marine weather facsimile receiver designed to receive and print high quality, high definition weather charts and satellite images transmitted from onshore stations located around the world. Source: www.furuno.com/en/products/weatherfax/FAX-410 Accessed March 12, 2020

302   JENNIFER M. SMITH

weather helm – The tendency of a sailing vessel to turn up in to the wind. [1]

winch – A mechanical device which uses sets of gears to turn a drum. A rope, cable, or chain is coiled on the drum to achieve purchase. The winch is then turned using a motor, a crank, or a handle, bringing the line taut and providing a substantial mechanical advantage for hauling and hoisting. [1, 3]

wind speed – The velocity of the wind; may be recorded in kilometres per hour or miles per hour, but typically measured in knots by mariners. [3]

windlass – A type of winch, typically situated on the bow of a vessel and used to raise and lower the ship's anchor. [1, 3]

windward – (noun) The direction from which the wind is blowing. [1]

windward – (adjective) The side of a ship or area that is exposed to the wind; the windward side; the side opposite the leeward side. [1]

windward – (adverb) Toward the direction from which the wind is blowing. [3]

wing-on-wing – Or wing and wing, describes a sailing vessel with sails extended on both sides, the foresail filled with wind on one side of the boat and the mainsail filled with wind on the other, used when sailing directly downwind. [1, 3]

zot/zotting – (verb) A term we adopted from Liza Copeland's book, *Just Cruising, A Family Travels the World: Europe to Australia*. In the book, the Copeland children coin the onomatopoeic term "zotting" to mean going for a high-speed trip in the dinghy.

Acknowledgements

It turned out to be true. Just as I'd suspected when I first met him, whenever Nik was around, something exciting was about to happen. There would have been no adventure to write about if it weren't for my husband, who so many years ago made the simple suggestion that we take sailing lessons. His love of adventure, his seamanship, his strength and bravery, his ability to come up with good ideas even as he vomited into a stockpot, all these things made our successful voyage possible while his good nature and playful spirit made our journey fun. Nik's skill in photography captured many memorable moments, including the cover photo, taken as we approached Sarawak (Malaysian Borneo) from the South China Sea. His unwavering support on this second journey – my solo journey, the writing of this book – has been a source of strength and encouragement for me. Alex "Nik" Nikolajevich, captain of my heart, thank you so very much.

I also thank my parents, David and Barbara Smith, who have loved me unconditionally and supported me in everything I've ever done. Growing up in their safe harbour is exactly what gave me the gumption to dare to sail beyond its limits.

To all those who contributed to our successful passage, from my sisters and their families, who sent mail packets and gear to faraway places and put us up in spare bedrooms when we flew in from God knows where, to our wider circle of family and friends who always welcomed us home with open arms, treating us like celebrities when we were near, and keeping us in their prayers when we were far: thank you.

I would also like to extend heartfelt thanks to my teacher, Brian Henry, who helped me develop my writing skills through his many valuable writing classes and workshops, with special thanks to my fellow students in the Burlington Thursday night Intensive Creative Writing class for their feedback on early chapters.

Thanks to beta readers Jean Richardson, John Batchelor, James Bryan Simpson, Paula Aicklen, Joseph McAdam, Beth Walpac, Liz Taylor Rabishaw, Pietro Galluzzo, Kimberley Bates, and Ann Marie Parkin, who waded through my first lengthy, error-strewn draft, providing me with honest feedback and many, many corrections. Thanks to my second cousin, Debby Seed, for her encouragement and copy-editing skills.

The Saturday morning Write Before Noon, Just Write! Burlington Meetup group, led by Cindy Towsley, lessened the loneliness of writing by welcoming me into their fold.

Many thanks to friend Kathie Jaworski for the beautiful and professional figures depicting our route around the world.

I also want to express my gratitude to publisher Lesley Choyce for his belief in my manuscript and the team at Pottersfield Press for helping to make my dream come true.

Finally, thanks to all those who supported and encouraged me to write a book about our journey aboard *Green Ghost*. To those who have anxiously waited and oh-so-often asked, "How's the book coming, Jenn?" here it is, finally finished.